THE
LITTLE BOOK OF
DERBY COUNTY

THE
LITTLE BOOK OF
DERBY COUNTY

PETER SEDDON

breedon **books**
PUBLISHING

First published in Great Britain in 2006 by
The Breedon Books Publishing Company Limited
Breedon House, 3 The Parker Centre,
Derby, DE21 4SZ.

A catalogue record for this book is available from the British Library.

Other titles by Peter Seddon

A Football Compendium
Steve Bloomer: The Story of Football's First Superstar
Football Talk
Tennis's Strangest Matches
Law's Strangest Cases
The World Cup's Strangest Moments

ISBN 1 85983 521 X

Printed and bound by Cromwell, Trowbridge, Wiltshire.

CONTENTS

ACKNOWLEDGEMENTS

The people who I would most like to thank for their help in compiling this book can't possibly be named individually – there are thousands of them. They are the countless players, officials, supporters and chroniclers of Derby County who have made the club tick or reported its daily deeds in three different centuries. It is they who have literally made the stories that set the Rams apart as a club so worth following, and without their vast collective contribution *The Little Book of Derby County* would have been a very small volume indeed. More specifically, though, I am grateful to a number of fellow supporters for clarifying facts, reminding me of incidents I might otherwise have overlooked, or simply for offering their interest and support – so sincere thanks to Andy Ellis, Kate Ibbitson, Ian Kellock, Richard, Rebecca and Rosemary Marshall, Ian Methven, Steve Perrins, Joyce Seddon and Steve Swanwick...and finally to Steve Caron and his editorial team at Breedon Books for steering a mere idea through to publication.

INTRODUCTION

From the moment Derby County were born in 1884 they began to make headlines which were by no means ordinary. They were formed from a cricket club, played their home games at a racecourse and later moved to a Baseball Ground. They lost their first ever game 6–0 on the 13th of the month and were thrashed 7–0 at home in their first FA Cup tie. Yet on their Football League debut they won 6–3 away and for one glorious but all too brief moment were the 'highest League scorers in the world'.

An early secretary ran off with the takings…a later one saved the club from extinction with a brisk bit of business conducted in a gents' toilet…a new pitch was laid with 'the wrong type of grass'…directors ousted two Championship-winning managers…a former chairman drowned at sea in mysterious circumstances…the club was bought for £3…then offered for sale on the internet…and a famous victory over Nottingham Forest was achieved with the aid of a plastic coffee cup.

That might be more than enough for a 'normal' club, but in the 'strange but true' world of Derby County it represents the mere tip of an enormous iceberg, and it is those hidden depths which have turned a great football club into the celebrated institution that it is today…much-loved, occasionally loathed, regularly a source of mirth and always widely cherished, but, above all, never ever dull.

And that's exactly the spirit in which *The Little Book of Derby County* has been compiled – other volumes have already presented the serious history and mind-boggling statistics…and expertly too… so this one embarks on a rather more light-hearted tour of 'planet Rams' with the accent on lesser-known stories, quirky facts, and endless nuggets of trivia…the more obscure the better!

The book makes no claim to be all-inclusive, and in fact is deliberately not so – that's why great days such as the Rams 1946 FA Cup triumph may grab less space than the team's epic victory on a vintage TV quiz show…and why centre-forward Bernard Vann, who few people have ever heard of, takes his place alongside Kevin 'The King' Hector and other true greats. Nor does the book adhere to a chronological approach – it's made to be dipped into and out of or even read back to front!

When I began putting the material together I had in mind a phrase much-used by those with an affection for the redoubtable Rams – 'It could only happen at Derby County' – a mild exaggeration perhaps, but one which had me nodding in agreement countless times as the book progressed. It's also said of Derby County that they are a 'real family club' and like all 'real families' they have enjoyed their proud moments and suffered some they'd rather forget – and alongside the many famous sons there are also some infamous ones and even a handful of genuine 'black sheep'.

But, despite it all, a sense of common purpose and an essential sense of humour somehow keep this particular football family together through thick and thin. *The Little Book of Derby County* is a nostalgic dip into the Rams family album – I hope it will be an entertaining one too.

Peter Seddon
Derby, June 2006.

ONE – THEY SAID IT...

Derby County have never been short of words. Since the club's formation in 1884 the varied media of newspapers, magazines, books, television, radio, official records, the internet and the terraces have all served the same end – the club has both 'spoken' and been 'spoken about' in equal measure. Whether composed of wise words, witty ones or just the plain daft, all these quotes have a Rams connection.

COMMENTATORS AND PUNDITS

'It is a club with a peculiar record for idiocy, it really is.'
  Veteran reporter Gerald Mortimer, Radio Derby, December 2005.

'How would I know? I've never seen a tin man run.'
  Clockwork Rams winger turned radio pundit Ted McMinn when asked if he got the nickname 'The Tin Man' because he ran like one.

'He's got a knock on the shin there, just above the knee.'
'You're not sure if the ball is going to bounce up or down.'
'A bit of retaliation there, though not actually on the same player.'
  Hat-trick of Irish wisdom from striker Frank Stapleton, who joined Derby from Ajax in 1988, here in his capacity as Sky TV summariser, 2005.

Ross Fletcher: 'I got that from the autobiography of Piers Morgan.'
Ted McMinn: 'Yeah, he's very good as James Bond isn't he?'
  Fletcher raises the tone, but a former Mirror *newspaper editor and 007 actor Pierce Brosnan are one and the same to Ted, Radio Derby, 2005.*

'If that lad makes a First Division footballer then I'm Mao Tse Tung.'
  Former Rams manager Tommy Docherty in 1989, prior to purchasing his chopsticks. The lad was Aston Villa's Dwight Yorke, who later won Premiership, FA Cup and Champions League medals.

'If he can find a ground where he scored a League goal I'll meet him there.'
  Wicked response of legendary Rams manager Brian Clough to pundit and former footballer Jimmy Hill's challenge to a 'serious debate', 1979.

'Jimmy Hill is to football what King Herod was to baby-sitting.'
  Tommy Docherty sustains the attack on the controversial pundit, 1992.

'If brains were chocolate, he wouldn't have enough to fill a smartie.'
  Alan Birchenall on Leicester City's Robbie Savage, 2000 – countless unsavoury incidents in games against Derby made the aptly-named midfielder extremely unpopular with Rams fans.

'I am not Pelé or Maradona.'
  Robbie Savage proves Birchenall's point in trying to give a clever reply.

'Michael Owen is not a diver. He knows when to dive and when not to.'
  Double-speak from Derby's 1994 midfielder Steve Hodge as 'expert' guest on Talk Sport radio.

'Bolton couldn't win even if they had Pelé and George Best in their side.'
  Sky Sports Frank McLintock on Derby's 4–0 Premiership victory over the Trotters – Pride Park, April 1998.

'The whole idea of playing football under artificial light is fantastical. Spectators need not let their imaginations run riot that one day they will have to wait until 9 or 10 o'clock for the results. That day will never come.'
  Columnist Steve Bloomer proves less adept at punditry than scoring goals – Derbyshire Football Express, *March 1930.*

'I propose the League lays it down that the home teams will always play in red and the visiting teams in blue, although perhaps I am treading on dangerous ground. I know that thousands of football followers have a conscientious objection to their favourites playing in anything other than their familiar raiments.'
  Another 'Bloomer' as Derby's greatest striker seeks to kill the replica kit market before it even takes off – Derbyshire Football Express, *March 1931.*

'Lee...interesting...VERY interesting! Look at his face...just look at his face.'
  Manchester City 1 Derby County 2 – Match of the Day *commentator Barry Davies hails the stunning winning goal by Francis Lee, playing against his former club for the first time, December 1974.*

'And this is extraordinary! We're going to have the penalty spot painted, are we, during the match?'

Incredulous commentator John Motson as the Baseball Ground mud works a disappearing trick – Derby County 4 Manchester City 0, April 1977.

'And here it comes now, circling in over Chaddesden……'
Radio Derby's Colin Gibson (to sound of chopper blades) unwittingly 'glams it down' during the live broadcast of the spectacular arrival by helicopter of Rams new manager Billy Davies, 2 June 2006.

THE GRAHAM RICHARDS COLLECTION

'One Graham Richards, there's only one Graham Richards.'
Tribute chant to the unconventional Radio Derby commentator who first covered the Rams in 1977 – frequent 'Grahamisms' made him a cult figure.

'If Carsley was a painter he would put the paint in the lawnmower…he'd be a good player on the moon though.'
Suggestion that Derby's hard-working 1990s midfielder Lee Carsley sometimes played his football in a parallel universe.

'He's a two-legged tripod, if you know what I mean.'
Classic contradiction in terms on the unorthodox loping style of Derby's Costa Rican striker Paulo Wanchope – Middlesbrough v Derby, August 1998.

Colin Gibson: 'He had his foot up…'
Graham Richards: 'Well he's Darryl Powell isn't he'?
On the Rams harum-scarum midfielder in the same match as above.

'Deane collapsed like the World Trade Centre…only less spectacularly.'
14 September 2002 – Leicester City 2 Derby County 1 – an unwise analogy to use at any time, let alone three days after the first anniversary of the terrorist attack on New York's twin towers. Radio Derby was swamped with complaints, and Richards issued a humbling apology.

'It's a penalty, I do not believe it. The referee has given a penalty – I do not believe it…Christie looking as cool as custard comes back…one, two, three, four…goal, goal, goal, goal…well you'll not believe this run in.'

A 'Victor Meldrew' moment ahead of its time – Trevor Christie scores the penalty that secured promotion from the Third Division for Arthur Cox's side – Derby County 2 Rotherham United 1 – Friday 9 May 1986.

'A thumping great tackle from Gascoigne...and it's goodnight Gascoigne. He has behaved like an oik from the beginning of the game to the end – a spoilt fat brat – and he has been sent off.'

An early dip in the Baseball Ground bath for Newcastle United's 'Gazza', Derby County 2 Newcastle United 1 – 4 April 1988.

AND FINALLY...

- ✪ First goal: 'Into the box...in goes Shilton...he's dropped it, he's dropped it... Shilton, oh a terrible error by Shilton...makes a complete hash of it, and he drops it straight into the path of a Derby forward who shoves it into the net.'
- ✪ Second goal: 'And Duncan's headed in the second one. Incredible...Forest all over the show, Forest absolutely in chaos...and Derby are two ahead.'
- ✪ Third goal: 'Emery's through...and he's scored...Emery clean through... Forest are in absolute ruins and Derby County are three up...and manager Brian Clough...I've never seen such an expression of disgust on his face.'
- ✪ Fourth goal: 'A superb header...oh a magnificent header from John Duncan diving in...and everybody is up...the entire crowd is up... ...Derby County 4 Nottingham Forest 1.'

   Graham Richards's finest hour – this strangulated, high-decibel delivery entered Derby folklore as a struggling Rams side trounced Brian Clough's high-flying Forest at the Baseball Ground, 24 November 1979.

MANAGERS

JIMMY METHVEN 1906–1922

'When I accepted the offer made by Derby County to become manager of the club, little did I dream of the trouble I was running into. The idea installed in my mind was that it was an easy job, but I assure you it is not. Even most Sundays a manager's time is pretty fully occupied on club business, and after doing his level best he seldom gets any thanks for it. If the results are satisfactory the players get the credit, likewise the bunce accruing from the gain of points, and if the results are not pleasing then the manager's share is the other stuff.'

The first to 'see the light' – From Forty Years in Football, *Methven's serialised memoirs, 1927.*

'The Rams once had a gay Hogmanay night in Edinburgh.'

Candid revelation that Bloomer and the 1890s lads had partied the night before a New Year's Day tour game against Dundee, although then a perfectly unambiguous reminiscence, Derbyshire Football Express, *1927.*

GEORGE JOBEY 1925–1941

'The strong shall live and the weak shall die.'

Jobey's favourite catchphrase – the no-nonsense Geordie ruled his players with a rod of iron, and to great effect. Although winning no major trophies during his tenure, Derby County came to be regarded as one of the top sides in the country while under his guidance.

TED MAGNER 1944–1946

'He was outstanding. His man-management was superb. He had an immense knowledge of the game. He would take us on to the pitch and hit the crossbar from the 18–yard line just to show us that he could play.'

Rams star Peter Doherty in Spotlight on Football, *1947. Magner is Derby's 'forgotten manager' – the Rams team that won the FA Cup in 1946 was effectively his. Magner left the club just three months prior to the Wembley triumph.*

STUART McMILLAN 1946–1953

'If you don't play golf, you'll have to caddy for them that do.'

Unusual directive to his players prior to the 1946 FA Cup Final – the Rams boss played golf for Derbyshire. The preparation worked – Derby beat Charlton Athletic 4–1, and McMillan remains the only manager to have won the Cup for Derby.

HARRY STORER 1955–1962

'The biggest crime in football is to give the ball to the opposition.'

Sign put up by Storer in the Baseball Ground home dressing room, later retained by Brian Clough. It so impressed Roy McFarland that he posted the same message on becoming manager of Cambridge United.

TIM WARD 1962–1967

'The job has been the toughest I have ever had and the shortage of money has been frustrating. The trouble with this club is that you can't put a twopenny stamp on a letter without consulting the board personally.'

T'was ever thus! Being told his contract would not be renewed, 1967.

Andrew Ward: 'What's your team for Saturday Dad?'
Tim Ward: 'Toogood, Nogood and Getgood, Freeman, Hardy and Willis, Greenhouse, Glasshouse, Doghouse, Sweetshop and Doorknob.'

Reminiscence from Armed with a Football, *1994 – no manager reveals his team sooner than necessary, even to his inquisitive young son.*

BRIAN CLOUGH 1967–1973

'Age doesn't count. It's what you know about football that matters. I know I am better than the 500 or so managers who have been sacked since the war. If they had known anything about the game they wouldn't have lost their jobs.'

An inexperienced 'young man' on taking his first managerial post at Hartlepools United, 1965, where he travelled to work on a pushbike.

'He is a kind of Rolls-Royce communist.'

Neat analogy from rival manager Malcolm Allison, 1973.

'He's worse than rain in Manchester – at least God stops that occasionally.'

Bill Shankly, former managerial adversary, on Clough's constant and often controversial pronouncements, 1979.

'A player can never feel too sure of himself with Clough, that's his secret.'

His assistant Peter Taylor in With Clough By Taylor, *1980. The book contained material which Clough seriously disapproved of and contributed to an acrimonious rift which was never healed.*

'We pass each other on the A52 going to work most days of the week. But if his car broke down, and I saw him thumbing a lift, I wouldn't pick him up. I'd run him over.'

Nottingham Forest manager Clough on Derby manager Peter Taylor after the former close partners had fallen out for good, 1983.

'It only takes a second to score a goal.'

No side has ever won 5,400–nil, but we knew what he meant, 1984.

'It's easy enough to get to Ireland – just a walk across the Irish Sea as far as I'm concerned.'

Clough mischievously confirms his application for the Republic of Ireland manager's job, 1985.

'I want to be manager of Scotland.'

Changing horses, 1985.

'I can't promise to give the team talks in Welsh, but from now on I'll be taking my holidays in Porthcawl, and I've bought a complete set of Harry Secombe albums.'

On hoping to become Wales manager, 1988.

'My wife says OBE stands for Old Big 'Ead.'

Self-deprecating swipe on receiving (and accepting) the award, 1991.

'If God had meant football to be played in the air, he'd have put grass in the sky.'

On his preference for sides to 'play to feet', 1992.

'Like all the great dictators, from de Gaulle to Thatcher, he stayed on a little too long.'

Italian sports newspaper Gazetta Dello Sport *after Clough's retirement, 1993.*

'I'm ill-tempered, rude and wondering what's for tea, same as ever.'

On what he was like at 4.45 pm on Saturdays after retirement, 1994.

'They didn't want an England manager who was prepared to call the Italians cheating bastards. They failed to understand that I would have curbed my language and revelled in the relief from the day-to-day grind of club management.'

Reflecting in 1995 on his unsuccessful application for the England manager's job in 1977.

'United have got into Europe thanks to the FA Cup. And where are they going? Brazil. I hope they get bloody diarrhoea.'

On Alex Ferguson's decision not to enter the FA Cup, 1999.

'At last England have appointed a manager who speaks English better than the players.'

On Sven-Goran Eriksson as England's first foreign coach, 2000.

'I want no epitaphs of profound history and all that type of thing. I contributed. I would hope they would say that, and I would hope somebody liked me.'

On 'being remembered' – Brian Clough died of stomach cancer, aged 69, in Derby City General Hospital, Monday 20 September 2004.

DAVE MACKAY 1973–1976

'I want to be judged on merit. It's up to me to buy and sell the right players and to get them to play well together as a team. I'm not setting any time limits, but we must win trophies. Managers who aren't successful should get out.'

Beginning of the 1974–75 season. Derby went on to become League champions for only the second time in their history, and they finished third and fourth in Mackay's other two seasons as manager. He was sacked in November 1976 after asking for a 'vote of confidence', which the board astonishingly denied him.

COLIN MURPHY 1976–1977

'Colin Murphy was quite excitable. If you could understand his London accent and slang you were halfway there, but he wasn't the best at giving pre-match talks. Largely because no one could understand him.'

Veteran physio Gordon Guthrie, 1999. 'Murph' suffered a double indignity at Derby – the sack and being replaced by Tommy Docherty.

'Of the keys on the ring at the moment, we should be selecting more correctly to unlock opposing mechanisms. However, there is not a lock that cannot be unlocked, so we shall continue to endeavour to unlock the lock, but in doing so we must not get locked out.'

Murphy lends credence to the story in his 'Murph's Message' programme column at Lincoln City – this garbled tactics talk earned him a 1989 'Golden Bull' award from the Plain English Campaign.

'You, me, we all of us have been forced to breakfast on travesty, lunch on objection and insult, and dine on inflicted pressure. High tea we daren't even sit long enough to take – and by supper we were still expected to be victorious.'

A final message from 'Murph', 1980s – not until the double act of Phil Brown and Murdo Mackay in the dark days of 2005–06 did anyone associated with the Rams come close to taking Murphy's 'Golden Bull' title.

TOMMY DOCHERTY 1977–1979

'All Derby will get here will be a cup of tea afterwards.'

As Aston Villa manager, 29 March 1969 – Result – Villa 0 Derby 1. The 10,000-strong contingent of travelling Rams fans sang 'Tommy put the kettle on' and some later sent him teabags through the post. Derby were promoted as Second Division champions. Villa finished a sorry 18th.

'It's a farm yard.'

As manager of Scotland Under-23s about the Baseball Ground pitch for the game against England there, February 1972.

'Your pace is very deceptive son. You're even slower than you look.'

Purported comment on first meeting Leighton James, 1977. Derby's Welsh international winger was a Dave Mackay signing and soon left the club, one of countless casualties of the 'Doc's' meddling.

'Come and see my three Van Goghs.'

On his midfield maestros Gerry Daly, Bruce Rioch and Don Masson, 1977. Twenty months of lunacy followed before Docherty was out on his ear.

'Lots of times managers have to be cheats and conmen. We are the biggest hypocrites. We cheat. The only way to survive is by cheating.'

Docherty in 1979. Despite following his own dictum he failed to survive what proved to be a nightmare stay at Derby – not least for supporters.

'All this talk about Tommy Docherty not being fit to run a football club is rubbish. That's exactly what he's fit for.'

TV critic and confirmed football-hater Clive James after the Rams manager's resignation in May 1979.

'He's gone 200 years too late.'

Anonymous manager on hearing Docherty had moved to Australia to manage Sydney Olympic, 1981.

'I've been in more courts than Bjorn Borg.'

Reference to his ongoing acquaintance with controversy, 1981. Shortly after leaving Derby, 'The Doc' was arrested in connection with allegedly 'dodgy' transfers between American clubs and the Rams.

'Football's a rat race – and the rats are winning.'
Explaining his reasons for leaving British football, 1982.

'When the TV people asked whether I'd play a football manager in a drama, I asked how long it would take. They told me 'about 10 days', and I said: 'That's about par for the course."
Having just left his final club Altrincham, Docherty takes to the after-dinner speaking circuit, 1989.

PETER TAYLOR 1982–1984

'I'm not equipped to manage successfully without him. I'm the shop front and Peter's the goods at the back.'
Brian Clough on Taylor's contribution when the two still worked together on friendly terms, 1973.

'My Missus could save this side from relegation.'
On his arrival in the 1982–83 season when he kept the Rams up.

'Top six by Christmas.'
Late 1983 after Brian Clough's former partner rejoined the ailing Rams. In fact they got nowhere near, and escaped relegation by a whisker. Taylor's comedic catchphrase became a fans' mantra, cheerily invoked whenever a bad first half of the season lowered the spirits.

ARTHUR COX 1984–1993

'You can find my secret by wringing out my shirt at the end of every working day.'
To Ram Magazine, May 1987, after taking Derby from Third Division to First Division in successive seasons. Cox played the 'work ethic' card throughout his reign, even after his earlier achievements were soured by later events – ironically he resigned from the club due to 'a bad back.'

'The next Kenny Dalglish – The next Ian Rush – The last piece of the jigsaw.'
Cox's observations in turn on Craig Ramage, Phil Gee and Martin Kuhl. Even 'King Arthur' didn't get it right all the time.

'You are under pressure in war zones, not in football.'
When asked if he was finding difficulty coping after Derby were relegated and striving unsuccessfully to regain the top flight, 1993.

'He'd just got a presence around him. You knew he was somebody. If you'd never seen him before, you'd say "Who's he? He's got to be someone in the public eye."'
Geraint 'George' Williams sings his former manager's praises, 1998.

JIM SMITH 1995–2001
'My chairman, Robert Maxwell, they ought to let him run football.'
Early moment of madness as manager of Oxford United, 1983.

'Paolo was way out of order, but I deny that I ever called him a poof. I'd never use that kind of language…even if it were justified.'
On one of several heated rows he had with Derby's Costa Rican international forward Paolo Wanchope, 1997.

'I understand that Walter Smith (Everton manager) described the ref as diabolical. I didn't think he was as good as that.'
28 August 1999 after Derby 1 Everton 0 – referee Andy D'Urso wielded nine yellow cards and one red.

'There is a definite place for agents but it's turning into a spivs' market place. There are people coming into the game who are accountants, solicitors, estate agents or whatever, telling you who these footballers are.'
The 'Bald Eagle' tunes into the fans' wavelength, 2000.

'Over there, sir, those lads in the tracksuits are all our apprentices.'
'Well they haven't got much hope here with all those foreigners, have they?'
Exchange between Smith and the Duke of Edinburgh at the opening of Pride Park Stadium, 18 July 1997– related in Smith's auto-biography It's Only a Game, *2000.*

'The old Roman emperors used to fall on steel swords. Jim falls on a rubber one then bounces back and blames everyone else.'
Supporter John Leeson on Radio Derby phone-in, October 2000.

'SMITH RESIGNS FROM RAMS'
Newspaper headline October 2001 after the Derby boss rejected a proposal to demote him to the nominal role of director of football.

JOHN GREGORY 2002–2003
'The players can get out of their brains every night as long as they're Man of the Match on Saturday.'
Cultivating a liberal regime as Aston Villa manager, 1999.

'Referees should be wired to a couple of electrodes and they should be allowed to make three mistakes before you run 50,000 volts through their genitals.'

After David Elleray awarded a controversial penalty, 1999.

'I remain convinced that I am a much, much better manager than when I started. But not half as good as I will be.'

The final sentence of the 2001 edition of his autobiography The Boss *boded very well indeed for his next club Derby County.*

'GREGORY SACKED AS RAMS MANAGER FOLLOWING INVESTIGATION INTO SERIOUS ALLEGATIONS'

Headline news, 9 May 2003 – after relegation from the Premiership in 2001–02, Gregory was mysteriously suspended by the club in March 2003 before the sorry end. The ever-confident 'Gregs' claimed damages and settled out of court in March 2004 – the full story has remained under wraps.

GEORGE BURLEY 2003–05

Q – 'Do you agree with Marco Reich that German cars are the best?'
A – 'Well he would say that wouldn't he. I don't know of many Scottish companies that make cars, so I'll probably agree with him there.'

Rare light moment from the careful Scot – Radio Derby, February 2005.

'It is with great regret I wish to announce my decision not to continue as manager of Derby County Football Club. My position has become untenable.'

Not such a light moment – the shock resignation followed a prolonged bout of internal politics, June 2005.

PHIL BROWN 2005–06

'Bruce Rioch without a shadow of a doubt. I played under him for three years at Bolton – he taught me a lot about psychology, new ideas and embracing modern technology.'

Brown's tribute to former Derby midfielder Rioch when asked which managers he'd learnt from, Radio Derby, 2005.

'There are a lot of good personalities in the dressing room. Some nice lads, some not so nice – but as a group of characters I think we can do something this season.'

The 'psychologist' uses an unusual technique to create a sense of togetherness – August 2005.

'It's a bad day at the office. To be beaten six by anybody, that's a bad day at the office. But I'll bounce back.'

Following Coventry City 6 Derby County 1, Radio Derby, 21 January 2006.

'We would like to thank Phil for the time and effort he has given to the job and wish him well for the future.'

Curt statement from the Derby County board after announcing Brown's sacking, 10pm Monday 30 January 2006 – the axe fell two days after a 3–1 FA Cup reversal at Colchester United.

BILLY DAVIES 2006

Shane O'Connor: 'Didn't he spend some time at Leicester City?'
Colin Gibson: 'Yes, but we won't hold that against him.'

First Radio Derby exchange seconds after it was revealed that Preston North End boss Billy Davies had become the Rams new manager, 2 June 2006.

Colin Gibson: 'Will you be supporting Sven's men at the World Cup?'
Billy Davies: 'No…yes of course I will.'

The canny Scot hedges his bets in his first Radio Derby interview on the day of his arrival, 2 June 2006.

SUPPORTERS

'They had no job, little food, rags to wear. But they scraped together the few pence it cost to come and watch us. It lit up just a small part of their dreadful lives. We had to turn it on for them, had to make that day more bearable than the rest. I was lucky. It could have been me.'

One that understood – Rams 1940s legend Raich Carter sensitively recalls his time at Sunderland in the depression-hit 1930s.

'I don't want to ask a question. I just want to make an observation. I would have given my right arm to be a professional footballer, but I wasn't good enough. I would give anything now to have memories like yours.'

Elderly supporter close to tears at a Derby County former-players' forum in the 1980s, touchingly articulating what so many modern footballers seem unable to grasp about the nature of fandom.

'DERBY, DERBY, DERBIES!! YOU'LL GO HOME LIKE SHEARED LAMBIES'

Banner at the Spartak Trnava v Derby County match, European Cup third-round, first leg, 7 March 1973. The Czech side fleeced the Rams 1–0 but were beaten 2–0 at the Baseball Ground in the return leg.

'YOU'VE ENJOYED THE MATCH – NOW LET HER ENJOY HERSELF'

Chauvinism rules the Baseball Ground – Ram *newspaper advert, 15 December 1976. Big treat for the stay-at-home ladies was '5 free games at Showboat Bingo – Jackpot prize a Goblin Teasmade!'*

'SHATTERSBURY'

Derby Evening Telegraph *headline after Nottingham Forest fans had smashed windows and broken down front doors in Shaftesbury Crescent outside the Baseball Ground, 33 were arrested, January 1978.*

'ROBERT MAXWELL WALKS ON WATER'

Not quite prophetic Baseball Ground banner pays homage to the club's wealthy new 'saviour' and owner, 1984. Maxwell's body was found in the Atlantic Ocean in mysterious circumstances on 5 November 1991, shortly before major financial irregularities were discovered in his business empire.

'He's fat, he's round, he's never at the ground.'

Regular terrace chant at the Baseball Ground in the late 1980s, as doubts about the well-built Maxwell began to surface.

'FAT CHEQUES NOT FAT CZECHS'

Punning fan's banner, 1990, after Czech-born Maxwell announced there was 'no more money available' and put Derby County 'up for sale'.

'PAUL McGRATH LIMPS ON WATER'

Derby fan's banner in homage to the injury-ravaged defender, 1997. Despite being regularly excused from serious training as a 'preservation measure', the Republic of Ireland international was one of the most exceptional talents ever to pull on a Rams shirt.

'We have some exciting players at Derby. Jim is building a great mix of youth and experience. And if some fans can't recognise that, they should stop going to football – or, better still, go and watch Nottingham Forest.'

Red rag to a bull (or a Ram), September 1999 – chairman Lionel Pickering on Radio Derby responding to fans' criticism of the board and manager Jim Smith. Many fans never forgave him for the Forest jibe.

'It's my seat. I've paid for it. I'm not coming to watch this lot again. I'll bring it back in the summer.'

Irate fan to stewards who manhandled him during Derby's 3–0 home defeat by Wolves, November 2005. The seat in question was stuffed up his jumper at the time.

'He's fat, he's round, he bought us for a pound.'

Golden oldie bitingly re-written for Pride Park, 14 January 2006 – Rams beat a woeful Crewe Alexandra 5–1, but chief executive Jeremy Keith still got a torrid barracking from sections of the crowd. They remained unhappy at his contribution after his purchase of the club with two others for the sum of £3! The trio were disparagingly dubbed 'The Three Amigos'.

'Five-one and we hate the board, five-one and we hate the board.'

Incongruous repetitive chant at the same above game shows the full extent of mounting anti-board feeling.

PLAYERS

'I've heard far worse than that – the roar of a pit falling in.'

Rams centre-half Jack Barker on coping with the 'Hampden Roar', ahead of Scotland v England, 6 April 1935. Despite the ex-miner's bravado, England lost 2–0 to goals scored by his Derby teammate 'Dally' Duncan.

'Courage isn't just tackling and winning the ball. Courage is when Alan goes down the wing and full-backs are sticking the studs up, and he crosses the ball and doesn't care about getting his leg broken, when they're all trying to get at him. That's courage.

Assistant manager Peter Taylor on legendary winger Alan Hinton in the late 1960s in a dressing-room speech that silenced Derby players

who had criticised Hinton's apparent distaste for hard physical
challenges.

'He's got more skill in his little finger than I ever had in my whole body.'
    *Brian Clough on his first Rams signing, August 1967. Centre-forward
    John O'Hare joined the club from Sunderland for £20,000.*

'Leave it, Terry son.'
    *16 years and 30 days old Steve Powell, on his Rams debut, to veteran
    Welsh international Terry Hennessey as he was about to take a throw-in
    during a Texaco Cup match – Derby 3 Stoke City 2 – 20 October 1971.*

'If you don't start belting that ball out of our penalty area, I'll get some big
ignorant lad who can do the job better.'
    *Brian Clough to three Rams defenders following a game against
    Birmingham City, 1973. The incompetent trio were cultured England
    internationals David Nish, Roy McFarland and Colin Todd!*

'If it had been his day, Roger could have scored 10.'
    *Manager Dave Mackay after Derby County v Luton Town, 29 March
    1975. Lanky striker Roger Davies scored a mere five in the Rams 5–0
    victory.*

'If he was a chocolate drop he'd eat himself.'
    *Graeme Souness on his Scotland teammate Archie Gemmill, 1978.
    Having just scored a wonder goal against Holland in that year's World
    Cup Finals, the Derby County legend was perfectly entitled to be so
    pleased with himself – shame he played for Forest at the time.*

'If some foreigner had done that we'd be talking about it for months.'
    *Rams manager Arthur Cox uncharacteristically enthuses over a
    sublime lobbed goal by Derby's Mick Harford – Chelsea 1 Derby
    County 1 – 31 March 1990.*

'Touch wood, I've never scored an own-goal in 10 years as a professional.'
    *Stockport County defender David Miller before a 1993 FA Cup game,
    Derby 2 Stockport 1. The Rams winner came 90 seconds into injury
    time – an unstoppable headed own-goal by David Miller.*

'Nobody ever won a tackle with a smile on his face.'
    Former Derby midfielder Bruce Rioch in 1994, justifying a robust

approach to managing Bolton Wanderers. Rioch's tackling at Derby
in the mid-1970s was at best fearsome and at worst bordering on the
psychopathic.

'Footballers are only interested in drinking, clothes and the size of their willies.'
Karren Brady, Birmingham City managing director, 1994, prior to
wooing a future Ram.

'He is the nicest person I have ever met – warm, funny and good looking.'
On Paul Peschisolido in Brady Plays the Blues, *1995. Karren married*
the future Rams striker on 10 June 1995 – Paul's best man Barry Fry
almost became Derby's manager the very same month. Blessedly, Jim
Smith was appointed instead.

'I didn't get too many women running after me. It was their f*****g husbands who'd be after me.'
One of Derby's all-time heroes Charlie George recalling his often
controversial 1970s heyday in 1995.

'I wouldn't give up football even if I won the £18 million jackpot on the National Lottery. I love this job, and I would even pay to play.'
Bolton Wanderers striker Dean Holdsworth, 1995. Ten years later he
became assistant manager-player at cash-strapped Derby County –
needless to say, the forgetful Deano didn't forgo his salary.

'One of the all-time greats – someone to compare to Bobby Moore.'
Jack Charlton on Republic of Ireland defender Paul McGrath, 1995.
Although playing only 25 games for Derby in 1996–97, he was highly-
ranked in the Greatest 100 Rams Players chosen by Gerald Mortimer
in 2005.

'I play anywhere.'
A shocked Igor Stimac on joining Derby County in October 1995.
Manager Jim Smith had foolishly asked if the super-confident
Croatian international defender played better on the left, right or in
the centre.

'TIN MAN IS WIZARD OF AUS'
From Lancashire Evening News, *April 1996, after former Derby and*
Burnley winger Ted McMinn had joined the Sydney club Joondalup City.

'When I was with Norwich my wife Dawn had a baby and we called it Darby. A month later I joined Derby. The Norwich lads told me they were all trying for babies and were going to name them Lazio or Barcelona.'

Derby striker Ashley Ward, 1996, best remembered for scoring the Rams last ever first-team goal at the Baseball Ground – Derby 1 Arsenal 3 on Sunday 11 May 1997.

'He was, for me, the best player. No question. You had your Todds and Gemmills, Hennessey and O'Hare, Hector, the whole lot. But to me he was the best player, no question.'

Dave Mackay assesses his former Derby teammates, 2000. His highest praise was reserved for classy centre-back Roy McFarland.

'Hello there, I'm Kinky, can I come in?'

Cult Rams hero Giorgi Kinkladze to a burly doorman at the Victoria Inn, Derby, arriving as invited guest at a music gig, 2001.

'During the match he insulted me 150,000 times.'

Mild exaggeration from Chelsea defender Marcel Desailly after a spat with Fabrizio Ravanelli, Pride Park, 28 October 2001. Only the Derby player was cautioned by referee Steve Bennett – Ravanelli waited outside the Chelsea dressing room after the game to continue the argument!

'I started the shirt-lifting thing, and I'm still the best at it.'

Macho Italian Fabrizio Ravanelli still struggling with English colloquialisms a year into his time at Derby, 2002.

'A mundane first half saw Everton nose in front thanks to a stunning strike from David Unsworth, whose swerving shot beat the despairing dive of 'keeper Patriot Fellatio.'

News of the World report – Derby County 3 Everton 4 – 23 March 2002. A computer spell-check was blamed for the interesting corruption of the name of Derby's debutant Swiss goalkeeper Patrick Foletti.

'I don't mind Roy Keane making £60,000 a week. I was making the same when I was playing. The only difference is that I was printing my own.'

Derby's mercurial 1986 midfielder Mickey Thomas in 2002, cheerfully alluding to the 18-month prison sentence he received in 1993 for passing fraudulent currency.

'We were going to fly out for my stag night from East Midlands airport. Now they've changed its name to 'Nottingham' we've all cancelled. They're Derby's biggest rivals. It's unthinkable.'

Steve Elliott takes his local-boy image seriously, 2004. The Derby County central-defender was born and bred in the city.

'I'm still a West Ham fan deep down because I was brought up there.'

New Derby County assistant manager-player Dean Holdsworth adopts an unusual approach to winning over sceptical Rams fans, Radio Derby, 2005.

THE BOARDROOM

'Is the club worth continuing or is it not?'

Chairman William T. Morley at a crisis meeting in July 1907 when mounting debts threatened the very existence of Derby County. The club was saved by additional investment, but the crisis was one of many yet to come.

'Even I could manage this lot.'

Chairman Sam Longson after watching Dave Mackay's first game in charge as successor to Brian Clough – West Ham 0 Derby County 0 – 27 October 1973.

'The ideal board of directors should comprise three men – two dead and one dying.'

Tommy Docherty on leaving Manchester United after a well-publicised affair with Mary Brown, wife of the club's physio Laurie Brown, 1977. In September the same year a Derby board that was either brave or naïve, but definitely still breathing, appointed Docherty as Rams manager.

'Football hooligans? Well there are 92 club chairmen for a start.'

Brian Clough upsetting at least 92 people, 1980.

'I've never been so insulted by anyone in football as this little upstart puppy.'

Denis Hill-Wood, Arsenal chairman and staunch Old Etonian, responding to Clough's above jibe, 1980.

'When I was a director at Sheffield United for six months, the chairman told me normal business standards didn't apply in football. It was the most stupid advice I ever had.'

Mike Watterson after being appointed Derby chairman, November 1982. The millionaire former snooker professional and promoter lasted only eight months before declaring 'I am resigning because I cannot devote sufficient time to the club.' Like other chairmen since, he had drastically underestimated the size and nature of the task.

'ARABS BUY OUT DERBY'

One of a number of newspaper headlines which got it wrong as the troubled club sought a saviour, Derby Evening Telegraph, *28 January 1984.*

'IT'S HONG KONG BUT NOT WONG'

A Derby Trader *headline incorrectly states that the Rams have sold out to a Far East consortium, January 1984.*

'I went into the gents' toilet with the Inland Revenue solicitor and slipped him a bank draft for £250,000.'

Rams charismatic director Stuart Webb describing the last-second deal at the High Court on 12 April 1984, which saved Derby County from bankruptcy and almost certain oblivion. Never have two men met in lavatorial circumstances to such good effect.

'I have played football since I was a toddler. Left-wing, as you would expect. I was very fast.'

Oxford United chairman Robert Maxwell, 1985, establishing his 'man of the people' credentials on assuming control of Derby County.

'Robert Maxwell has just bought Brighton & Hove Albion, and he's furious to find out that it's only one club.'

Quip by Tommy Docherty at the expense of the Rams ever-acquisitive chairman, 1988.

'What I do with my money is my business. Haven't I already done enough for Derby? They were in the knacker's yard when I was invited to help them.'

Chairman Robert Maxwell on the sudden transfer freeze he imposed at Derby in 1990, from which relegation and many future difficulties ensued.

'Football in Britain could not be in a sorrier state. Sport is dying. The future lies in culture, spirituality and religion.'

Chairman Robert Maxwell airs further disenchantment, 1990. A year later football and Derby County were still alive, but Maxwell wasn't.

'Normal business principles don't apply in football.'

Rams chairman-owner Lionel Pickering, 1992, after investing almost £10 million of his personal publishing fortune in the ailing club within a year of taking the hot seat.

'For years I've been saying that football should be run by football people. Then along came Franny Lee at Manchester City. Oh well, back to the drawing board.'

Jimmy Greaves in his Sun *column, 1995, after the former Derby striker Francis Lee became City chairman in 1994, one of very few former players to fill such a role. It all ended in tears as Lee found the job much more difficult than he ever imagined.*

'My worst f*****g nightmare.'

Anguished utterance from Rams chief executive Keith Loring overheard in the Pride Park directors' box as a floodlight failure plunges the ground into darkness during the abandoned first ever League game there, 13 August 1997.

'There just aren't enough raving lunatics out there with cheque books.'

Belper-born Carlisle United chairman and former Rams youth player Michael Knighton on investing in a football club, 2000. Knighton had earlier revealed a soft-spot for Derby County – at a Christie's football memorabilia auction in Glasgow on 26 October 1994 he paid what proved to be a bargain £8,000 for 19 international and trial caps awarded to Rams striker Steve Bloomer.

'I just can't go on with this torment in my head. I don't want blaming simply for going about my job which I love so much. I am going to end it all.'

Sensational statement by John Sleightholme, who became Derby County chairman on 20 October 2003. Not quite what it seems, however – barrister Sleightholme was reading out a suicide note to court in his capacity as assistant coroner for North Yorkshire.

'Jeremy is a talented individual, but I do not think his talents lie in football.'
Derby's director of football Murdo Mackay talking publicly and out of turn about the club's chief executive Jeremy Keith, September 2005.

'I thought I'd go in there, turn it around, get it promoted and sell it for a fortune. But I've fallen in love with the train set.'
Chief executive Jeremy Keith reveals all in the Derby Evening Telegraph, *December 2005. The 'it' likened to a plaything was Derby County Football Club. Few statements in the Rams long history so angered sectors of the club's supporters.*

'The simple reason myself and my fellow directors haven't put money into Derby County is because it might cloud our judgement in making the right decisions.'
All for the good of the club – Derby chief executive Jeremy Keith, Radio Derby, December 2005.

'It is with deep regret that I resign from Derby County. My position has been made untenable.'
Another one bites the dust – chairman John Sleightholme, 13 April 2006. His fellow directors Jeremy Keith and Steve Harding soon followed him.

'And finally I would like to thank my wife Sharon...'
After a local consortium led by Peter Gadsby had assumed control of the club, Rams' managing director Mike Horton enjoys an Oscar moment in his stirring 'I've got my man' speech at the packed press conference to announce the arrival of new boss Billy Davies, 2 June 2006.

TWO – PEOPLE AND PLACES

————————————— WELL TRAVELLED —————————————

The phrase 'well-travelled' is something of a football cliché, but a number of personalities connected to Derby County suit it perfectly.

- ✪ In April 1986 **Jim Smith** became the first man to visit all 92 Football League grounds as a manager. He achieved the feat with Colchester United, Blackburn Rovers, Birmingham City, Oxford United and Queen's Park Rangers. When he joined Derby County in 1995, he really had seen it all.

- ✪ When people said Derby's prolific striker **Ray Straw** 'knew his way around the game,' they weren't exaggerating. Over a period of eight seasons from 1952–53 to 1959–60 he played in all six Divisions of the Football League. The epic journey began when he turned out for Derby County in the First, Second and Third Division North. It continued with Coventry City in the Third Division South followed by the newly-formed Fourth. Straw completed his work-experience programme when Coventry were promoted back to the re-consolidated Third Division in 1958–59.

- ✪ There was no blade of grass in the entire Football League that Derby's Welsh international **Alan Durban** hadn't covered. He was 22 when Tim Ward signed him for Derby County from Cardiff City in 1963, and he finished his playing days with Shrewsbury Town in 1978. It was not an exceptionally long career – which made it all the more remarkable that Durban played on all 92 Football League grounds.

- ✪ At the tender age of 19, **John McGovern** became the youngest player ever to turn out in all four Divisions of the Football League. The midfielder reached the milestone when he played for Derby at home to Burnley in the opening Division One fixture of 1969–70.

- ✪ When **Terry Curran** joined Derby from Nottingham Forest in 1977, it was his fourth League club in as many years. But the itinerant winger was merely warming up – by the time he retired as a Chesterfield player in 1988, Curran had appeared for 13 different League clubs.

✪ A change of name by deed poll in 1979 earned **Mick Derby** a reputation as the club's most committed fan. Not that his loyalty was ever in doubt – he has travelled to as many as 140 Derby County games in a season, taking in everything from junior matches to overseas friendlies. On one occasion in the early 1990s his ruling passion even cost him his job when he was sacked after returning late from an Anglo-Italian Cup away leg. Mick was subsequently re-instated but only after his employers set the date for his appeal to clash with another Anglo-Italian away trip.

———————————— DYNAMIC DUO ————————————

When Middlesbrough visited the Baseball Ground on 11 April 1959, they beat Derby County 3–0. The game was quickly forgotten, but years later it acquired a renewed curiosity. The Boro centre-forward that day scored two fine goals. The 'keeper did very little, but the men became great friends, and eight seasons later they returned to Derby to make a more permanent mark and claim their place in trivia books like this one. The razor-sharp front man was Clough, and the quiet man behind him was Taylor.

———————————— JUST ANOTHER DAY ————————————

The perfect illustration of the status of Derby County in the local community came on 21 July 1969 when Brian Clough suffered a setback in his bid to sign Hull City striker Ken Wagstaff. Elsewhere that day an American took the steps that re-wrote the history of mankind. The two major headlines in the next edition of the *Derby Evening Telegraph* were 'WALK ON MOON' and 'BLOW FOR RAMS – HULL KEEP WAGSTAFF'. Not a hint of irony was intended.

———————————— HONOURED GUESTS ————————————

Sheffield United were one of the first clubs to produce a substantial match programme. Their inaugural issue was for 1 September 1897 to mark a Football League game against highly-respected opponents from an adjacent county. Evidently not wishing to cast a shadow over the programme launch, Derby County contrived to lose the game by two goals to one.

Anyone lucky enough to own a copy of the rare publication is sitting on quite an investment – the original price was 'One Penny,' but programme dealers now estimate its conservative value at 'several thousand pounds'.

———————————— HIGH-FLYERS ————————————

West Bromwich Albion and Derby County hit new heights on 3 September 1900. The Rams were the visitors for a League game which marked the grand opening of Albion's brand new Hawthorns ground. The elevated status of the game arose from the curious fact that The Hawthorns is the highest Football League ground in England – at 551ft above sea level.

Derby failed to respect the lofty occasion – Steve Bloomer rudely scored the first ever goal at The Hawthorns to put the Rams ahead. Only an equalising strike from 'Chippy' Simmons saved Albion's historic day.

Albion's altitude record would be almost doubled at a stroke should the Derbyshire club Buxton ever attain League status. Teams visiting their Silverlands ground might benefit from oxygen masks – as the highest in the non-League pyramid, it stands at 1,000ft above sea level!

WELSH WIZARD

Few Derby County players have had prouder full international debuts than Lewin Nyatanga. On 1 March 2006 the Rams defender crowned a memorable St David's Day with a Man-of-the-Match performance in his first appearance for Wales in a 0–0 draw against Paraguay in Cardiff. It was also a proud moment for the Rams Academy staff who had developed the player – the centre-back became his country's youngest ever international at 17 years and 195 days. Even so, Nyatanga's reign as a record holder was short-lived – on 27 May 2006, in a friendly game against Trinidad and Tobago in Austria, Wales brought on the Southampton youngster Gareth Bale as a substitute...aged 16 years and 315 days...while old man Nyatanga also came on for his third cap.

SPARKLING ENCOUNTERS

Baseball Ground regulars saw Derby County in a whole new light on Monday 16 March 1953 when 15,585 were present for a friendly game which kicked-off at the then unfamiliar time of 7.30pm. The occasion was the official switch-on of the club's floodlights. Notts County provided the opposition, and the Rams won the game 3–0. A week later Derby returned the favour by playing in the first ever floodlit match at Meadow Lane.

After the big switch-on Derby went night match crazy. Doubtless encouraged by the fact that the home side were picking up the electricity bill, a procession of Scottish clubs visited the Baseball Ground for floodlit friendly games – East Fife, Partick Thistle, Hibernian, Stirling Albion and St Mirren all made the trip during the 1953–54 season.

In time the Baseball Ground floodlights became towering landmarks on the Derby skyline, but they finally bit the dust at 10.30am on Thursday 8 April 2004 when the final remnants of the Rams' long-standing home were demolished. Social historians suggested that with more foresight the famous old stadium might have been preserved as a heritage site. It was certainly a dark day for the club's most nostalgic supporters when the lights were lowered forever.

SIMPLY THE BEST

On 4 August 1998 a prestigious list of 100 League Legends was announced by the Football League in celebration of its centenary. No fewer than eight Derby County players were included in the illustrious 100.

JOHN GOODALL (1889–99)
STEVE BLOOMER (1892–1905 & 1910–13)
HUGHIE GALLACHER (1934–35)
RAICH CARTER (1945–48)
PETER DOHERTY (1945–46)
DAVE MACKAY (1968–71)
PETER SHILTON (1987–92)
PAUL McGRATH (1996)

Since five of the players failed to live long enough to see their names honoured, only the final trio could legitimately claim to have become legends in their own lifetime. It is only fair to point out that the list also included a number of players from Nottingham Forest – that number was three.

Five Rams players also figure in other lists regarded as particularly worthwhile, although only two were with Derby at the time of their inclusion. Nottingham Forest's Kenny Burns was voted the 1978 Football Writers' Player of the Year in the same season as his teammate Peter Shilton won the PFA equivalent, and Paul McGrath also won the PFA award in 1993 while an Aston Villa player. The two to lift that same title while with Derby were Dave Mackay – jointly with Manchester City's Tony Book in 1968–69 – and Colin Todd, who in 1974–75 won the coveted PFA Player of the Year award outright. The pair are the only Derby County players to be so honoured, and many observers consider Todd's near-faultless season to be the best individual showing in Rams' history, and possibly in the life of the award itself.

──────────── TURFED OFF THE PARK ────────────

Queen's Park Rangers introduced Derby County to a whole new field game on 20 February 1982. The Division Two fixture was played on Rangers' recently-laid 'Omniturf' – popularly dubbed a 'plastic pitch'. John Newman's Rams were beaten comprehensively by three goals to nil, and even Gerald Mortimer was moved to whimsy in his report: 'The Rams were simply brushed off the carpet.'

John Newman put matters in perspective: 'I'm not blaming the pitch. We can't win away on grass either.' The Derby line up tells a better story than a thousand words: Yakka Banovic, Brian Attley, Steve Buckley, Glenn Skivington, Frank Sheridan, John McAlle, Kevin Hector, Barry Powell,

John Clayton, Kevin Wilson, Paul Emson – possibly not the strongest side ever.

MEN IN BLACK

When Derby played Brighton at the Withdean Stadium on 26 November 2005, a minute's silence was observed in memory of George Best who had died the day before. Observers may have concluded that the Rams players were taking their mourning seriously as Derby wore all black for the occasion.

In fact, the club were shamelessly promoting the limited edition black strip which had been recently launched in the Pride Park shop. The money-spinning idea was dreamt up to commemorate an unusual incident which had occurred in the fixture at Brighton the season before.

On that occasion Derby were forced to adopt their all-black training kit when referee Fred Graham bizarrely decreed that both their first strip (white) and change strip (blue) clashed with Brighton's blue and white stripes. The shirts were rushed into town to be numbered, but because someone forgot the squad list this was completed in the 1–11 style redolent of the old days.

Derby won that game 3–2 and (according to the club!) the strip acquired cult status. But its second outing at Brighton was entirely in keeping with the funereal garb – after a sombre 0–0 draw Derby stood 17th in the Championship table.

DOUBLE TROUBLE

Many Derby County players have struggled to cope with one referee, but when Jack Barker and Sammy Crooks were selected to play for the Football League against West Bromwich Albion at The Hawthorns on 8 May 1935 their task was doubly hard. The unusual match was a celebration of the Jubilee of King George V, and the Football League decided to use the game to test a system of two referees and no linesmen. One of the whistlers certainly had the intellect to grasp the concept – Derby man Dr Arthur Willoughby Barton, Head of Physics at Repton School – but the experiment was formally abandoned by the Football League the following month because it had proved 'unworkable'. At least the twin 'men in black' kept the game flowing – it finished Football League 9 West Bromwich Albion 6.

MILE HIGH CLUB

On 13 July 1999 the entire Derby County squad joined the 'Mile High Club' – but this had nothing to do with amorous antics in an aircraft. The Rams played a transatlantic friendly against the United States national side in Denver's 'Mile High Stadium' – so named because it stands at exactly 5,280ft above sea level. The unusual fixture was an acclimatisation exercise for the USA side ahead of their Confederations Cup games in Guadalajara, Mexico, which stands at 5,000ft above sea level. Few English club sides ever get the chance to take a national scalp, and the Rams came close. Dean Sturridge put them ahead and twice they hit the bar, but the USA emerged eventual winners by two goals to one.

NATIONAL MANAGERS

A number of Rams men have managed a national side, although not always the most expected one. Here are some who could say that they once led a nation.

✪ **Arthur Latham** joined Derby County in 1886 and later became trainer to both the Rams and England. On 11 February 1911 he was made honorary 'manager for the day' when Derby's Baseball Ground hosted the game between England and Ireland. Latham's fleeting tenure in the days before England had a formal manager proved very satisfactory – his side won 2–1.

✪ **Ted Magner**, Derby manager from 1944–46, holds a unique place in Danish football. He was appointed national team manager for two games in June 1939, steering Denmark to a 5–0 win over Finland and a 6–3 victory against Norway, both in Copenhagen. Of the 22 men to manage Denmark up to 2006, Ted Magner is the only one to boast a 100 percent record!

✪ **Peter Doherty** is the longest serving national manager connected to Derby County. The 1940s inside-forward was in charge of Northern Ireland from October 1951 to February 1962 – his finest achievement was taking them to the quarter-finals of the 1958 World Cup in Sweden.

✪ The wealthy Arab state of Qatar is still finding its football feet, but Derby's charismatic forward **Frank Wignall** (1968–71) helped them in their early days – he was appointed national coach in October 1974.

✪ **Tommy Docherty**, Derby County manager from 1977–79, was in charge of Scotland from September 1971 to December 1972. His record – played 10, won 5, drew 3 and lost 2 – makes him a 'better' manager than Alex Ferguson, Jock Stein, Craig Brown and Willie Ormond, all of whose win ratios while in charge of Scotland were worse than the mighty Doc's.

⊕ **Frank Upton** (272 games for Derby in the 50s and 60s) became an intrepid globetrotter after his playing days. In May 1989 he became national coach to Borneo but lasted only nine months before taking charge of Burton Albion. But he soon left the brewery town and in January 1994 again went in search of exotic climes, spending 17 months as national coach of India.

⊕ **Colin Murphy**'s brief spell as Derby County manager (November 1976 to September 1977) was an unhappy one, but in far-flung parts he achieved more success. In 1997 Murphy led Vietnam to the bronze-medal position in the South-East Asian Games, and two years later he was in charge of Myanmar (formerly Burma) – although he won no silverware there he is still remembered in that remote outpost as 'the eccentric Englishman'.

⊕ On Thursday 4 May 2006 Derby County were able to bask in reflected glory when their former midfielder and one-time assistant manager **Steve McClaren** became the only Rams man to land the ultimate job in football – after a protracted recruitment procedure the then Middlesbrough boss was appointed full-time England manager as replacement for the departing Sven-Goran Eriksson.

MANAGING ABROAD

A number of men linked to Derby County have managed club sides overseas. Here are some of the most notable.

⊕ Inside-forward **Jimmy Hagan** played 31 games for Derby County before they unwisely let him go to Sheffield United in November 1938. But 34 years later, on 25 October 1972, he returned to the Baseball Ground as manager of the Portuguese giants Benfica for a European Cup game famously won 3–0 by the Rams. Hagan also managed Sporting Lisbon and Oporto and remains the most revered overseas manager connected to Derby County – in each of his three seasons at Benfica they won the Portuguese Championship, a record all the more remarkable considering how he joined them. When he was appointed in March 1970, he had already 'left football' and taken a job as a driving instructor.

⊕ Legendary 1960s and 1970s winger **Alan Hinton** later became equally admired as a manager across the Atlantic. In the North American Soccer League he was in charge at Tulsa Roughnecks (1979), Seattle Sounders

(1980–82) and Vancouver Whitecaps (1984) and later managed Tacoma Stars in the Indoor Soccer League and then Seattle again. Hinton was Coach of the Year in 1980 and 1994 (both with Seattle), and when he won the Championship for Seattle in 1980 he shrewdly included three former Rams players in his side. Bruce Rioch and David Nish both performed steadily, but the real star was the winner of the League's Most Valuable Player award – who was the man who scored 27 goals in 34 games? Ex-Derby striker Roger Davies.

⊕ **Dave Mackay**, a giant at Derby County as both player and manager, had one of the longest overseas exiles of anyone connected to the club. He left his post as Walsall manager in May 1978 to take over at the Kuwaiti side Al-Arabi Sporting Club, where he remained for nine years. From there, in 1986, he moved to the Dubai side Alba Shabab, and after spells at Doncaster and Birmingham he moved to Egypt to manage the Cairo side Zamalek before ending his globetrotting with three years in Qatar running the national Youth team. All in all, Mackay's Arabian travels lasted 16 years.

⊕ Few Englishmen have managed more overseas sides than Derby County's **Colin Addison** (manager 1979–82). He began in South Africa at Durban City (1975) and continued with El Ali in Qatar (1985–86). His first Spanish sojourn took in Celta Vigo (1986–87), Atletico Madrid (1988–89) and Cadiz (1989–90). That was followed by a move to the Kuwaiti side Al-Arabi (1992–93) before a return to Spain saw him manage Cadiz for a second time (1993–94) followed by a stint at Club Deportivo Badajoz (1995–96). By 2006 Addison had managed 20 clubs at home and abroad...and still rising!

CROWD HIGHS AND LOWS

⊕ The most spectators to watch Derby County in any match is the 120,000 for the second round of the European Cup game (second leg) against Real Madrid in the Santiago Bernabeu Stadium on 5 November 1975. On the night it was the Spanish fans letting off the fireworks – Derby contrived to squander a 4–1 first-leg lead, losing 5–1 and crashing out of the tournament 6–5 on aggregate.

⊕ The highest crowd to watch Derby County in this country is 98,215 at Wembley for the FA Cup Final against Charlton Athletic on 27 April

1946. That remains the greatest number of people ever to witness a Rams victory – Derby lifted the Cup after a 4–1 win.

✪ Aside from the 1946 Cup Final, the biggest domestic crowd for a Derby County game was that year's semi-final replay against Birmingham City at Maine Road, Manchester. Derby won 4–0 after extra-time and the 80,407 attendance remains a record for a midweek game between two Football League clubs outside an FA Cup Final.

✪ Written attendance figures suggest that the lowest crowd for a competitive Rams match is 500. It was recorded twice – for the 1–1 draw at Glossop on 5 September 1914 and at the Baseball Ground on 22 April 1903. On that occasion the loyal 500 saw a 2–2 draw with Grimsby Town in the final home game of the season, which seemed odd considering the previous home game had attracted 10,000. But there was a ready explanation for the huge fall off, since in between Derby had been humbled 6–0 by Bury in the FA Cup Final – no wonder the fed up supporters voted with their feet. Not far behind was an Anglo-Italian Cup game in December 1992 when only 598 saw Derby win 3–0 at Reggiana – and quite a few of those were Rams fans!

✪ When Derby Boys played the second leg of their 1949 English Schools' Shield semi-final, a remarkable Baseball Ground crowd of 22,000 saw them knocked out on aggregate by their under-15 counterparts from Barnsley.

✪ Several ground attendance records still stand for games in which Derby County were visitors. Three occurred in sixth-round FA Cup ties – 2 March 1946 v Aston Villa at Villa Park (76,588), 8 March 1933 v Sunderland at Roker Park (75,118) and 26 February 1949 v Portsmouth at Fratton Park (51,385). The others were also Cup games – the League Cup fourth-round tie on 15 November 1967 v Lincoln City at Sincil Bank (23,196) and the FA Cup fifth-round tie on 20 February 1937 v Millwall at The Den (48,672).

✪ In March 1973 a crowd of 1,500 Czechs watched Derby County at Spartak Trnava. What might seem a disappointing attendance for a UEFA Cup game was nothing of the sort – the awe-struck locals had turned out to watch the Rams in a training session.

✪ On Sunday 9 May 1993 the Baseball Ground played host to the oldest aggregate crowd in its history when 12,000 mostly senior citizens from all over the county gathered for a parade and concert to celebrate the 50th anniversary of the legendary Dambusters' raid on German reservoirs. As 76-year-old songstress Vera Lynn delivered all the old favourite melodies, the famous stands had never been so alive with movement (largely due to the unprecedented level of 'comfort breaks'), and all present agreed it was a day they would never forget. That said, there were chaotic scenes at the concert's close when many of the happy throng disgorged into the streets unable to remember where their coaches were parked.

☻ Unusual circumstances on Monday 1 May 2006 saw a record attendance established at Pride Park. A crowd of 33,475, boosted by around 12,000 from Scotland, saw Derby Legends draw 3–3 with Rangers Legends in a benefit match for **Ted McMinn**, a former player at both clubs who had recently undergone the amputation of his right leg just below the knee. The record was even more remarkable because only the day before a crowd of 30,391 had watched Derby's home League game against Sheffield Wednesday. So Pride Park had hosted 63,866 spectators in successive days, a rare record which seems likely to remain intact for all time.

CAP THAT

☻ Surely only Scotland could drop a man who scores a goal for his country every 22.5 minutes, but it happened to the Rams forward **Sandy Higgins**. In March 1885 when at Kilmarnock he was given his Scotland debut and scored four times in an 8–2 thrashing of Ireland...but there his international career ended!

☻ **Steve Bloomer** scored on each of his first 10 England appearances, netting 19 goals in the process. In 23 internationals from 1895–1907 the Rams striker scored 28 goals, equivalent to one every 73 minutes. No English professional has bettered that rate, and if the fixture list had been as full then as it is now Bloomer would top the all-time England international scoring charts by a mile.

☻ A curious landmark was attained on 4 March 1899 when the Rams defender **Archie Goodall** made his international debut for Ireland against Wales. Although it was Ireland's 51st international it was the first time they had included a player from an English Football League club.

☻ Derby stalwart **Jimmy Methven** never played in a full international but was so proud of his Scottish representative cap that he wore it during his last home game as a player, the 1–0 win against Middlesbrough on 6 October 1906.

⊙ The highest number of Derby players taking part in an international match while actually with the Rams is four. The record was set on 24 May 1972 at Hampden Park when **John O'Hare** and **Archie Gemmill** played for Scotland in their 1–0 win over a Wales side including **Alan Durban** and **Terry Hennessey**. The record was matched on 11 May 1974 in England's 2–0 win over Wales at Ninian Park when **Roy McFarland, David Nish** and **Colin Todd** played for England and **Rod Thomas** for Wales. The hat-trick was completed at Hampden Park on 15 May 1976 – **Bruce Rioch** and **Archie Gemmill** helped Scotland to a 2–1 victory over an England side including **Roy McFarland** and **Colin Todd**.

⊙ A great international future was predicted for **Steve Powell** when in June 1973 he captained England to victory in the International Youth Tournament in Italy. Sure enough, the Rams prodigy looked set for a full call-up just a year later when the new England manager Don Revie called together his first squad of 'possibles' in a Manchester Hotel. But Powell's hopes were soon dashed – on arrival he discovered Revie's 'squad' contained a ludicrous 85 players – Powell failed to make the cut and never did win that coveted England cap.

⊙ The most talent-filled contest involving Derby County was their home game with Liverpool on 11 September 1976. The Rams had nine capped players in their side – **David Nish, Roy McFarland, Colin Todd, Charlie George** and **Kevin Hector** for England; **Bruce Rioch** and **Archie Gemmill** for Scotland; **Rod Thomas** and **Leighton James** for Wales. Only one Liverpool player was uncapped, making 19 of the 22 players on show internationals. Liverpool emerged 3–2 victors and went on to win the League Championship.

⊙ In 1977–78 Derby fielded a club-record 16 capped players during the season – **Roy McFarland, David Nish, Colin Todd, Kevin Hector, Charlie George, Jeff Blockley** and **Gordon Hill** for England; **Archie Gemmill, Bruce Rioch** and **Don Masson** for Scotland; **Rod Thomas** and **Leighton James** for Wales; **David Langan, Gerry Daly, Tony Macken** and **Gerry Ryan** for the Republic of Ireland. The manager for most of that season was also an international – **Tommy Docherty** of Scotland – but he was unable to mould his multi-capped men into a winning outfit. Derby finished an average 12th in Division One.

✣ No Derby County player has won more international caps than goalkeeper **Peter Shilton**, who played 125 times for England. For many years Shilton also held the record for winning the most international caps while at Derby (34), but this was eventually beaten by striker **Deon Burton**, who played 42 games for Jamaica while with the Rams from 1997–2002.

BALLS

✣ When Derby played Preston North End at the County Ground on 29 September 1888, they tried out an experimental ball which was bonded together in two halves. But the novel orb lasted only a few minutes before a huge punt by the Preston defender Jimmy Ross saw it split clean in two. Preston went on to win 3–2 using a conventional sphere, and the 'ball of two halves' became nothing but a Victorian novelty which had failed to hit the mark.

✣ Derby County might well wish to draw a veil over the 1899 FA Cup Final, but their opponents Sheffield United won't let it lie. The Blades triumphed 4–1 after hot-favourites Derby had led 1–0 at half-time, and the ball from the game now takes pride of place in the Hall of Fame at Bramall Lane. Nor can the 1903 Cup Final be conveniently 'buried' – the ball from that is on permanent display at the National Football Museum in Preston and, much to the amusement of thousands of visitors, is inscribed with the record score – 'Bury 6 Derby County 0.' Will they never let us forget?

✣ **Frank Sugg**, centre-forward in the Rams' first ever season, was still calling 'my ball' years after he had finished playing. In the 1890s the Ilkeston-born all-round sportsman set up his own sports equipment company and the patent 'Sugg's Football King' ball was used in many FA Cup Finals and international matches. Sugg died in Liverpool in 1933, but the firm lived on until it finally ceased trading in 2002.

✣ It was weak bladders all round just after the war. Derby's 4–1 extra-time win against Charlton Athletic in the 1946 Cup Final might have been clinched in normal time had the ball not burst as Jack Stamps shot from close range moments before the end. Strangely, the two teams again suffered a burst four days later when Charlton visited the Baseball Ground for a Football League South game, and an uncanny treble was completed when exactly the same thing happened during Charlton's 1–0 win over Burnley in the 1947 Cup Final. Before that game, the 1946 Final referee had been asked about the chances of another burst – his reply of 'a million to one' was a bad call, for wartime material shortages had led to the manufacture of inferior quality balls, which actually went pop quite often. Even so, few hat-tricks have been stranger.

⊕ Welsh international **Alan Durban** scored four hat-tricks as a Derby player but failed to appreciate the feat being performed by others. On 2 September 1985 Reading's Trevor Senior netted three times against Cardiff at Ninian Park, but City manager Durban refused to give him the traditional gift of the match ball. 'We need the money,' said the stingy Welshman – 'he can have it for £40'. In January 1993 the same fate befell Derby's Welsh international midfielder **Mark Pembridge**, who was denied the ball after scoring an away hat-trick for the Rams in a 5–1 FA Cup victory against his former club Luton Town.

⊕ An unusual post-match ball presentation took place after Derby's away game against Benfica in November 1972. Yorkshireman Ernie Clay, manager of the Hotel Miramonte where Derby were staying, lent strength to the Rams European Cup quest by laying on a half-time surprise of a commodity rare in Portugal – an urn of steaming-hot tea. The refreshed players held out for a famous 0–0 draw, and Mr Clay's wife Marie was presented with the autographed matchball by Derby's grateful assistant manager Peter Taylor, who added a typical aside – 'even my missus can't make tea like that'.

── INFLUENTIAL PLAYER ──

It's often said that great players can directly influence the result of a game. This was particularly true of Derby's 1940s inside-forward Raich Carter, who was still dictating the outcome of matches when well into his 60s. Nor did he need boots to swing a game his way – in the early 1970s the former England international was a respected member of the Football League Pools Panel!

PENALTIES!

⊕ Rams defender **Jack Nicholas** suffered a costly double aberration in the 1909 FA Cup semi-final when he conceded a penalty against Bristol City in both the first match and the replay as Derby were beaten 2–1 just a step short of possible glory. To his eternal credit, Nicholas manfully redeemed himself a year later by fathering his son Jack junior, who in 1946 became the only Derby captain to hold aloft the FA Cup.

✪ The penalty offence that many Rams fans consider the most irresponsible of all time was committed by **Bobby Saxton** in the home leg of Derby's 1967–68 League Cup semi-final clash against Leeds United. Under no pressure, the Rams centre-half lept basketball-style to palm away the ball, and the resulting penalty condemned Derby to a 1–0 first-leg defeat from which they failed to recover. They lost 4–2 on aggregate and the hapless Saxton is remembered for little else but that one moment. Clough never picked Saxton again and soon transferred him to Plymouth Argyle.

✪ In 1974 Derby signed a striker dubbed the 'Penalty King' – but **Francis Lee** failed to score a single League spot-kick while with the Rams because Derby's regular penalty takers were **Bruce Rioch** and **Charlie George**. It was a far cry from Lee's days with Manchester City – in 1971–72 he scored 13 League penalties in a season, which remains a record. Although many critics attributed the feat to Lee's 'diving' ability, only two of the penalties were awarded for fouls on himself.

✪ On 6 November 1974 Derby suffered a brand new form of agony when the second leg of their UEFA Cup game away to Atletico Madrid ended 2–2. That made the score 4–4 on aggregate, and Derby were subjected to the ordeal of a penalty shoot-out for the first time in their history. Rams fans listening on the radio had their nerves torn to shreds before **Colin Boulton** saved the 16th kick to put Derby through by seven penalties to six.

✪ The Baseball Ground witnessed its first penalty shoot-out on 3 September 1980 in a League Cup tie against Queen's Park Rangers. After two 0–0 draws and extra-time the Rams were beaten 5–3 when **Barry Powell** missed Derby's opening spot-kick and Rangers made sure with all of theirs.

✪ Should any youngsters from Mickleover Lightning Blue Sox or Chellaston Boys become Derby County players, they will arrive with a peculiar shoot-out pedigree. In an under-10 Community Cup game in December 1998 the sides set an all time record of 66 spot-kicks before the contest was resolved. Many efforts barely reached the goal and only three were con-verted as the farcical marathon ended at a nail-biting 2–1!

REFEREE!

☉ Countless Derby County players have fancied themselves as referees, but one actually achieved the position for real. In November 1899, when an FA touring team whitewashed Germany in a series of four away games, the Rams wing-half **Jack Cox** took part in three and took charge in the other!

☉ 'Play to the whistle' is an adage which sometimes backfires. In a League Cup tie against Aston Villa on 29 October 1986 Derby players stopped as they heard a piercing blast. Villa's Tony Daley went on to score, and the goal stood – the whistle had come from the Baseball Ground crowd. It cost the Rams dearly as the game finished 1–1 and they lost the Villa Park replay 2–1.

☉ Most players feel momentarily aggrieved if they have a goal disallowed, but **David Nish** is still moaning 30 years after the event. When Derby played Manchester United at Hillsborough in the semi-final of the 1976 FA Cup, the Rams classy full-back worked out the perfect way to beat the United offside trap. At 1–0 down Nish chipped the ball over the advancing defence and ran on to his own 'pass' to score what would have been Derby's equaliser – but stubborn referee Jack Taylor disallowed the goal because retreating Derby forwards well away from the action were deemed offside. United scored a cruelly-deflected second, and Derby's 2–0 defeat remains one from which the club never truly recovered – many supporters still regard the referee's decision as the most controversial in Derby's history.

TALES OF THE UNEXPECTED

☉ In 1895 Derby County's new home the Baseball Ground was visited by a celebrated gypsy curse, but in the same year the ground they were leaving was visited by a celebrated gypsy. On 9 March 1895, when England played Ireland at the County Ground in a Home International Championship game, the debutant Robert 'Rabbi' Howell became the only full-blooded Romany gypsy to play for England. The Sheffield United right-half, who was born in a caravan, certainly didn't curse the side – Howell nabbed a goal and another debutant, Derby's **Steve Bloomer**, bagged two. The Rams and England captain **John Goodall** also scored a brace as the home nation ran out 9–0 winners in the only full international staged at the County Ground.

✪ The third-round FA Cup replay between Derby and Blackpool on 19 January 1977 produced a fantasy result for Rams fan John McGuiness. He had dreamt that Derby would win the game 3–2, and so clear was the premonition that he visited a Chaddesden bookmaker to place a whacking £70 bet on the outcome. Icy weather put the match in doubt, but the club hired heaters, laid 10,000 sacks on the Baseball Ground pitch and employed an army of volunteers to clear the ground for the game to go ahead. Goals from **Derek Hales**, **Leighton James** and **Charlie George** earned the Rams a famous 3–2 victory and a delighted McGuiness collected £2,304.60 from the stunned bookie.

✪ In August 1975 an anonymous fortune teller known only as 'Ivy of Ilkeston' caused a sensation when she made several football predictions that astonishingly came true. Included on her list was Derby to win the 1976 FA Cup, and several players believed so strongly in the mystery soothsayer that they had substantial bets to that effect. Ivy said the Rams would knock out a team beginning with 'L', and when Liverpool fell 1–0 at the Baseball Ground in January 1976 things began to look spooky. When Derby reached the semi-finals against Manchester United, press coverage of Ivy reached fever pitch. But alas the Derbyshire mystic was exposed as nothing more than a lucky-guessing housewife when the Rams were beaten 2–0. Although quickly dubbed 'Poison Ivy,' she contrived various reasons and made a new prediction that Derby would be relegated the next season. When they weren't she went completely to ground...the only truly predictable thing in the entire strange saga.

✪ When **Arthur Cox**'s Derby County won only three of their first 12 home League games of 1992–93 a clairvoyant named Aveline Lee stepped in to lift the gypsy curse she believed still plagued the Rams. After the mysterious and exotic Romany (from Skegness) had burnt a scroll, chanted a strange incantation and buried herbs around the Baseball Ground for the benefit of TV cameras, she promised that Derby's home game against Peterborough on 6 February 1993 would end in victory. It did...to Peterborough, who won 3–2 after Derby had led 2–0 in 18 minutes. After the game, 'COX OUT' placards were stuck on board members' cars, and the vehicle of associate director Peter Gadsby was trashed and had to be towed away. All a far cry from April 2006 when

Gadsby was fêted as a hero on becoming chairman of the club – maybe Aveline Lee's good luck spell worked after all.

⚽ In a city dubbed the 'Ghost Capital of England' it had to happen sooner or later. Very early one Sunday morning in September 2005 two late-night revellers returning home claimed to have spotted the spectral form of **Steve Bloomer** shimmying his way around Pride Park. It is worth noting that Derby is also renowned for a pub and club scene dispensing an endless supply of mind-bending alcoholic beverages...especially on a Saturday night.

GRASSED OFF

⚽ At the end of the 1974–75 Championship season Derby County decided to replace the notorious Baseball Ground quagmire with a brand new pitch and at the same time proved that clever marketing can achieve anything. It wasn't a case of 'coals to Newcastle' or even 'fridges to Eskimos' but something more ingenious still. The Baseball Ground centre circle was dug up and 10,000 pieces of the famous turf were reserved to be encapsulated and mounted on commemorative certificates made available to Rams fans – countless of the faithful paid the going rate and many have hung on to their precious prize ever since...a glorious brown piece of authentic Derby mud.

⚽ The re-seeded Baseball Ground was an oasis of fresh green grass as the 1975–76 season kicked-off, but only a season later there were 'leaves on the line' style excuses as the once sodden pitch resembled an arid desert. The embarrassed contractors Chipman Ltd. confessed to having sown 'the wrong type of grass,' and in April 1977 a spokesman issued a classic statement: 'Unfortunately the roots grew sideways rather than down so the grass became a shallow covering instead of real turf and the players' boots just rubbed it off – literally the grass evaporated. During the drought we were only allowed to water the surface rather than use deep irrigation so the grass, being intelligent, reacted by growing sideways...we really needed a more resilient strain.' In the face of 'evaporating grass,' Rams supporters were once again heard to mutter that 'it could only happen at Derby County.'

⚽ On 21 February 1996 **Darryl Powell** scored for Derby as they drew 1–1 with Luton Town at the Baseball Ground. The match was unremarkable, but it proved to be one of the most historic days in the life of Derby County as before the game the club's chief executive Keith Loring announced that, for the start of the 1997–98 campaign, the Rams would be installed in a new 30,000–seater state-of-the-art stadium. As the construction progressed, 75,000 visitors went to the site and were shown actual photographs of what the ground would look like when completed – in reality pictures of its clone, Middlesbrough's Riverside Stadium, with the red seats digitally changed to black and white.

✪ In 1997–98 Derby County began their first season at Pride Park with a pitch that at last stood up to scrutiny. The club's head groundsman won awards for his husbandry of the turf, but not without sheer hard work. It is a seven-and-a-half-mile trip to mow the grass one way, while cutting it both ways plus marking out the lines is equivalent to a 19-mile journey. The pitch is five yards longer and four yards wider than that at the Baseball Ground, and to guard against cold-weather cancellations there are 26 miles of undersoil heating. As for the state-of-the-art floodlight system…well, that's another story.

STRANGE COMINGS AND GOINGS

✪ Most men would jump at the chance to sign for Derby County, but not **Bill Roberts**. When he played for the Rams in 1890–91 the club asked him to sign on permanently. But the 'transfer' never took place – Roberts was a drummer in the Sherwood Foresters regiment and steadfastly refused to be bought out of the Army.

✪ No player has dictated more cheeky terms than **Jack Atkin**. When Jimmy Methven signed him for Derby in 1907, the full-back said he wouldn't play unless his brother Harry was signed too. Methven knew Harry had no chance of making the first team but shrewdly agreed to the request, and the brothers shared the 15 shillings per week wages. Atkin also wangled another odd perk – in 15 years with the Rams he was excused from all formal training. Instead Atkin pursued a rigorous personal fitness regime which worked a treat – he made 325 appearances for his one and only League club.

✪ When trainee teacher **Alick Grant** signed for the Rams he only thought of the money. But Grant's demands were unusual – when he left the club in 1948 his wages were just 3d (1.25p) a week, the nominal sum requested by Grant so that he could remain eligible for a full government family allowance while continuing his teacher-training. The conscientious but canny goalkeeper is believed to be the lowest-paid professional footballer of all time.

✪ Although no fee was involved, no transfer deal ever stunk so much as the one that bought **Angus Morrison** to Derby. When he signed for the club in 1944, he was in the RAF, and the scout who gave the Rams the first whiff of his talent received a discreetly-wrapped package for his recommendation – a box of cigars.

✪ Force of habit seemed to rule the Rams manager Harry Storer when in 1955 he signed **Martin McDonnell** for the third time. Storer had previously taken the centre-half to Birmingham and Coventry, and his ongoing faith in the player was rewarded as the ever-reliable McDonnell clocked up 99 appearances in three seasons with the Rams.

✪ No signing can have been more prudent than that of **Gordon Brown**. When he joined the cash-strapped Rams from Scunthorpe in 1957 the club paid not a single penny since the entire £5,150 transfer fee was generously donated by the Supporters' Association. In the circumstances, Brown might easily have tested the fans' patience, but he fully proved his worth by scoring nine goals in 17 games as Derby clinched promotion from Division Three North.

✪ When young **Andy Crawford** made his Derby debut, sharp-eyed critics said the striker would go far. They were right – in May 1979 the club arranged for him to go out on loan to gain further experience...at Manawatu in New Zealand.

✪ Before Derby's home game with Manchester City in April 1980 the Rams on-loan striker **Dave Swindlehurst** signed for the club on the Baseball Ground pitch for a then record fee of £410,000. But even that wasn't the club's most unusual transfer ceremony – when Jack Howe joined Derby from Hartlepools United in 1936 the England full-back signed the forms on Lincoln railway station.

✪ A fortuitous ticket allocation oiled the wheels for one of Derby's best managerial signings. **Jim Smith** was languishing as chief executive of the Football League Managers' Association when on 3 June 1995 he travelled to Wembley and saw England beat Japan 2–1. More importantly, he spent much of the game chatting to the erstwhile 'stranger' seated next to him, the Derby director Stuart Webb. A few meetings later Smith received a phone call from his friendly Wembley neighbour offering him the manager's job at Derby.

✪ Derby County signings have been labelled daft, disastrous or merely unwise, but that of **Esteban Fuertes** surpasses the lot. After a lengthy wait for international clearance, the Argentinian with an 'Italian passport' joined the Rams for £2.3 million in August 1999 – he played 10 times, scored only twice and was sent off once before leaving the club in bizarre circumstances. As the Rams returned from a mid-season break in Portugal in November 1999, the player was refused re-entry at Heathrow Airport because his EU passport was exposed as a forgery. Barred from playing in the UK, he returned to Argentina and was quickly labelled the most unwise signing in Derby's history.

✪ When the Norwegian international **Björn Otto Bragstad** arrived at Derby in July 2000 it soon became apparent that the club had been 'sold a pup'. The Rams farmed him out on loan to Birmingham City, but Bragstad's nightmare form continued and the Birmingham fans booed him off the park. Football's most unwanted gift was dispatched back to Derby marked 'return to sender'.

IT'S OFF

✪ Although the County Ground was said to possess 'the finest patch of turf in English football,' the Rams first home was so exposed to the elements that a game against Liverpool in the 1890s was abandoned solely on account of a gale-force wind.

✪ For a club formed as an off-shoot of a cricket club, the outcome of Derby's first-round FA Cup replay at Chesterfield in January 1906 seemed quite appropriate – in front of a then record Saltergate crowd of 14,000 Derby led 2–1 seven minutes from the end of extra-time when the under-pressure referee abandoned the game with the dramatic proclamation 'bad light stopped play'.

✪ On 8 May 1963, while with Spurs, the future Rams legend **Dave Mackay** captained Scotland in a 'friendly' against Austria. The Hampden Park crowd of 94,596 watched open-mouthed as the

Austrians cut up rough and had two men dismissed and one carried off. The eight remaining battlers were only counted out when the English referee Jim Finney abandoned the game 11 minutes from time with Scotland leading 4–1.

✤ During the 'big freeze' of 1962–63 football fans in England and Scotland gave up checking to see if matches were off and instead were pleasantly surprised if a game was on. After 22 December 1962 Derby didn't play another League match until 23 February 1963 when the thaw finally came. The nine week lay-off caused a major fixture pile-up in what was a relegation-threatened campaign for the Rams, but their skipper **Jack Parry** led by magnificent example – he played 20 games in 12 weeks as Derby survived by five points.

✤ The Rams full-back **Mark Patterson** had every reason to forget the FA Cup replay against Burnley in January 1992, but he still goes on about it today. Patterson hit a screaming shot from outside the Osmaston End box to score what is considered to be one of the best ever goals seen at the Baseball Ground – or not seen as the case may be. It was scored as thick fog descended on the ground, and the game was later abandoned with Derby 2–0 up. To compound Patterson's woeful night, he finished it needing an operation on damaged knee ligaments.

✤ New Year's Day 1997 was freezing cold but much hard work had gone into the preparation of the notorious Baseball Ground pitch and it was perfectly playable. Derby fans looked forward to the traditional year-opener, and their Premiership counterparts from Sheffield Wednesday were up for it too, as were both sets of players and their managers. But somewhere giant hangovers must have been being nursed, for one key group didn't fancy working that day – only a few hours before kick-off the game was called off at the behest of the police for 'safety reasons'......icy pavements!

✤ There are seldom shockwaves when a reserve game is called off, but when Derby's match against Ipswich Town was cancelled in November 2005 there were certainly some raised eyebrows – out of the blue the Rams had announced they were disbanding their second string forthwith and pulling out of all their remaining reserve-team fixtures. Instead their squad players would play friendly games behind closed doors.

―――――――――――――――BLOOMER'S BEST―――――――――――――――

Steve Bloomer was 57 when he played his last game of football. On 31 September 1931 he captained Belper British Legion in a charity match against Herbert Strutt School. His side were defeated 4–3, but Bloomer scored from a penalty. At an after-match dinner the Rams striker named his 'best-ever' side and the clubs with which he considered the players reached their peak. The 'Bloomer's Best XI' was Jack Robinson (Derby), Howard Spencer (Aston Villa), Billy Williams (West Bromwich Albion), Ben Warren (Derby), Alex Raisbeck (Liverpool), Ernest Needham (Sheffield United), Billy Meredith (Manchester City), Bobby Walker (Hearts), G.O. Smith (Corinthians), Joe Bache (Aston Villa) and Fred Spiksley (Sheffield Wednesday). Although few dared to openly question the great man's judgement, eyebrows were certainly raised at the curious omission of Bloomer's early mentor at Derby, the England international John Goodall.

WORLD CUP WOES AND WONDERS

Most players regard an appearance in the final stages of the World Cup as the ultimate career achievement – relatively few with Derby County connections actually made it and none have appeared in the World Cup Final itself, but here are some who tasted the action – plus a few who narrowly missed out.

☺ **Switzerland '54** saw the future Rams manager Tommy Docherty forge the club's first World Cup link when the Preston wing-half played in both Scotland's games. He had a hot time of it as they lost both, failed to score, and were 'back before the postcards'. Docherty explained the debacle in inimitable fashion – 'It was the thick shirts. We thought Switzerland would be cold because it had mountains, but it was 100 degrees. Against Uruguay we melted away and their short sleeves were the deciding factor – honestly that's the only reason we lost 7–0.'

☺ **Sweden '58** saw two Rams players, one former and one future, representing Scotland. Neither Stewart Imlach (Nottingham Forest) nor Dave Mackay (Hearts) could prevent a familiar pattern developing – once again Scotland failed to win a game. Northern Ireland made their World Cup Finals debut under the management of former Rams legend Peter Doherty, his team creating quite a surprise by reaching the quarter-finals.

☺ **Chile '62** and **England '66** were sadly bereft of Derby players, although the hero of England's '66 victory later made an appearance at the Baseball

Ground. Strangely he went largely unnoticed because it wasn't the hat-trick hero Geoff Hurst at all, it was Tofik Bakhramov, the 'Russian' linesman, who gave the nod to Hurst's infamous 'was it over the line?' second goal. The legendary Azerbaijani official ran the line when Derby beat Real Madrid 4–1 in October 1975, and once again he demonstrated his English allegiance, this time helpfully flagging offside a Real strike when they trailed only 3–1.

☺ **Mexico '70** afforded the Welsh international Terry Hennessey the mischievous boast that he had been selected for the Finals despite Wales failing to qualify. In a national poll the Rams midfielder had been nominated for a Great Britain Select XI and won a prize of a trip to Mexico to watch the Finals! There by rights was Francis Lee, then of Manchester City, in the England side that lost a heartbreak quarter-final 3–2 to West Germany.

☺ **Germany '74** proceeded without England when they failed to qualify after an infamous 1–1 draw against Poland at Wembley in which the 'keeper Jan Tomaszewski – labelled 'a clown' by Rams manager Brian Clough – emerged the Polish hero. The Rams striker Kevin Hector, on as a late substitute, almost clinched England's place when his last-second header was shovelled off the line by a Polish knee. Also in the England side on that fateful night were future Rams goalkeeper Peter Shilton and central-defender Roy McFarland.

☺ **Argentina '78** saw Scotland again fall at the first hurdle, but they finally won a game when an Archie Gemmill wonder goal helped them to beat Holland 3–2. Both Gemmill and Bruce Rioch captained the side and Kenny Burns, Don Masson and John Robertson all got games – no bigger bunch of Rams-linked names have ever graced a single World Cup squad.

☺ **Spain '82** saw England's Peter Shilton and Scotland's John Robertson get another crack, but both returned empty-handed once more.

☺ **Mexico '86** will forever be remembered for England's quarter-final defeat by Argentina, a game in which the two England players at the centre of the infamous 'Hand of God' goal by Diego Maradona were both destined to play for the Rams. Captain Peter Shilton was the beaten 'keeper, and a horribly sliced clearance by Steve Hodge gave Maradona the opening.

☺ **Italia '90** saw England's tragic semi-final defeat by Germany when two

Rams personalities were again involved in a crucial incident. Germany's only goal in normal time was a huge deflection off former Ram Paul Parker, which left 'keeper Peter Shilton stranded – a third Rams man in the side, defender Mark Wright, could only stand and watch as England lost 4–3 on penalties. England fielded Tony Dorigo in their third-place Play-off defeat by Italy – the future Rams full-back had hedged his bets...he was an Australian with both English and Italian passports! The cosmopolitan flavour was completed by the USA midfielder John Harkes.

☻ **USA '94** gave John Harkes a second chance to impress, and he was joined there by two more men who appear in the Rams archives, the Republic of Ireland's Paul McGrath and Norway's Lars Bohinen.

☻ **France '98** saw both Christian Dailly and Craig Burley play in Scotland's humiliating 3–0 defeat by Morocco, a game in which Burley, his hair dyed a bizarre yellow, was sent off. Aljosa Asanovic and Igor Stimac fared much better for Croatia, the team heroically reached the semi-finals after earlier beating a Jamaica side that included Rams players Darryl Powell and Deon Burton. While Burton was able to walk down any Derby street virtually unrecognised, in Jamaica he was routinely mobbed and became the country's Sports Personality of the Year. Also taking part were Taribo West (Nigeria) and Jacob Laursen (Denmark).

☻ **Japan–South Korea '02** gave two former Rams players their first World Cup experience – Paulo Wanchope and Mauricio Solis played in each of Costa Rica's three games, and Wanchope had the rare distinction of scoring against eventual winners Brazil. Taribo West again turned out for Nigeria, while Branko Strupar played for Belgium and Tomasz Hajto for Poland. But the unluckiest man in the Japan–South Korea tournament was surely the former Rams stalwart Lee Carsley – the Everton midfielder's World Cup lasted just 60 seconds after he came on as a last-minute substitute for the Republic of Ireland.

☻ **Germany '06** kicked-off with a cracker as the hosts beat Costa Rica 3–2, both the underdogs' goals being scored by Paulo Wanchope, which earned Derby County multi-mentions in the commentary, including reference to his sensational debut goal against Manchester United at Old Trafford in 1997. Mauricio Solis again played for Costa Rica, and the much-reviled Rams loanee Stern John stole a march on countless true Derby greats by appearing for Trinidad and Tobago.

ALL CLEAR

On 3 January 1948 the Baseball Ground witnessed an unusual piece of football history. A few weeks before that day's third-round FA Cup tie with Chesterfield, the Rams manager Stuart McMillan had noticed that his full-back Jack Howe had developed a tendency to misjudge headers, so he arranged for a series of eye tests. Thus it was that Howe played in the 2–0 win against the Spireites wearing his brand new £70 contact lenses, the first League footballer so equipped. A few months later, making his England debut in a difficult game against Italy in Turin, he again wore the expensive items of kit. Clearly they did the trick as the Rams man demonstrated perfect vision throughout a famous 4–0 victory and became the first England footballer to play an international match wearing his lenses.

THREE – THE NAME GAME...

Long after the details of stirring victories and tragic defeats have become a muddled mass, one thing remains clear in supporters' minds – the names of the men who wore the shirt. What a dull affair football would be if those identifying labels were banished from the game overnight – the on-field action might not change a bit, but taking full enjoyment from a game played by nameless souls would be pretty well impossible for fans.

Consider a world with no 'today's line up', no nicknames, no Player of the Year, no 'Best All-time XI', no 'rumour mill' and no team names or fixture lists. Anonymous football simply wouldn't work because names are the points of reference by which all fans relate to their club and indulge in reminiscence.

Each football club has its own unique archive in which many crossovers exist, but no two are alike. Here's a dip into the Derby County lexicon and the club's uniquely personal family history...warts and all.

WE ARE DERBY

Derby County is a perfect name. The team represents the city and the county. The club were very privileged to be so christened, since local authority approvals for the 'county' tag were rarely granted. It was considered presumptuous and politically incorrect for mere football teams to assume such grandeur.

Yet it might never have been. They were formed in 1884 as an off-shoot of Derbyshire County Cricket Club, and the football section simply adopted the most obvious name. So reports of their first ever game (a 6–0 defeat at Great Lever on 13 September 1884) referred to the team as Derbyshire County Football Club. The 'shire' was only dropped after a pompous protest by the Derbyshire Football Association – 'Only we can truly represent the county' – thus the newly-shorn Derby County were born. The rest is history.

UP THE RAMS

When Derby County were formed the town had already long been associated with the creature which would in time give the club its nickname. The 16th-century folk ballad known as *The Derby Ram* told of a giant mythical beast which was a sight to behold. One stanza contained the first link between the ram and the game, an allusion to the age-old tradition of Derby Shrovetide football.

'The little boys of Derby sir, they came to beg his eyes.
To kick around the streets sir, for they were football size.'

The county of Derbyshire had also been linked with the ram since 1858, when the 95th (Derbyshire) regiment of Foot captured a particularly fine specimen during their Indian Mutiny campaign and adopted it as their mascot. The beast was christened 'Private Derby' and marched 3,000 miles through Central India with the regiment. Like the football club he later inspired, the ram fought countless winning battles but had a tendency to self-destruct – in 1863 he jumped into a well in Hyderabad and was drowned.

It was only natural that journalists dubbed Derby County 'the Rams' soon after the club formed. Cartoonists also represented the club as a ram, and supporters liked the idea. The club are thought to have formally accepted the nickname in 1900. Many more 'Private Derby' mascots subsequently served the regiment, and prior to the debut of official club mascot Rammie in 1991 the incumbent beast was occasionally paraded around the Baseball Ground in its full regimental regalia.

The *Bloomsbury Dictionary of Word Origins* states that *ram* derives from both the Germanic for 'male sheep' and the Old Norse *ramr* meaning 'strong'. So far so good – but it also says that *ram* gave the English language the word *ramble*. The *Oxford English Dictionary* defines that as 'to make one's way in a free, unrestrained manner and without definite aim or direction' – again that has a certain resonance with the club. But Derby fans might well baulk at the original meaning of *ramble* stated in *Bloomsbury* – 'to wander around like a randy ram looking for ewes to copulate with'. Considering the unsavoury 'sheep-s******s' tag given to the Rams faithful by rival supporters, we'll leave it at that.

───────── WHAT THEY ANSWERED TO ─────────

Footballers and nicknames go together. The unusual word derives from 'an eke name', which simply means 'another name'. Maybe it's not manly to address a teammate by his real title – at any rate, the re-christening game has been around forever. All of this composite XI were born before World War Two.

Jack '**String**' Fryer – 6ft 2in goalkeeper, lanky as a string bean.
Jimmy '**Logie**' Methven – Forever reminiscing about Logie Park, home of his former club Edinburgh St Bernards.
George '**Cock**' Kinsey – It wouldn't be polite to ask.
William '**Tiddler**' Murray – Again we can only surmise.
Ken '**Rubberneck**' Oliver – The giraffe-necked defender headed the ball further than some players could kick it.

Jack '**The Spondon Squire**' Cox – Being the only footballer in the village made him quite a celebrity.

George '**Corkscrew**' Richards – Great dribbler made defenders feel giddy.

Lionel '**Spud**' Murphy – 'Murphy' is slang for a potato – as is 'spud'.

Lewis '**Kid**' Cooper – Very young debutant with a cute baby face.

Ray '**Toffee**' Straw – The prolific striker was always eating sweets.

Steve '**Paleface**' Bloomer – The goal-ace looked a sickly youth.

NOT WHAT THEY SEEMED

The origins of most nicknames can be readily traced to the dressing room, but a few have been more mysterious. That of Alf 'Snobby' Bentley suggests he might have been somewhat aloof, but in fact he was the friendliest of souls. Jimmy Methven, the manager who signed the centre-forward for the Rams in 1906, once explained 'In those days a shoe-maker was known as a "snob". Alf spent so much time as a lad playing in the yard of a local cobbler that he acquired the boyhood nickname "Snobby". We saw no reason to part with tradition.'

Another nickname carried from boyhood into the dressing room belonged to Douglas Duncan, a member of Derby's 1946 FA Cup-winning side. The outside-left was universally known as 'Dally', and it was generally said this was because he delayed his crosses until exactly the right moment. It took Duncan himself to correct the misconception: 'When I was a child I had a habit of "dallying" behind my father kicking stones – that's why they called me "Dally" and it just stuck.'

AN INDIGESTIBLE QUESTION

When the Italian star Fabrizio Ravanelli signed for Derby County in 2001, it caused quite a sensation. But punning fans who knew the meaning of the player's surname were quick to sound a note of caution – 'have too much of him and you'll soon be suffering'.

All was revealed when the name featured as an answer in the TV quiz show *University Challenge*. In a grand final between Magdalen College Oxford and Open University the teams were neck and neck when a pivotal question arose: 'Which footballer's name means 'radishes' in Italian?'

The Open University's Mrs Courtney scored a memorable own-goal by lunging in with 'Radiccio' – the howler cost her team the trophy. Unlike the red-faced contestant, the budding linguists among Rams fans were proved absolutely right. By the time 'the radish man' departed Derby County in September 2003 many fans had had their fill of Signor 'Ravanelli'.

Brian Clough had an entirely different take on the name. Asked on Century 106 Radio about how the new signing would fare in the Premiership, the former Rams manager replied 'The nearest I've got to Ravanelli is in the Co-op. They sell it in tins.'

The Italian isn't the only Rams player to have a name with 'lost-in-translation' possibilities. For what it's worth (not a lot), the word for 'now' in the Manx language of the Isle of Man is 'nish', while a number of Derby's overseas players take on a new identity if translated. Steve Strong doesn't appear in the Rams *Who's Who,* but Esteban Fuertes (literally 'fortifications') does, and one wonders if Derby would have been quite so keen to sign a player named Horace Coalman if he hadn't come with the more glamorous Argentinean label Horacio Carbonari, literally a 'charcoal burner' or 'fuel merchant'.

But perhaps the most misleading name in Derby's history was that belonging to 2003 loan signing Daniele Salvatore Dichio – Rams fans expecting a cultured Italian international were disappointed...he joined Derby from West Bromwich Albion, was blessed with a middle name Ernest and was born in Hammersmith.

Even Derby County themselves have been the subject of a bizarre translation. When bookies in China noticed in the 1990s that punters betting on English football matches had trouble pronouncing the team names, they re-christened the major sides with a more accessible approximation. Thus it was that Derby County became Tah Pei Gan and their two East Midlands rivals took on the names Lok Ting Ham Su Lam and Lei Si Tat Sing.

FASHION VICTIM

Nicknames move with the times. But for linguistic change, Warren Barton would probably have been nothing more than a 'Fancy Dan' – in the swinging 60s that meant a player whose attention to his wardrobe went that little bit too far.

Alas for Barton, his career came later. By the time he arrived at Derby from Newcastle United in February 2002, he had already acquired an updated name to reflect his sartorial elegance. Once his Newcastle teammate Rob Lee also arrived at Derby, no time was lost in introducing Barton's nickname to the dressing room – 'everybody calls him "Dogs",' asserted Lee.

The unusual tag is derived from 'The Dog's Bollocks', that unsavoury phrase which suggests in the modern vernacular that a man rates himself in the fashion stakes. It perfectly reflected Barton's snappy-dresser image – his penchant for crisply pressed shirts, silk ties and an immaculate bouffant coiffure. Even in the thick of the action, Barton could have doubled for a shop-window mannequin – indeed his fiercest critics claimed he was about as fast as one. That is a matter for debate, but what is certain is that Warren Dean Barton remains the only Rams player named after these particular canine attributes.

COMMON MEN

Up to 2006–07 the top 10 most common surnames of players having made a first-team appearance for Derby County were as follows:

There have been 11 players named Smith, six named Hunt, Moore, Powell, Wilson and Wright, and five named Davies, Robinson, Robson and Thompson. A healthy rash of four-timers includes Cooper, Walker, Taylor, Mills, Thomas, Richards and Ritchie. As for the mere hat-trick squad, they could make several teams between them.

Here is the 'Smiths XI' laid out according to correct positions – a 5–3–2 formation being preferred by the side's illustrious manager.

Goalkeeper:	John William Smith (1903–07)
Defence:	Joshua Smith (1914)
	Herbert Smith (1907)
	Mike Smith (1957–61)
	J. Smith (1888–90)
	Frederick Smith (1909)
Midfield:	Tommy Smith (2004–)
	Albert Smith (1884–86)
	Valentine Smith (1925–27)
Attack:	Frederick Edward Smith (1947)
	Sydney Joseph Smith (1922)
Manager:	Jim Smith (1995–2001)

Albert and Herbert won full England caps while Mike and Tommy won England international honours at Schoolboy and Under-21 levels respectively.

But the overall make-up of the side suggests it is badly lacking in strength in depth. It's just as well that the Smiths XI remains a team on paper only.

CALLING CHINA

Every letter of the alphabet but one is represented in the who's who of players who have appeared for Derby County in a first-team game, but getting there hasn't been easy. The club was already 30 years old when Steve Bloomer's son-in-law Alf Quantrill manfully filled the difficult 'Q' spot in December 1914. Andy Quy later joined him – but only just. The 'keeper's entire Rams career comprised a miserly eight minutes – a substitute appearance in a League Cup tie at Portsmouth in October 1994.

It took until 1954 for Stewart Imlach to fill the surprisingly difficult 'I' berth. Fifty years later the Spaniard Inigo Idiakez made doubly sure. Ted Udall and Frank Upton jointly resolved the 'U' dilemma, and the club took a giant step towards alphabetic completeness in 2001 when Colin Todd obligingly signed the Argentinean player Luciano Zavagno after his optimistic approach (allegedly!) for the French international Zinadine Zidane had been strangely rebuffed.

But the Rams are still looking for the elusive 'X-men'. Scouting reports suggest that a centre-forward currently playing in China is the complete article. Will we ever hear the chant 'There's only one Xin Xin Xiong'?

WOULD YOU ADAM AND EVE IT?

Two Derby County players enjoy a rare distinction. They are the midfielder Gary Ablett (1984) and the Danish international striker Mikkel Beck (1998–2000). Both figure in contemporary dictionaries of cockney rhyming slang.

Although hardly likely to be used in everyday 'Derbyshire', here's how the distinguished pair might be employed: 'No alcohol for me, I'm on the Gary Abletts' and 'Oi ref, want to borrow me mikkels?'

For the uninitiated, that's Gary Ablett = 'tablet' and Mikkel Becks = 'specs'.

The only other Rams personality officially admitted to the cockney lexicon is manager Brian Clough, who figures twice. The phrase 'Give us a Brian' would generally be heard between smokers, while 'I'm feeling a bit Brian today' serves for the morning after the night before. Again the root of the rhymes is simplicity itself – Brian Clough = both 'puff' and 'rough'.

THE CHOSEN ONES

Most footballers have nicknames. Only the privileged few are given a *soubriquet*.

That is a rather grander label usually bestowed by journalists to reflect the prowess or particular characteristics (not always good) of a legendary character.

The term is French in origin – *soubriquet* literally means 'under the chin', a reference to the sort of affectionate 'chuck' one might give to a well-loved child. This Rams XI looks tough to beat – the famous management team elected to play a 4–3–3 formation. The infamous board did very little.

Goalkeeper	'The Cat'	Reg Matthews (1961–68)
Defence	'The Rock'	Steve Powell (1971–85)
	'The Black Pearl'	Paul McGrath (1996)
	'The Iron Man'	Dave Mackay (1968–71)
	'The Tank'	Frank Upton (1954–61 & 1965–66)
Midfield	'The Tin Man'	Ted McMinn (1987–93)
	'The Gleaming Dome'	Terry Hennessey (1969–73)
	'The Silver Fox'	Raich Carter (1945–48)
Attack	'Magic Feet'	Hughie Gallacher (1934–36)
	'The White Feather'	Fabrizio Ravanelli (2001–03)
	'The Destroying Angel'	Steve Bloomer (1892–1906 & 1910–14)
Manager	'Old Big 'Ead'	Brian Clough (1967–73)
Assistant Manager	'The Sergeant Major'	Arthur Cox (1984–1993)
Director of Football	'The Bald Eagle'	Jim Smith (1995–2001)
Board Members	'The Three Amigos':	John Sleightholme (2003–06), Jeremy Keith (2003–06) and Steve Harding (2003–06)

No explanation is needed save perhaps in the hair department – Terry Hennessey had very little and both Raich Carter and Fabrizio Ravanelli went prematurely grey.

The inclusion of Reg Matthews as 'The Cat' may prompt debate – he received the name while with Chelsea in the 1950s, superseding that club's better-known goalkeeper Peter 'The Cat' Bonetti by several years.

As for Steve Bloomer, he had more *soubriquets* than anyone – he was variously dubbed 'The Twisting Tormentor', 'The Hammer of the Scots' and 'The Ghost in Boots', but a much shorter name best reflected the England striker's fame – in countless match reports he was referred to throughout only as 'Steve'.

MISTAKEN IDENTITY

Sales placards advertising the *Derby Evening Telegraph* were once the cause of much chagrin to ever-optimistic Derby County supporters. Countless near-delirious Rams fans bought copies of the newspaper after seeing the signs displayed outside newsagents' shops one day in September 2002 – 'RAMS SIGN NICKY BUTT' was a truly sensational headline.

The England midfielder had been voted by Pelé as 'best player of the 2002 World Cup'. He'd won every trophy in sight with Manchester United, and now he was joining John Gregory's mid-table Division One side – it defied logic.

That was because the *Telegraph* had been very naughty indeed. Nicky Butt was 10-year-old local girl Nicola Butt, who had just signed for Derby County Ladies under-12s. A collective sound of 'Doh!' engulfed Derby that night as feverish Rams fans turned to the back page and realised they'd been well and truly had.

SCRAPING THE BARREL

Discretion proved the better part of valour when a Derby County internet forum invited supporters to nominate an 'appropriate' all-time Rams XI. In the event the webmaster wisely restricted the competition to five-a-side:

Ernest Ramsell (1905)
Peter Ramage (1928–36)
Alan Ramage (1980–81)
Craig Ramage (1989–93)
Marino Rahmberg (1997)

Despite making only one substitute appearance in a 4–2 defeat away to Leicester City in 1996–97, Swedish international Marino Rahmberg was made captain on the additional grounds that his name is an anagram of A BIGHORN RAMMER.

Other suggestions for the squad were Sam Lamb, George Shepherd, Sammy Crooks and Thomas Shanks, but none were admitted to the fold. The sheepish submission of an entire XI made up of Barbour, Barclay, Barrowcliffe, Bartlett, two Barnes's, three Barkers, and two Bartons was considered far too woolly and was butted into touch with a wittily appended comment – 'baa'd for stating the bleating obvious'.

MISSION IMPOSSIBLE

In the opening years of the new millennium Derby County supporters faced an ever-increasing struggle to put names to faces. In both 2002–03 and 2003–04 they fielded 36 different players in the first team. That was a club record few expected to be beaten.

But in 2005–06 it was exceeded even before the season ended. On 26 February 2006 in the 1–0 home win over Plymouth Argyle 18-year-old Lionel Ainsworth became the 37th player used by the club to that date when he came on as substitute for the final few minutes – and nothing was more certain than that the tally would increase further by the season's end. It did, to a mind-numbing 41.

Ainsworth's fleeting appearance had been his debut, a fact which also established another record. He was the 21st debutant for the club that season, of which 11 had been players taken on loan. Only the most gifted or saddest Rams fan could have given chapter and verse on Derby County's most unstable team of all time.

A WORD OF PRAISE

Goalkeeper Jack Robinson holds a unique distinction. He is the only Rams player to achieve linguistic celebrity in an overseas dictionary. In his book *Soccer Revolution* (1955) the former Austrian goalkeeper Willy Meisl explained:

'When the English goalkeeper Jack Robinson played against a Viennese City XI in the late 1890s he foiled a series of raids by spreading himself at the feet of onrushing forwards and stealing the ball with ease in a manner never before witnessed by the Vienna crowd. The exhilarating technique made such an impression that in Austria and Central Europe that type of save is still known as a 'Robinsonade' to this very day.'

HEAD SCRATCHER

Supporters often argue about team formations. Should Smith play on the left or right? Is Bloggs a defender or midfielder? The fans expect the manager to get this right, and it's a common assertion that writing names on a team sheet is an easy task. But statistics suggest otherwise.

Leaving the goalkeeper aside, a football team can be altered a staggering 3,628,800 ways using the same 10 outfield players – the figure is calculated by the sum 1x2x3x4x5x6x7x8x9x10. No wonder a succession of Rams managers have torn their hair out trying to achieve exactly the right blend.

UNUSUAL MIDDLE NAMES

Footballers are no different to anybody else in one respect. Many have had parents who blessed their offspring with middle names which try to make a point. Most common is a mother's maiden name, but the Rams squad below includes several exoticisms which remain a mystery.

Benjamin **Ward** Spilsbury (1885–88)
Percy **Ollivant** Francis (1893–95)
Arthur **Docwra** Turner (1902)
Elijah **Solomon** Tremelling (1905–07)
Ernald **Oak** Scattergood (1907–14)
Henry **Doxford** Leonard (1911–19)
Archibald **Teasdale** Scott (1927–33)
Samuel **Dickinson** Crooks (1927–46)
Errington **Ridley** Liddell Keen (1930–37)
Hugh **Kilpatrick** Gallacher (1934–35)
Horatio **Stratton** Carter (1945–47)
Reginald **Alphonsus** Ryan (1955–58)
George Hedworth Darwin (1957–60)
Peter **Aylmer** Daniel (1965–78)
John **Prescott** McGovern (1968–73)
John **Pearson** Duncan (1978–80)
Marvin **Leon St Clair** Robinson (1998–2002)

The only Derby County player whose middle name remained unknown for all time was Arnold R. Warren, who played eight games at outside-right in 1901–02. That was because he had no second Christian name at all – the 'R' was a mere affectation added to distinguish him from one of his brothers.

WHO DID THEY THINK THEY WERE?

Three men in Derby County history have used 'false names' for three different reasons – here they are unmasked.

☀ The inside-forward **George Antonio** signed for the Rams from Stoke City in 1947. He was actually born George Rowlands but took the surname Antonio when he was adopted as a child by an Italian family of that name. Nor was that his only identity crisis. In 1937–38 Antonio was selected to play for Wales but had the honour snatched away from him when his birthplace was revealed as Whitchurch in Shropshire – just the wrong side of the border. Nowadays he'd probably be eligible for Wales, England and Italy!

☀ The goalkeeper **Ernest Hoffman** played once for Derby in the final match of 1922–23, but he had earlier played for another club as Ernie Holt. When he joined South Shields in 1919 bitter memories of the wartime enemy were still so fresh that the player swiftly effected a change from the Germanic Hoffman to avoid abuse from the terraces. Whether he called out 'Hoffman's ball' or 'Holt's ball' in his solitary game for Derby remains unrecorded – but neither were effective anyway. The club's only truly pseudonymous player failed to keep a clean sheet as Derby were beaten 1–0 at Leeds United.

☀ When the infamous Rams chairman of the 1980s **Robert Maxwell** was born to a poor Yiddish-speaking Jewish family in Czechoslovakia on 10 June 1923, he was actually named Jan Ludvik Hoch. He only changed his name 'for cosmetic reasons' in 1945, becoming Ian Robert Maxwell before later dropping the Ian to avoid being confused with his son Ian Robert Charles Maxwell, also a one-time Derby chairman. No wonder people suggested Maxwell senior wasn't all that he seemed, an observation fully validated only after his death when the true extent of his many financial misdemeanours were shockingly exposed.

CENSUS NONSENSE

☀ Enthusiasts who trace their family history are often warned to prepare themselves for potential shocks and this holds very true for Derby County. The two men who were the driving force behind the formation of the club in 1884 were William Morley and his son William junior, but as the senior

of the two it was 'Old Man' Morley who became known as the Rams'
patriarch and founder and who was for years thereafter revered as their
greatest and at one time oldest supporter. The 1881 census shows him
living in the Litchurch area of Derby, but it is the 'place of birth' column
that carries Morley's awful secret – the founder of Derby County was born
in Nottingham!

✪ The Rams wing-half **Shirley Wray Abbott** holds several distinctions of
dubious merit. His appearance in an away game against Huddersfield
Town in 1911–12 was his only Rams outing, he is the very first entry in
the *Derby County Who's Who*, and he is the only player with a truly
girlie name to turn out for the club, although the Frenchman Lilian
Martin runs him close. His unusual christening certainly caused
confusion when the 1891 census returns were digitised – Abbott appears
in the electronic records as his father's 'daughter' and his sex is listed
boldly as 'female'...the only 'official' transgender player in the Rams'
history.

✪ Although Derby's prolific scorer **Steve Bloomer** made his Rams debut in
1892, he had seemingly anticipated his future career a year earlier. On the
1891 census his occupation is listed as 'striker'. Naturally the word didn't
carry the same connotation then – Bloomer wielded a huge hammer at the
local iron foundry, where he cultivated a sinewy physique striking hot
metal into shape.

✪ The 1890s Derby full-back and later manager **Jimmy Methven** was fond
of what he called 'my little leverage trick' in the tackle, but was hardly
known for his trickery in the ball-juggling department. All the more
reason to be amused by his census entry, which lists his occupation as
'football exhibitionist'. Then again the rock-steady Scot did have his
moments – when the Rams were saved from relegation in 1894–95 by a
last-minute winner Methven celebrated the goal by standing on his head
in the centre-circle.

THAT ELUSIVE QUALITY

Over the years a number of phantom players, mystery men and mere fleeting
acquaintances have been associated with Derby County. Here is a selection of
personalities who were imbued with what is normally a great attribute to a
footballer – 'that elusive quality'.

✪ **Henry Harbour** is listed in *The Who's Who of Derby County* despite never having signed for the club. His solitary appearance came on 27 October 1888 at Everton, a game to which Derby had travelled with only 10 men. Adopting an 'any port in a storm' philosophy, they agreed to borrow the lowly Everton reserve for the afternoon. Harbour floundered badly and Derby were sunk by six goals to two. It was the only League appearance Harbour ever made, and he boasts the oddest 'career details' in Derby County history.

✪ An inexperienced statistician once listed a player called Scrimmage as having netted several goals for Derby in the 1890s – he had picked up the name from early records and failed to realise it was simply the term used for 'scorer unknown' whenever a goalmouth scramble made identification unclear.

✪ So much uncertainty surrounded team selection during World War Two that 'fictitious' names were often listed in the programme. Men named A.N. Other, S.O. Else and A. Newman were regulars in the Derby line up.

✪ The England international **Phil Boyer** pulled on a Rams first-team shirt but never played for the club. He was an unused substitute when Derby beat Cardiff City 5–1 at Ninian Park on 23 September 1967. Derby's manager Brian Clough decided the young striker was surplus to requirements and let him go. But Boyer became a prolific scorer wherever he went and remains the best player on Derby's books never to have got a first-team start.

✪ England international **Ian Storey-Moore** was never a Rams player despite being introduced as such to 33,000 cheering fans. Prior to kick-off at Derby's game with Wolves on 4 March 1972, the stylish winger from Nottingham Forest was paraded on the Baseball Ground pitch as 'our new signing'. But the paperwork remained incomplete and the transfer caused such an uproar that Forest withdrew on a technicality. Moore went to Manchester United instead – no 'Derby career' was ever more fleeting.

✪ In January 1989 the Derby chairman Robert Maxwell announced he had signed the two Czech internationals **Ivo Knoflicek** and **Lubos Kubic**. Both were introduced to the Derby crowd before a Cup tie against Southampton. They trained with the club and became popular figures, but neither played a single game – FIFA refused to sanction the move. Knoflicek and Kubic are the most celebrated double 'signings' never to play for the Rams.

❦ In 2001 a book called *The Final Whistle* imparted the following sad news: 'On 17 February 1998 the former Derby County player-manager Reg Watson died aged 80.' Watson has both the worst record and the lowest profile in Derby County's entire history. He never played for them and never managed them!

DO THEY MEAN ME?

A number of Derby players became widely known either by their middle names or by one which didn't appear on their birth certificate at all. Here's a pretty useful squad.

Real full name	Known as
Walter Urban Musson (1945–53)	Chick
William Alan Durban (1963–72)	Alan
Edward Curran (1977)	Terry
Roy Greenwood (1978–79)	Reggie
Vjekoslav Banovic (1980–83)	Yakka
Francis Mark Wallington (1985–86)	Mark
David Geraint Williams (1984–91)	George
Kevin Clifton McMinn (1987–92)	Ted
Rowan Lee Mills (1994)	Lee
Robertus Petrus van der Laan (1995–97)	Robbie
Hendrick Andries Ronald Willems (1995–97)	Ron
Francesco Baiano (1997–99)	Ciccio
Georgiou Kinkladze (1999–2003)	Giorgi
Manuel Martinez Fernandez (2003)	Manel
Guimaraes Sanibio Jose Luiz Junior Fortaleza (2003)	Junior
Paolo Pasquale Peschisolido (2004–)	Paul
Muhamed Konjic (2004–06)	Mo

The most obscure reason for a re-christening belongs to Ted McMinn, who spilt the beans in the *Scottish Evening Times* in November 2004.

'When I was a boy my mates used to wind me up about my running style. According to them it looked as if I had a teddy bear under my arm. So they called me 'Teddy'. It got shortened to 'Ted' and stuck. Now it's even on my driving licence and bank statements.'

But the reason for some names may never be known. The Derby winger Reg Harrison once said of Musson – 'I shared a room with him for seven years and still have no idea why he was called Chick.'

WE'LL TAKE EACH GAME AS IT COMES

After computers were first used to compile the fixture lists in 1967, clubs often complained that gremlins seemed to be at work. But the Football League stubbornly refused to admit that a computer could possibly get confused. Yet consider the huge odds against this sequence happening purely by chance.

Derby's first six League opponents of 1988–89 were selected by the machine in perfect alphabetical order – Middlesbrough, Millwall, Newcastle United, Nottingham Forest, Queen's Park Rangers and Southampton – even those high up in the Football League must have suspected a malfunction on that one.

But the fates have sometimes delivered unusual runs that can't be put down to technical error. The 'balls out of the bag' system used for the FA and League Cup draw is as random as it gets, but an odd sequence for the Rams began in 1999–2000. That season they lost in the FA Cup to Burnley and the League Cup to Bolton, then were dumped out of the FA Cup in the next three seasons by Blackburn Rovers, Bristol Rovers and Brentford. When they again drew Burnley in the 2005–06 FA Cup competition it was feared the curse of the 'B' teams might continue, but the spell was broken when a Paul Peschisolido brace clinched a 2–1 win.

QUICK CHANGE ACTS

✪ On Boxing Day 1989 Derby's joint leading scorer **Paul Goddard** was one of the first names on the team sheet for the home clash with Everton. But five days later on New Year's Day 1990 he appeared in the Millwall side that played *against* Derby County at The Den. While the fans had been busy polishing off the turkey leftovers, the Rams manager Arthur Cox had sold the popular player for £800,000. Few outgoing transfers ever prompted more criticism than this shock end-of-year sale.

✪ Popular midfielder **Bruce Rioch** played the last League game of his first spell with Derby County in a 2–0 defeat at Everton on 20 November 1976. Two weeks later he was sold to the Goodison Park club, but in less than a year Derby bought him back from Merseyside, and he made his second Rams debut at the Baseball Ground on 5 November 1977 – against Everton! Some part-time supporters attending their annual game had no idea Rioch had ever been away.

TWO TIMERS

Players held in high regard are occasionally signed twice by the same club. Here are the most celebrated Derby County two-timers.

Steve Bloomer (1892–1906 & 1910–14) is Derby's most successful two-timer. After the striker's shock move to Middlesbrough in 1906, the club entered a period of decline. His return in 1910 was greeted with euphoria. He scored two on his second debut and in 1911–12 skippered the Rams to a famous promotion.

Kevin Hector (1966–78 & 1980–82) was a prolific striker in his first spell and still had star quality when Colin Addison brought him back in 1980. In the final game of 1981–82 Derby needed to beat Watford to ensure their Second Division place. Hector scored in a stirring 3–2 victory – still the king in his last ever game.

Roy McFarland (1967–81 & 1983) led Derby to their 1971–72 League Championship success. But his return from Bradford City as assistant to Peter Taylor was a sorry affair. Derby were heavily fined for an illegal approach and then McFarland was pressed into emergency action for nine games. His final appearance was as a substitute for Graham Harbey during a 3–0 drubbing at Portsmouth on 10 December 1983 – an inglorious end to a glorious career.

Archie Gemmill (1970–77 & 1982–84) starred in the 1971–72 and 1974–75 Championship-winning sides, but his return turned sour. He worked tirelessly helping Derby escape relegation in 1982–83 and was voted Player of the Year in 1983–84, but in the same year he was dropped by manager Peter Taylor after a fall out. The next manager Roy McFarland reinstated him to the side, but Gemmill's career ended with a disastrous relegation to Division Three.

Roger Davies (1971–76 & 1979–80) was a regular in Dave Mackay's 1974–75 Championship-winning side and scored all five goals that season against Luton at Derby. However, the return of the cult-hero ended unhappily – he played 22 League games in 1979–80 but scored only three goals. Derby were relegated to Division Two.

Bruce Rioch (1974–76 & 1977–80) was leading scorer with 15 League goals when Derby won the Championship in 1974–75. Tommy Docherty brought him back for a disastrous second spell. Rioch fell out with Docherty and was twice sent off in 1977–78. Then he fell out with Docherty's successor Colin Addison. In 1979–80, his final season, Derby were relegated to Division Two.

Charlie George (1975–78 & 1982) had a brilliant first season and quickly became a cult hero. When John Newman brought him back in March 1982, George helped Derby to stay up, but it is the 'old George' that fans remember.

Bobby Davison (1982–87 & 1991) was the goalscoring hero when Arthur Cox's side won two successive promotions. His brief return was almost heroic again – on loan from Leeds in 1991–92 – when he scored eight goals in 10 games but Derby missed promotion to Division One after a Play-off defeat against Blackburn.

Nigel Callaghan (1987–89 & 1990) played a key part in 1986–87 when Arthur Cox's side were promoted to Division One. The winger's brief second coming on loan from Aston Villa was less inspirational – he returned to Villa Park mid-season, and Derby were relegated to the Second Division, although results did improve during his loan spell.

Seth Johnson (1999–2001 & 2005–) failed to reach his full potential in his first spell, and when Leeds United offered £7 million for him Derby gleefully accepted. It remains the highest fee the club has ever received. When he again signed for the Rams in 2005, Johnson set about becoming one of the few returnees whose second spell proved better than their first.

RAMAGRAMS

According to an internet website listing football anagrams, the following were considered appropriate to Derby County.

ENTER HOT LIPS – One-time subject of racy press stories PETER SHILTON

A NIGHT OF TORMENTS – Usual drill for fans of NOTTINGHAM FOREST

NICE FLARES – The fashion style of seventies icon FRANCIS LEE

MYTH – COMEDY – ROT – The chaos-ridden legacy of TOMMY DOCHERTY

GROUND SALE BLAB – Leaked rumour from the BASEBALL GROUND

DON HOWLED TRASH – One regular's reaction to DEAN HOLDSWORTH

OR IT'S MAGIC – Alternative explanation for the rare skill of IGOR STIMAC

OUTCRY BY END – Typical outcome of a season following DERBY COUNTY

EARLY DROP – Not always first on the team sheet, RORY DELAP

RETAINED DRUGS – Unfounded rumour concerning DEAN STURRIDGE

GO JOHN…GERRY – One fan's written plea to JOHN GREGORY

POETRY ALERT – Warning of another odd interview with PETER TAYLOR

LONG GOODBYES

Most players depart from a club with absolute certainty, but a few linger on unexpectedly. Others 'retire' completely, only to pop up again when least expected. Here are some who weren't sure whether they were coming or going.

❂ When the Derby-born schoolboy prodigy **Fred Flanders** made his last Football League appearance for the Rams in April 1911, he drifted into the non-League game before making a remarkable time-warp comeback. His next League appearance was for Newport County more than 10 years later.

❂ On Boxing Day 1946 Huddersfield Town fans looked forward to seeing their new signing **Peter Doherty** make his debut following his 'transfer' from Derby. The inside-forward was listed in Huddersfield's programme for their game with Aston Villa, but the paperwork had yet to be completed – instead Doherty was summoned by police to the Baseball Ground, where, to his total surprise, the unsettled Irishman played one last game for the Rams and scored twice in a 5–1 home win over Everton.

❂ Few players have been given fonder farewells than **Stefano Eranio**. After announcing his plans to retire at the end of 2000–01, the Italian midfielder was given an emotionally-charged send-off against Ipswich Town by a full Pride Park Stadium. So there were more than a few double-takes when Eranio reappeared for training the following season – the generous-hearted player had returned as a special favour to manager Jim Smith. But Eranio was soon saying a second and more distressing farewell – he left in disgust after Smith lost his job early in the season.

BEARDED WONDERS

The 60 team and squad photographs in the Rams official history *The Derby County Story* feature close to 1,000 different players, yet only one is sporting a beard. Either footballers have plenty of shaving time at their disposal, or they simply fear a dressing room ribbing. Nevertheless, a handful of brave or lazy souls have cultivated some sort of chin whiskers while with the club – here is a hirsute squad and accompanying style notes.

Mick Brolly (1982) – Shades of William Shakespeare.
Francesco Baiano (1997–99) – Natty 'musketeer'/Italian nobleman.
Roy Greenwood (1979–80) – Neat and ginger 'photofit' style. *
Malcolm Christie (1998–2002) – Devilish 'Beelzebub'.
Robbie Van Der Laan (1995–98) – Dutch-style 'mannequin' gone haywire.
Derek Hales (1976–77) – The W.G. Grace of football. **
Archie Gemmill (1970–77 & 1982–84) – Behold the son of werewolf.
Charlie George (1975–78 & 1982) – Authentic 'Neanderthal'.
Kenny Burns (1982–84) – Classic cave-man look.
Dave Langan (1976–80) – Known as a 'Guinness' – smooth and dark.
Marcus Tudgay (2002–06) – A wisp of the Oriental.
Igor Stimac (1995–99) – Elegant and silky smooth, as one would expect.
Peter Taylor (manager) (1967–73 & 1982–84) – Jazz club/beatnik retro.

* When Roy Greenwood was at Sunderland prior to joining the Rams, manager Bob Stokoe banned him from the club's official 1976–77 team photograph because he was growing a beard at the time and 'looked scruffy'.
** In 1977 Derek Hales won an expensive prize at a Kevin Hector testimonial pro-am golf event – a state-of-the-art electric shaver!

OWN-GOAL KINGS

When Derby beat Bolton Wanderers 4–0 at the Baseball Ground on 5 May 1950 they were aided by an own-goal from an appropriate source. The red-faced Trotter was the aptly-named M. Barrass. A total of 81 own-goals were scored by visitors to the Baseball Ground from 1895–1997, but only one other player came close to Barrass for a suitable name – the Bristol City man who netted in the Rams 2–0 win on 27 March 1967 was Low before the game and none too chuffed after it.

A SINISTER SQUAD

Because most footballers are strictly-speaking dextrous – that is naturally right-footed – it's the sinister ones, the left-footers, who often linger in the memory for that very reason. Here is a Rams XI plus substitutes – the more than useful squad is made up entirely of players whose right legs were used mainly for standing on.

Mart Poom (1996–2002)
Alan Wright (2006)
Dave Mackay (1968–71)
Steve Buckley (1978–86)
Seth Johnson (1999–2001 & 2005–)
Giorgi Kinkladze (1999–2003)
Archie Gemmill (1970–77 & 1982–84)
Aljosa Asanovic (1996–98)
Bruce Rioch (1973–76 & 1977–79)
Paul Simpson (1992–97)
Lee Holmes (2002–)

Andy Oakes (2000–05) *
Paul Boertien (1998–)
Tony Dorigo (1998–2000)
Lewin Nyatanga (2006–)
Shane Nicholson (1992–96)
Mark Pembridge (1992–95)
Danny Higginbotham (2000–03)

*'Keeper Andy Oakes was party to a curious snippet of trivia when he kept goal for the Rams at home to Wolves on Monday 26 August 2002. His opposite number was Michael Oakes. Wolves won the game 4–1, but the most assiduous statisticians were more interested in posing a crucial question – had two left-footed 'keepers named Oakes ever played in the same game previously? Informed opinion suggested probably not!

WHERE HAVE ALL THE BROTHERS GONE?

Two brothers played in Derby County's first ever League game and eight pairs in all are known to have played first-team games for the club. Here is the full squad from that rare breed of Ram which appears to have become a dying one.

✪ **Lawrence 'Lol' Plackett** scored twice in Derby's opening League game against Bolton Wanderers at Pike's Lane and was the first Rams player to complete an ever-present season in the Football League. Alongside him that day, and for much of 1888–89, was his brother Harry. Two other brothers also played in that first League season, Walter and Scotch Selvey, but the extent of their Rams career was just a single game each.

✪ Budding footballers **Charles** and **Walter Rose** were like two peas in a pod. Each joined Derby County from Derby Midland in June 1891, both left the Rams to join Loughborough Town and both ended their careers with a move to Ilkeston United in September 1904. Just to keep things even, each played five senior games for Derby and neither scored a goal.

✪ No brothers have had more contrasting Rams careers than **Steve** and **Phillip Bloomer**. One played for Derby 525 times and scored 332 goals, the other played only once and drew a blank. Phillip's only edge over his older brother was that he never finished on the losing side – his solitary game at home to Sheffield Wednesday in 1895 finished 3–1 to Derby.

✪ The worst double-transfer mistake in Derby's history concerned the **Forman** boys. **Fred** was sold to bitter rivals Nottingham Forest in 1894, and **Frank** followed him there a few months later as well. The brothers played only a handful of games for the Rams but both became Forest legends and were the last brothers to play for England before Jack and Bobby Charlton in 1965.

✪ No brothers had a bigger impact on Derby's history than the **Goodall** lads, the fiery one an Irish international and the thoughtful one an England legend. They called one the 'incorrigible **Archie**' and the other 'gentleman **John**'. From 1889 to 1902 they notched up 661 Rams appearances between them.

✪ An injury to **Johnny May** during the 1899 FA Cup Final against Sheffield United was said to be a key factor in Derby's defeat, and Steve Bloomer considered the Scotsman 'one of the finest half-backs who ever kicked a ball.' Bloomer's assessment of May's brother **Hugh** might well have been less glowing – in his six games for the Rams in 1902 the centre-forward failed to produce a single goal.

✪ No greater lookalikes have played for Derby than the **Hazledine** brothers. However, the finest hour of **Don** and **Geoff** came 'against' the Rams when both played in the non-League Boston United side that won 6–1 at the Baseball Ground in December 1955. It was a massive FA Cup shock, one made all the more newsworthy by Geoff's heroic hat-trick…in his sole senior start for the Rams he had barely mustered a single shot.

NAMES TO CONJURE WITH

Derby began the 1897–98 season with a new goalkeeper, the unfortunately-named **Joe Frail**. The custodian proved reasonably true to his name, finishing on the winning side only three times in 10 games. Other Derby players' surnames of the not entirely convincing kind have included goalkeepers of both the **Camp** and **Green** persuasion, a Short central-defender, a **Cross** midfielder, several **Walkers** and a worrying-sounding, all-era forward-line of **Gamble, Daft, Little, Long** and **Hope**. Suggesting something rather better are the dogged half-backs **Hardman** and **Keen** and the wise defender **Sage**, who would have been joined by the perfect pro **Goodlad** had the Rams reserve been given a well-earned chance. An interesting sound-alike and namesake clan, although in some cases only retrospectively so, includes political heavyweight **Gordon Brown**, mad-cap comedian **Tommy Cooper** and *Animal Magic* legend **Johnny Morris**. **Bill Haley** was hardly a star, let alone a rock 'n' roll comet, but he was once kept company on the music front when **Eddie Nelson** appeared in the programme notes as Nelson, Eddy. On a more erudite front, the very first man to score on his Derby County debut, in 1886, might well have fancied that he did so with religious zeal, for he shared his name with the 16th-century reformer **John Knox**. Nor must the book world be overlooked, with **Tom Sawyer** the pick of the Rams library, while railway buffs are well served by the daddy of them all, **George Stephenson**. Undoubtedly the most pleasant-sounding side ever fielded by Derby was one from the 1890s in which **Rose, Garden** and **Bloomer** lined up together, and along with **Flowers, Swallow, Summers, Bird, Greenwood, Cherry, Hill** and **Wood** they might have made up the most idyllic Rams XI of all time. Certain natural pairings failed to come off – neither **Tate** and **Lyle** nor **Fox** and **Hunt** ever played together, nor **Lamb** with **Shanks**, **Money** with **Penney**, or **Tinkler** with **Bell**. The classic literary trio of **Holmes, Watson** and **Doyle** ought to have thrilled the Rams crowds together, but never quite made it, just as **Thomas** and **Hardy** missed each other too. Finally, the vagaries of the fixture lists denied those rare 'team players' **York, Oxford, Scarborough** and **Morton** the singular pleasure of playing against their namesake sides…and after 122 years the Rams have still not had the foresight to sign a single player named Derby.

PLAYERS OF THE SEASON

Footballers see their names in print so often that they become immune to it. But one place any Rams player does value seeing his name is at the top of the list for the Supporters' Player of the Year Award. Inaugurated in 1968–69, the coveted annual prize is now known as the Jack Stamps Award – here are the men who impressed the fans and were proud to win it.

1968–69	Roy McFarland	1987–88	Michael Forsyth
1969–70	John O'Hare	1988–89	Mark Wright
1970–71	Dave Mackay	1989–90	Mark Wright
1971–72	Colin Todd	1990–91	Dean Saunders
1972–73	Kevin Hector	1991–92	Ted McMinn
1973–74	Ron Webster	1992–93	Marco Gabbiadini
1974–75	Peter Daniel	1993–94	Martin Taylor
1975–76	Charlie George	1994–95	Craig Short
1976–77	Leighton James	1995–96	Dean Yates
1977–78	David Langan	1996–97	Chris Powell
1978–79	Steve Powell	1997–98	Francesco Baiano
1979–80	Steve Buckley	1998–99	Jacob Laursen
1980–81	Roger Jones	1999–2000	Mart Poom
1981–82	Steve Buckley	2000–01	Chris Riggott
1982–83	Steve Cherry	2001–02	Danny Higginbotham
1983–84	Archie Gemmill	2002–03	Giorgi Kinkladze
1984–85	Bobby Davison	2003–04	Youl Mawene
1985–86	Ross MacLaren	2004–05	Inigo Idiakez
1986–87	Geraint Williams	2005–06	Tommy Smith

✪ The only two players to win the award twice were defenders **Steve Buckley** and **Mark Wright**, the latter in consecutive seasons. The list suggests the ability to stop opponents scoring is the attribute most highly-valued by supporters, while it is most difficult to impress from the in-between world of midfield – the award has gone to defenders 23 times (including four 'keepers), nine to forwards and on only six occasions to midfielders. In Derby's 1974–75 Championship-winning season **Peter Daniel** and **Colin Todd** tied for first place, but Todd generously conceded to the man who had stood in so valiantly for the injured **Roy McFarland**. The proliferation of overseas winners since 1997–98 reflects a major change in transfer patterns, but players wishing to land the award in future should consider gaining what appears to be a very marginal advantage by changing their name to Steve.

THE WRONG KEVIN

If ever a story proves that names really do matter, it is the one told by Kevin Keegan concerning England's 1–1 draw with Poland at Wembley in October 1973. The infamous result denied Alf Ramsey's side a place at the 1974 World Cup, but it was a game that the Rams legend Kevin Hector might have had a real chance to influence had he been brought on earlier. Here's what his fellow substitute Keegan had to say in his autobiography: 'Alf Ramsey proved he was uncomfortable with substitutions by waiting until the 85th minute to make a change, but Poland were under extreme pressure and there was still time for someone with fresh legs to help grab the vital winner. Alf called over his shoulder to the substitutes sitting in a row behind him – "Kevin, get stripped." It was panic stations as goalkeeper Ray Clemence tugged at my tracksuit bottoms to help me get ready, and he was so eager for me to get on that he pulled down my shorts as well. My embarrassment was complete when Alf then made it clear his command had been meant for Kevin Hector, not this Kevin, and there were only 90 seconds left when the Derby man eventually got on...talk about "Don't panic Captain Mainwaring"...even then Kevin nearly scored, and given those vital few minutes more who knows?'

ENGLAND SNUB

Derby County are perhaps the only club to be truly snubbed by England, as on 1 March 1975, despite much pleading, England refused to play against the Rams.

In actual fact the true culprit was a Welshman, the international defender Mike England. He shocked his Irish manager Terry Neill by declining to appear in the League game against Derby County at the Baseball Ground because he had decided, after already being selected, to announce his immediate retirement. The visitors took full advantage of Spurs defensive disarray as Bruce Rioch, Peter Daniel and Roger Davies scored the goals which earned Dave Mackay's seventh-placed Rams a vital 3–1 win worth two points. Boosted by the victory, Derby went on to win the Championship by just two points from Liverpool, who had a superior goal average – but for Mike England's surprise refusal, the Rams might never have clinched that second League title.

ONE-MAN TEAM

Derby's 0–0 draw at Brighton on 26 November 2005 was achieved against a 22–man opposition – that's 11 Brighton players plus the entire QPR side. The explanation for this apparent impossibility is that the Brighton midfielder Charlie Oatway is a 'one-man team' in himself, his parents, fans of Queen's Park Rangers, having blessed him with the names of the Rangers promotion-winning side of 1972–73. He was born on 28 November 1973 and christened Anthony Philip David Terry Frank Donald Stanley Gerry Gordon Stephen James Oatway – 'Charlie' is merely a nickname bestowed by a kindly aunt who thought the whole idea made him look a right Charlie. Some very big names have played against the Rams in their time, but none bigger than the remarkable Mr Oatway.

WHO?

Many Derby supporters 'of a certain age' pride themselves on remembering every player to have made a first-team appearance. But some players make so little impact that it is difficult to recall their face or anything about the games they appeared in, or even sometimes the name itself. Here is a memory-taxing squad of the 'once seen quickly forgotten' variety, all of whom turned out for Derby County in at least one senior game in the last 35 years.

Goalkeepers	Jack Findlay
	Patrick Foletti
Defenders	John Lovatt
	Eamonn Deacy
	Kevin Ratcliffe
	Simon Webster
	Paul Ritchie
	Peter Kennedy
	Dave Walton
	Justin Phillips
	Ray O' Brien
	Daniele Daino
	Alan Lewis
	Gary Caldwell
	Alex Watson

Midfield	Ian Ashbee
	Brian Launders
	Avi Nimni
	David Preece
	Thordur Gudjonsson
Forwards	Aidan Gibson
	Sean Lane
	Nick Chadwick
	Andy Thomas

Even so, the forgettable squad includes two Republic of Ireland internationals, one Northern Ireland cap, one Welsh, two Scottish, an Israeli and an Icelandic international, one player capped at England 'B' level and three who played for the England Youth side. Doubtless there is at least one keen-brained Derby County fan out there who will remember all the faces, places, appearance dates and much more besides.

MEMORY LANE

Purely in the interests of nostalgia, here without explanation is a further 'Top 40' selection of the less routine nicknames variously enjoyed or endured by Rams players of the not-too-distant past.

Michael Johnson	'Magic'
Paul Peschisolido	'Pesky' or 'Pesch'
Marco Gabbiadini	'The Pie Man'
Paul McGrath	'Ooh Aah'
Jacob Laursen	'Cracker'
Lee Morris	'Brooklyn'
Tom Huddlestone	'Mr T'
Mart Poom	'Poooooooom'
Candido Costa	'Toothless'
Branko Strupar	'Super Strupar'
Rory Delap	'Jug Ears'
Seth Johnson	'Sethlad'
Horacio Carbonari	'Bazooka'
Deon Burton	'D' or 'Banjo Boy'
Dean Sturridge	'Studger'
Francesco Baiano	'Banana'

Igor Stimac	'God'
Paulo Wanchope	'Choppy' or 'Legs'
Esteban Fuertes	'Gloria'
Chris Powell	'Cat'
Aljosa Asanovic	'Ace'
Gordon Cowans	'Sid'
Alan Hinton	'Gladys' or 'Noddy'
Michael Forsyth	'Bruce'
Kevin Hector	'Zak' or 'The King'
Peter Daniel	'Ticker'
John O'Hare	'Solly'
Paul Williams	'Jossie'
Gary Charles	'Ray'
Gary Micklewhite	'Weasel' or 'Bobble'
Rob Hindmarch	'Rocky'
Mel Sage	'Parsley'
Ian Ormondroyd	'Sticks'
Kevin Francis	'Bruno'
Geraint Williams	'Leaky Bun'
Jesse Pye	'Auntie'
Grzegorz Rasiak	'Rodders'
Sean Flynn	'Errol'
Colin Boulton	'Bernie'
Leighton James	'Taffy'

IDENTITY CRISIS

✪ In the dark days before television, players' faces were much less familiar than they are now, even to opponents. Once when the Rams played a friendly against lowly opposition a keen but green young defender asked a Derby forward as they lined up – 'I'm marking Bloomer, which one is he?' After the Rams player casually indicated the wrong man, the gullible youngster spent some time doggedly marking his 'famous' man out of the game until he was alerted by a teammate – by then it was too late...elsewhere on the field a sickly looking 'unknown' had already wreaked havoc.

✪ After the Derby manager Tim Ward was continually urged by one of the directors to switch the positions of **Jack Parry** and **Mick Hopkinson** during a poor run in the 60s he decided on a devious experiment. Ward asked the players to change shirt numbers but not positions or roles – yet after the Rams had carved out a 3–1 win the beaming director approached Ward and said – 'There you are...I knew it would make a difference.'

✪ Soon after **Charlie George** signed for Derby in July 1975, the ex-Arsenal man introduced his wife Susan to the Rams chairman Sam Longson, a man prone to somewhat addled thinking. When Longson blurted out to Susan 'And how did you enjoy Wimbledon?' she was as confused as her husband. It turned out that Derby's senior board member thought he was talking to Susan George the film actress, her namesake, who had been splashed all over the papers for having a passionate affair with the US tennis player Jimmy Connors. The story is told in Charlie George's autobiography, and the player ended it thus – 'Who knows where the old boy thought I stood in all of this. They don't make them like Sam any more...who said "Thank Gawd for that?"'

✪ But for a classic case of mistaken identity, the Rams defender **Michael Johnson** would surely have been red-carded in the opening day 1–1 draw at home to Brighton on 8 August 2005, manager Phil Brown's first game in charge. The replacement referee Martin Harris (Brian Curson had limped off early in the second half) somehow missed a blatant pull-back by Johnson on the Seagulls forward Colin Kazim-Richards as he bore into the box. But the linesman did spot it, and as he briefed the referee Johnson prepared for the worst. But the incompetent Harris instead pulled over Rams debutant **Andrew Davies**, and only when his teammates wildly protested did Harris back off and sheepishly put away his cards – by then the official was so flustered he did nothing at all, and nor did the linesman step back in. Michael Johnson, who is small, dark-haired, wiry and black, heaved a huge sigh of relief...and Andrew Davies, big, stocky, straw blond and white, must have prayed he would never be confronted in an identity parade by the visually-challenged Martin Harris.

✪ The only man able to compete with the above Mr Harris, and impressively so too, is the Radio Derby commentator Graham Richards, who seemed to be caught cold by an early Derby goal in their 3–1 defeat at Newcastle in April 1997. Richards had become rather fixated with the obvious threat of Newcastle's England striker Alan Shearer, but after only 32 seconds **Dean Sturridge** broke clear to give Derby a shock lead. Not that the Radio Derby listeners would have known it – 'It's Shearer, Shearer is through, and Shearer has buried it', shrieked Richards – wrong name, wrong team, wrong end, wrong shirt, wrong colour…not exactly his finest hour.

WHO ARE YA?

A glance through the fixture lists of old reveals how many changes have occurred in the make-up of the Football League. The following teams, shown in the order in which the Rams first met them, are either defunct, changed their name to something more familiar or are no longer playing at Football League level – but all have at some time faced Derby County:

ACCRINGTON (A different side to the celebrated Accrington Stanley, who the Rams also faced on several occasions, and in 1955 lost to 2–0. The original Accrington resigned from the League in 1893.)
DARWEN (Dropped out of the League in 1899.)
NEWTON HEATH (The original name under which Manchester United played from 1878 until 1902.)
SMALL HEATH (Became Birmingham in 1906.)
GLOSSOP (NORTH END) (The smallest town to produce a First Division side, dropped out of the League in 1915.)
WOOLWICH ARSENAL (Re-christened The Arsenal in 1914 and then simply Arsenal in 1927.)
CLAPTON ORIENT (Changed their name to Leyton Orient in 1946, Orient in 1966 and back to Leyton Orient in 1987.)
BRADFORD PARK AVENUE (Dropped out of the League in 1970, four years after they had sold Kevin Hector to Derby.)
GAINSBOROUGH TRINITY (Left the Football League in 1912.)
LEEDS CITY (Expelled from the League in 1919 due to financial irregularities and reincarnated as Leeds United.)
LEICESTER FOSSE (Became Leicester City in 1919.)
SOUTH SHIELDS (Became Gateshead in 1931 after moving to the town nine miles from their original home.)
NELSON (The Lancashire club dropped from the League in 1931.)
SWANSEA TOWN (Changed their name to Swansea City in 1969–70.)
WORKINGTON (Dropped out of the League in 1977.)
GATESHEAD (Dropped out of the League in 1960 after failing to be re-elected.)
BARROW (Left the League in 1972 after their 11th re-election request.)
SOUTHPORT (Dropped out of the League in 1978.)
NEWPORT COUNTY (Dropped out of the League in 1989.)

MUGS AWAY

Most players would be delighted to see their names listed in a Top 100 poll, but three Derby men who fell foul of a 2005 internet survey might feel differently – Gordon Cowans, Paul McGrath and Mo Konjic were all voted into the Top 100 Ugliest Footballers list, and Mo Konjic, whose nose, cheek, jaw and just about everything else has at one time been broken, made the All-time Ugly Mug XI.

HIS WAY

On 19 September 2005, the day before the first anniversary of his death, the late Brian Clough was honoured in a rare fashion when road signs were officially unveiled re-naming part of the A52 between Derby and Nottingham Brian Clough Way. The former Derby County and Nottingham Forest manager had spent much of his travelling time on the dual carriageway, and an appropriate slogan added to the signs read 'Linking Derby and Nottingham'.

However, Clough wasn't the first ex-Derby man so honoured – a street near Manchester City's Maine Road ground was earlier named Horace Barnes Close after the striker they signed from Derby in 1914. In 2004 developers planning to build new houses on the site of the demolished Baseball Ground asked for suggestions for street names. Several Derby County greats should get the nod once the homes are built, although the developers had to weed out a crop of spoof suggestions – one waggish non-starter was Hector's House for the development itself and Maxwell House for the sewage plant.

BILLY'S THE KID

When Billy Davies was appointed Derby County manager in June 2006 he became the 28th man to occupy the post, but the third named Billy. That puts the name top of the charts for Rams managers – there have been two each named Harry, George, Colin and John, but only the Billys can boast a hat-trick.

The first was the Rams earliest named manager, William D. 'Billy' Clark – he joined the club from Burton Wanderers in 1896, and although often omitted from the official lists is clearly named as manager in that season's prospectus, although his duties would have been more limited than the tag now implies.

Next up was Billy McEwan who actually had two spells as caretaker manager but took charge for only three games in all – first in 1995 after the departure of Roy McFarland and again in 2002 after Colin Todd had left.

Whether the 2006 arrival of the third Billy will be a 'Billy Whizz' or 'Silly Billy', only time will tell – the only certain thing is that newspaper headline writers will have a very easy time of it.

FOUR – SAINTS AND SINNERS...

Benjamin Ward Spilsbury – the Repton-educated son of the rector of Findern and gifted graduate of Jesus College Cambridge scored Derby County's first ever goal. The unstoppable effort came at the County Ground against Blackburn Olympic on 27 September 1884, but the England forward's lofty connections were not enough to prevent the Rams losing 4–3.

John Barrington Trapnell Chevalier – a clergyman's son, the aptly-initialled J.C. scored a hat-trick in Derby's first ever meeting with Nottingham Forest, a thumping 6–1 'friendly' away win on 31 January 1885. A pen picture describing Chevalier as 'a busy and intelligent forward' seemed an understatement. When he signed for Derby County he had already played in four FA Cup Finals with Old Etonians and by profession was a commercial fruit grower who also served as a leading Justice of the Peace. Nor was the scourge of Forest an educational slouch – he was an Old Etonian, Cambridge University graduate and a master at Repton School, and in his spare time he bred prize cattle!

Llewellyn Henry Gwynne – perhaps the most saintly act of the Derby curate was his 'discovery' of the angelic 12-year-old Steve Bloomer playing for his St Chad's Choir team. But the sporty cleric played centre-forward for the Rams himself during 1887–88, dispensing with seasonal goodwill to hammer four goals past Eckington on Christmas Eve. He was later a missionary and became Bishop of Egypt and the Sudan. No Rams player had a grander farewell – when he died aged 94 in 1957 there were 1,300 gathered in Westminster Abbey to pay tribute to the one-time deadly striker who became known as 'The Flying Bishop'.

Charlie Morris – the Welsh international full-back was jester-in-chief of the Rams' early-1900s 'Crazy Gang'. He once carried a donkey into the Baseball Ground dressing room and on a training trip to Blackpool joined up with 'keeper Harry Maskrey to win a 10-shilling wager from the rest of the lads – both of them walked along the sea-front dressed as women, loudly hooted and pelted with eggs by their teammates as innocent passers-by stood agog.

But Morris was no alcohol-fuelled yob – he was a strict teetotaller and became a Methodist lay-preacher in his native Chirk.

Taribo West – the Nigerian international defender made some classy appearances for Derby in 2000–01 but his 'disappearances' were also legendary. The deeply religious West had founded his own church in Milan and regularly took refuge there without telling a soul. When he failed to return for an away game against Charlton Athletic, Rams manager Jim Smith was left nonplussed – 'I've had to change the team. Taribo has his mobile switched off. Where to play him isn't the problem. I don't even know what country he's in.'

Brian Clough – who but the self-professed 'water-walker' could cause a church service to be switched to a football ground? Following his untimely death, the memorial service for the legendary Rams manager was due to be held in Derby Cathedral, but demand for tickets was such that the venue was changed to Pride Park. On 21 October 2004 around 15,000 fans of both Derby County and Nottingham Forest gathered with Clough's friends, family and celebrity admirers to say farewell in style.

THE BOY DONE BAD

Believe it or not, footballers are mere mortals who sometimes fall foul of the law. Here are some Rams players who appeared in the press for the wrong reasons.

- ☻ Many Rams forwards have been urged to work harder, but outside-right **Arnold Warren** was the only one truly commanded to. Soon after Derby sold him to Brentford in 1902 the right-winger – also a talented Derbyshire and England Test cricketer – was involved in a violent pub brawl. He was convicted of assault and sentenced to two months' hard labour.

- ☻ **Errington Keen** was slightly too keen when it came to gambling. Despite earning a £650 benefit cheque in March 1936, the Rams and England half-back struggled after investing in a tea room. Having 'borrowed' from the till to fund frequent visits to Derby Greyhound Stadium, Keen kept on hoping his number would come up – it soon did…in Derby Bankruptcy Court.

✪ Few Rams strikers have been fierier than 1970s legend **Francis Lee**. Nor did age mellow him – on 28 May 2005 the 61-year-old spent a night in custody after vigorously defending his wife when she was arrested for drink-driving.

✪ The Rams 1980s winger **Mickey Thomas** always lived life to the full, but the Welsh international truly tickled the tabloids in 1992 when he was stabbed in the buttocks with a screwdriver by his wife's brother after being found in a compromising position (also known as a 'Shilton') in the back of a car. A year later things got even worse – Thomas received an 18-month jail sentence for wayward passing...of fake banknotes to Wrexham trainees.

✪ England full-back **Gary Charles** cut a quiet figure with the Rams in the 1990s, but no Derby player has fallen from grace so dramatically. After serial convictions for drink-driving and alcohol-fuelled assault, he was jailed for 6 months in 2004 and was back inside soon after his release following a farcical episode at Derby Crown Court when he appeared drunk before the judge. He was jailed again in the summer of 2006.

✪ Four days before Derby's May 1993 Play-off Final against Leicester City, left-back **Shane Nicholson** telephoned manager Roy McFarland from prison after a drinking binge ended in arrest. He was dropped and ultimately sold to West Bromwich Albion, where in 1998 he was banned from football for life for drug and alcohol abuse. Only after an FA reprieve was he given the most unlikely of new starts at Chesterfield – their manager was Roy McFarland.

✪ On 20 April 2000 striker **Marvin Robinson** took Derby one step closer to a full 'Lags XI' when he admitted breaking his ex-girlfriend's nose by head butting. He was sentenced to eight months in prison, but Derby County courted huge controversy by saying they would 'stand by him'. His playing strike rate was equally unimpressive – one goal in five seasons as a registered Rams player.

✪ In March 2000 the Rams 'keeper **Russell Hoult** was sold to Portsmouth after he had been accused of slowing down. In February he had suffered the indignity of being arrested for kerb-crawling in Derby's Red Light district and was convicted two months later.

STICKY FINGERS

Few football clubs have a history as strewn with financial misdemeanour and controversy as Derby County. For each indiscretion listed here there are many more in a catalogue of bad housekeeping which has consistently dogged the club.

- In 1889, when Derby County and Derbyshire County Cricket Club were still linked, the accounts revealed unusually high losses in the football section. The secretary **Sam Richardson** was found to have been quietly embezzling the takings. As the Rams entered their first crisis era, the disgraced club servant forged a new life abroad and was last heard of as court tailor to the king of Spain.

- A public meeting on 17 February 1919 resolved to 'save Derby County from the very threat of extinction'. The aim was achieved only when supporters dipped into their pockets to buy shares, and the owner of the Baseball Ground, **Sir Gordon Ley**, agreed to waive substantial arrears of rent.

- A bombshell hit the club in 1941 when a joint FA–Football League commission discovered that from 1925–1938 the club had habitually made illegal payments to players. They had been concealed by devices such as paying the manager for bogus journeys and inventing a fictitious groundsman. The club was fined £500 and five directors plus manager **George Jobey** were suspended from football.

- In November 1949 chairman **Ben Robshaw** and former secretary **Jack Catterall** were suspended when a further commission revealed that in 1945–46 payments due to the Inland Revenue had been surreptitiously withheld.

- In 1969–70 Derby finished fourth in the top flight and qualified for the European Fairs Cup, but they were fined £10,000 and banned from competing in Europe after a joint FA–League commission again revealed 'gross negligence' in the books.

- On 3 February 1984, as debts spiralled out of control, the Inland Revenue issued Derby County with a winding-up order. The club was saved only when chief executive **Stuart Webb** secured the backing of millionaire publisher **Robert Maxwell**, an alliance which brought its own alarming consequences.

✪ In October 2003 Derby County were put into receivership with debts of £34 million. Thousands of small shareholders were left with nothing but obsolete certificates as the club was hastily sold to an outside consortium in a matter of minutes. The purchase price agreed was a nominal £3, despite a group of wealthy local investors waiting in the wings to consider a bid of their own.

✪ On 13 April 2006 chairman **John Sleightholme** resigned after it was revealed that police were inquiring into allegations that chief executive Jeremy Keith and others had agreed to split a curious £375,000 'consultancy fee' paid as a commission to a company known as Streamline Management. Sleightholme himself was not implicated but stated his position to be 'untenable'.

DISAPPEARING ACTS

✪ Goalkeeper **Thomas Harrison** made his Derby debut in a 2–0 win at Liverpool in April 1902. Everything looked rosy as he was picked again for the away trip to Blackburn Rovers five days later, but disaster struck when he missed his train en route, and the Rams were forced to play their reluctant 39-year-old trainer Arthur Latham in goal. Derby were beaten 3–1, and Harrison had missed his big chance as well as his train – he was never selected again.

✪ For four seasons in the early 1920s **Jimmy Lyons** was a reliable source of goals, netting 33 in 86 senior games. Unfortunately the inside-forward's behaviour was rather less reliable, and the game at Clapton Orient in April 1923 proved to be his last in a Derby shirt – he became the only player permanently suspended by the club for a misdemeanour described as 'gross insubordination'.

✪ The Republic of Ireland international **Dave Langan** refused to travel with Derby's team to a third-round FA Cup tie at Bristol City on 5 January 1980. After a simmering bust-up with manager Colin Addison reached a flashpoint, the full-back travelled alone by train. But Addison was in no mood to compromise. Langan was dropped, sent straight home, fined two weeks' wages and invited to put in a transfer request. Bruce Rioch was also fined for taking Langan's side and using 'foul and abusive language' towards the manager. The spat hardly helped the team – Derby were hammered 6–2.

✪ Many players have failed to get on 'with' the team coach, but on 10 September 1983 the Rams striker **Bobby Davison** varied the theme by failing to 'get on' the team coach. He had overslept and missed the bus for Derby's away game at Blackburn Rovers. Without the heavy-lidded leading scorer the Rams went into a deep sleep themselves and suffered a nightmare 5–1 thrashing.

✪ The non-appearance of the Rams winger **Lee Morris** in a 1–0 home defeat by Crystal Palace on 6 March 2003 gave conspiracy theorists a field day. Morris was selected and came out for the warm-up but failed to start the game. Officially he had 'strained a hamstring' in the kick about, but rumours later circulated that his jaw had been broken during a dressing room 'tactical discussion' with the Rams manager John Gregory. Nothing was ever proven, and the Lee Morris mystery remains exactly that to this day.

RIGHT SIDE OF THE LAW

✪ The first player to be signed after the formation of Derby County in 1884 was **Haydn Arthur Morley**. His contract negotiations went particularly smoothly, and despite being very short in stature he quickly established an uncanny respect in the dressing room – Morley was a solicitor by profession, and his brother William happened to be chairman and co-founder of the club!

✪ Popular Side regulars at the Baseball Ground gave hard-as-nails defender **Jack Nicholas** the name 'Owd Nick'. In the event, it proved a suitable moniker as during the war the 1946 Cup-winning captain joined the Derby Borough Police Force. Even then the full-back's combative football spirit didn't go to waste – playing centre-forward for the Derbyshire Constabulary against Nottingham Borough Police, he preserved local supremacy by scoring all four goals in an easy win over the boys from Nottingham.

✪ Few Derby County players have sold their soul as comprehensively as **Leslie Bailey**. He was quite a favourite just before World War Two, but in 1939 he gave up the game and spoilt it all. The more roguish of Derby County fans considered his choice of new career almost a crime in itself – the former Rams defender joined the Nottingham City Police.

✪ But for a keen-eyed scout, **Colin Boulton** might well have spent more time guarding a 'gaol' than a 'goal'. He was a police cadet in his native Cheltenham when Tim Ward signed him for the Rams in 1964. It proved a sound move – his 344 games is a record for a Derby County 'keeper.

✪ A former Rams midfielder once helped shape the law. After **Brian McCord** left the club in March 1990, he had his League career tragically cut short. In March 1993, while playing for Stockport County, he was the victim of a reckless challenge by Swansea City player John Cornforth, and McCord decided on litigation. He finally won his case in London's High Court in December 1996, becoming the first footballer to successfully pursue such a claim. The landmark judgement by Mr Justice Ian Kennedy saw the player receive an interim award of £50,000 pending a full assessment of damages.

SINFUL SUNDAY

For many years the playing of professional football on a Sunday was considered unthinkable and even a mere mention of the game on a day reserved for worship was thought to be almost sinful by many religious leaders. But all that changed during the power and transport crisis of 1974 when a limited number of Sunday games were permitted because the day afforded better availability of electricity. Derby's first ever shameful Sunday came in the FA Cup fourth-round game at Coventry City on 27 January 1974, where they drew 0–0. But three days later in the Baseball Ground replay they paid for their sins – the Rams were beaten 1–0.

Now Sunday football is common and even religious leaders embrace the game. When Derby County won promotion to the Premiership in 1995–96, manager Jim Smith received this message of goodwill from a faithful admirer, the Provost of Derby Cathedral, the Very Reverend Ben Lewers: 'Mr Smith, may I add the congratulations of all of us here at Derby Cathedral. When I mentioned your promotion to the Premiership in my sermon last Sunday, there was an audible growl of glee and approval.'

BIBLICAL STRIKERS

Even Derby County can't attempt to match the mischievous claim of 'Queen of the South' to be the only football club mentioned in the Bible (actually a reference to the Queen of Sheba), but the Rams do have one Biblical boast of sorts – an unlikely trio of centre-forwards whose first names show a healthy nod to the testaments. The archaic threesome of Burton, Lane and Tremelling were in turn named Noah, Moses and Elijah – a saviour, a leader and a handsome prophet...Derby could do with them now.

ALWAYS HORSING AROUND

It's been said that the most troublesome player to represent the Rams is the Irish international Archie Goodall, and that despite his brother John being the saintliest. What an astrologer would make of it is anybody's guess, for the 'chalk and cheese' pair shared the same birthday – a year apart on 19 June.

Archie unnerved the Rams committee from the moment he arrived in 1889 – they never knew what he'd do next. Consider these extracts from the Archibald hall of shame:

- **11 January 1890** – Refused to travel to Preston because his wife was ill. Derby played with 10 men and were thrashed 5–0.
- **3 September 1892** – Suspended for the first four games of the season following 'a spot of bother at Sheffield.'
- **30 April 1894** – Refused to play extra-time against West Bromwich Albion in the United Counties League Play-off Final – Archie told the directors 'my contract finishes at 90 minutes...I'm off home.'
- **16 April 1898** – FA Cup Final v Nottingham Forest – Frayed the team's nerves by 'disappearing' close to kick-off to sell his surplus tickets outside the ground. After he returned, an unsettled Derby lost 3–1.
- **15 April 1899** – FA Cup Final against Sheffield United – Refused to play after being accused of 'inattention to training'. He told the committee 'Better not select me then...too many mischievous and idle rumours going about'. Without him Derby were beaten 4–1.

And so it went on. Among other things, Archie had fisticuffs with a spectator, put a dead rat in teammate Jack Cox's kit bag (found by Cox's pregnant and hysterical wife) and had a nice turn of phrase whenever brother John was badly fouled – 'do that again chummy and I'll lean on you' – and he did...many times.

His oddest jape of all was an epic journey from Derby to Kilmarnock and back, the town where the Goodall boys were raised. Archie completed the 600-mile round trip in five days on his favourite bay cob – 'the horse wore out four pairs of shoes but one lasted 300 miles and became my proudest possession', he said.

No one asked Archie why. They daren't. He played 423 games for Derby

County including a run of 167 consecutive appearances, which remains a record today. The truth is that the 'arch villain' had a heart of gold.

NEVER ON A SATURDAY

The reverend Ben Crockett was very reverential when it came to supporting the Rams. The vicar of All Saints, Mickleover, a season-ticket holder for 20 years, made national headlines in 1984 when he refused to conduct a marriage ceremony because it clashed with a Derby County home game.

When bride-to-be Helen Warner and her fiancé Robert Madeley named the big day as 13 October 1984 at 3.30pm, the Rams-mad cleric said he would have to wait for the fixtures to come out before he could commit himself. Unluckily for the young couple, the Football League also named 13 October as the day Derby would play Plymouth Argyle at the Baseball Ground.

Crockett stuck to his guns, saying 'It has long been my policy not to marry couples after 1pm on Saturdays when Derby are at home.' Miss Warner, who had attended the church since she was four, was not impressed and promptly complained to a higher authority – first the Bishop of Derby and then the Archbishop of Canterbury. She said, 'They say God's house is always open but in this case only if Derby are playing away.'

The 70-year-old Reverend Crockett was unrepentant though, and on 13 October, while the lovers exchanged their vows at Aston-on-Trent, he took his usual seat at the Baseball Ground to see his team win 3–1 with two goals by Bobby Davison and a penalty from Steve Buckley. The new Mr and Mrs Madeley declined to celebrate the victory and later that night were strangely unavailable for comment.

MARKED MEN

Of the countless bad tackles on Derby County players, the majority are quickly forgotten. But a handful of truly dreadful ones linger in the memory – here are some x-rated clashes for which the sinful perpetrators were never forgiven.

⚽ **Derby v Grimsby Town** – 10 March 1956 – the 'bodily assault' which effectively decided the Third Division North promotion issue was committed by hatchet-man Ray de Gruchy. The Mariners' full-back calmly disposed of 27-goal Jack Parry, the Rams key man, by means of a flying kung-fu kick to the back. As so often seems to happen, the villain profited from his crime – Derby lost 3–1, Parry missed the rest of the season, and Grimsby were promoted at the Rams' expense.

⚙ **Rotherham United v Derby** – 2 February 1982 – a terrible day as Derby were beaten 2–1, and a wild tackle by Rotherham's Gerry Gow broke the leg of the Rams midfielder Steve Emery, ending his Derby career at a stroke. Gow was sent off and roundly barracked on all his subsequent visits to Derby.

⚙ **Derby v Charlton** – 13 April 1983 – Steve Buckley was playing his 200th game for the Rams when he was the victim of an 80th minute over-the-top lunge by Mark Aizlewood. The diabolical tackle left Buckley limping badly, but the tough-nut left-back played on for five minutes before leaving the field – the 'knock' was later confirmed as a broken leg!

⚙ **West Ham v Derby** – 17 January 1990 – this Wednesday night League Cup tie was only four minutes old when George Parris cynically took out Derby midfielder Steve Cross, who left the ground on crutches. West Ham also had a go at his replacement Mark Patterson, who early in the second half just managed to evade an ugly, two-footed lunge by Martin 'Mad Dog' Allen, who was sent off for the challenge. The game ended 1–1, but Derby eventually went out 2–1 in a second replay at Upton Park after losing a toss for the choice of venue.

⚙ **Tottenham Hotspur v Derby** – 25 November 1990 – Derby's 2–1 win was marred by a serious knee-ligament injury to Ted McMinn, who fell awkwardly after being unceremoniously bundled over the touchline by the Spurs full-back Pat Van Den Hauwe. It was 14 months before the Rams winger played again.

⚙ **Southend United v Derby** – 16 October 1994 – in the 51st minute of this Division One clash the Southend striker Dave Regis launched himself studs-up for what only he saw as a fifty-fifty ball with the Rams 'keeper Martin Taylor. The reckless challenge left Taylor with a double fracture of the left leg, but referee Graham Pooley meekly awarded a corner as the stricken 'keeper was stretchered off. Southend won 1–0 via a sickening last-minute goal...by Dave Regis.

⚙ **Derby v Aston Villa** – 7 February 1998 – a last-minute goal by Dwight Yorke robbed Derby of their unbeaten home League record, but the Villa striker should not have been on the pitch. After only 15 minutes, he made a terrible tackle on the Rams defender Dean Yates, but timid referee Paul Alcock (of Paolo Di Canio 'pirouette' fame) shamefully allowed Yorke to remain on the field. The ligament damage to Yates ended his Derby career.

☻ **Liverpool v Derby** – 6 November 1999 – after 20 minutes, Liverpool's Finnish international defender Sami Hyypia left a boot in on Derby's stylish Italian midfielder Stefano Eranio. The Rams man suffered a broken leg, but referee Uriah Rennie failed to produce a card. Derby were beaten 2–0 and fuming manager Jim Smith described the tackle as 'unbelievable'.

☻ **Burnley v Derby** – 27 August 2005 – the Rams were trailing 2–1 after 55 minutes when full-back Marc Edworthy was on the receiving end of a shocking high-kick routine by the Clarets' Graham Branch close to the corner flag, which he later claimed was 'accidental'. Branch was merely booked, but after a long delay Edworthy left the field with a severe facial injury which kept him out for some time. Justice was done five minutes into the 11 minutes of added time when Rasiak equalised for Derby.

―――――――――――――― UNLUCKY BREAK ――――――――――――――

On 26 February 1995 defender Simon Coleman returned to the Baseball Ground for the first time since leaving the Rams 13 months earlier. The Bolton Wanderers player was carried off with a broken left leg in the 13th minute following a nasty challenge by his former teammate Marco Gabbiadini. Bolton were beaten 2–1 and their manager, ex-Derby favourite Bruce Rioch, was quick to condemn the home club's forcible approach – a classic case of 'boot on the other foot' syndrome from a Rams man whose own tackles once carried a health warning.

―――――――――――――― PACKING A PUNCH ――――――――――――――

Goalkeepers need a strong punch, but Colin Boulton took things too literally when Derby won the Texaco Cup against Airdrie on 26 April 1972. After being kicked in the back by Drew Jarvie, the Rams 'keeper landed a solid right hook on the Airdrie striker's jaw. Amazingly, World Cup referee Jack Taylor merely delivered a stern word, and Boulton stayed on the pitch to celebrate the Rams 2–1 victory. But he did not get away entirely unpunished – when the Derby directors saw the televised highlights Boulton was quickly fined, the first Derby player to suffer trial by television.

❧ The oddest bout of fisticuffs involving a Rams player concerned striker **Derek Hales** after he had left the Baseball Ground and rejoined his former club Charlton Athletic. In an FA Cup tie against Maidstone United in January 1979 he and **Mike Flanagan** were sent off for fighting following an argument over a free-kick. The double dismissal was the first of its kind in football history as it reduced Charlton to nine men – both players were on the same side!

❧ At Everton in 1997–98 Derby's Costa Rican striker **Paulo Wanchope** was jostling with Duncan Ferguson in his own area (Everton unsuccessfully claiming a penalty) when the big Scot, known for his temper and prison record, laid Wanchope on the Goodison canvas and was sent off after only 16 minutes. Despite Ferguson receiving warm applause from the Everton blind-faithful, justice was done as Derby beat the 10–man Toffees 2–1.

❧ Derby's Croatian international **Igor Stimac** never suffered referees gladly, but after leaving the Rams in 1999 his disdain for officials finally backfired. On 10 April 2004, while Sporting Director at Hajduk Split, he was accused of 'slapping' referee Miroslav Jedvav during the half-time break of an away game at Rijeka. Despite typical protests of boyish innocence, Stimac was found guilty of assault and banned by the Croatian FA for six months.

───────────────── AND THEY'RE OFF ─────────────────

Countless Derby players have been 'given their marching orders', 'taken an early bath', 'walked', been 'shown red', 'dismissed' or 'sent to the dressing room'. However it's dressed up, being sent off is part of the game – most of the incidents fade in time but a few were more noteworthy than others.

❧ Despite being a constant target for the cloggers, **Steve Bloomer** seldom lost his rag. But on the one occasion he was dismissed – for retaliation after being kicked 'between the legs' by Bert Sharp at Everton in 1901 – he was so aggrieved that he wrote a four-page letter of appeal to the FA, but the FA jury bottled it, and Bloomer was suspended for two weeks.

❧ No player with Derby connections ever caused more mayhem than **Geoff Hazledine**. After leaving the Rams in 1954, he entered non-League football and was playing for Loughborough against Belper in 1961–62 when he caused the abandonment of the game by refusing to leave the field when sent off. When the game was replayed, he was determined to repent, and in a sense he was true to his word – this time when he was again ordered off he went quietly!

☻ **Charlie George** had a 'consistent' season from start to finish in 1976–77. He was sent off for throwing a punch late in Derby's opening day draw at Newcastle and repeated his familiar walk nine minutes from the end of the final game of the season, a draw at home to Ipswich Town, this time making doubly sure with a combined head-butt and punch on John Wark.

☻ Rams manager Tommy Docherty once described midfielder **Jonathan Clark** as 'the best thing to come out of Wales since coal' – so his first League appearance in his native Swansea in October 1980 should have been a particularly proud occasion. But instead the young midfielder was left in the pits of despair – Clark was booked after four minutes, conceded a penalty after 33 and was sent off after 66. Derby's 10 men were beaten 3–1, their former winger Leighton James adding insult to injury by notching a hat-trick.

SUNDAY WORSHIP

Derby's churches suffered unusually low congregations one sunny Sunday morning in May 1972 when many of the town's citizens headed instead for another place of worship, the Baseball Ground, where a packed crowd had turned out at the unaccustomed time to see the Football League Championship trophy being presented to Brian Clough's triumphant Derby side.

FIVE – A QUESTION OF SPORT...

ALL-ROUNDERS

On 14 August 1896 Derby County became a Limited Company. But no one could have accused them of having limited objectives. Clause three subsection two of the club's 'Memorandum and Articles of Association' stated their aims as follows:

'To promote the practice and play of football, cricket, baseball, lacrosse, lawn tennis, hockey, bowls, bicycle and tricycle riding, running, jumping, physical training and the development of the human frame.'

Although only the football arm of the club made permanent headway, Derby County have always had a close association with the wider sporting community. In the spirit of that first mission statement, all the following tales have a link to sports other than association football, but each preserves a Rams connection.

THE SPORT OF KINGS

From 1884 to 1895 the regular home of Derby County was the County Ground. It was also known as 'Derby Racecourse', and race meetings were held there until August 1939. Considering the unusual early alliance, it's only fitting that Derby County should have some lasting acquaintance with the 'Sport of Kings'.

☉ But for the popularity of racing, a legendary era in Rams history might never have come to pass. At Easter 1895 the Derby Racecourse owners stubbornly prevented Derby County from fulfilling a prestige friendly against the crack amateur side Corinthians because a race meeting was scheduled 'for the same week'. Realising that sharing a stage with horseracing (and cricket for that matter) had become impossible, the club relocated to the Baseball Ground and stayed there for the next 102 years.

☉ Oswald 'Ossie' Jackson, president of Derby County when the club won the FA Cup in 1946, was a keen racing enthusiast. In honour of the Rams his registered owner's colours were always black and white. Unfortunately Jackson was also a gambler in his approach to running the club and was suspended in 1941 after the FA uncovered serious irregularities in the books.

✪ After his final game in 1976, Derby's bustling forward **Francis Lee** enjoyed great success as a racehorse trainer. He and his Rams colleague, leggy full-back Rod Thomas, co-owned a horse named Clydebank. Mischievous punters were quick to suggest that the unpredictable nag had inherited the combined attributes of its owners – an upright style and loping stride gave it a surprising turn of speed, but the horse invariably carried too much weight and fell when least expected.

✪ While researching a book, the former player Ian Hall quizzed **Willie Carlin** about Peter Taylor, assistant manager during Carlin's time at Derby. The no-nonsense midfielder delivered straight from the horse's mouth.
Hall: 'Did Peter Taylor go down to the training ground?'
Carlin: 'Who? Peter Taylor? You're joking. He used to give us tips, but not the sort you think. The only training he knew was racehorses.'

✪ A horse named Charlie George ran at a number of meetings in 2005. The handsome chestnut male – by Idris out of Faithful Beauty – was owned by chartered surveyor Peter Monteith. However, Rams fans resisting the urge to back it proved wise students of the turf, as 'Charlie George' seldom produced the brilliant form on the track that his namesake showed on the field.

ANYONE FOR TENNIS?

—————————————— OH I SAY! ——————————————

Two of Derby County's most outstanding players when they won the FA Cup in 1946 were Raich Carter and Peter Doherty. Yet only a quirk of fate enabled them to sign for the Rams at all. The story is told in Carter's autobiography *Footballer's Progress*.

In 1944 Sergeants P.D. Doherty and H.S. Carter were appointed as PT instructors to the No. 3 Medical Rehabilitation Unit based at Loughborough College. They were persuaded to go there following a chance meeting with a Squadron Leader from the unit. Both footballers settled in well.

It was the Squadron Leader's regular habit to take groups of his patients to watch Derby County at the Baseball Ground, and he agreed a neat deal with the club – his fitness instructors Carter and Doherty would make regular guest appearances for the Rams in exchange for free tickets. Both players so impressed the club that they were signed-on permanently for the Cup-winning season. The 'Mr Fixit' later made his name as a tennis coach and legendary commentator – the Squadron Leader was 'the Voice of Wimbledon' Dan Maskell. But for his persuasive nature, Derby County might never have lifted that coveted FA Cup.

WHAT HAPPENED NEXT?

When the budding young tennis starlet Sue Barker was interviewed on Radio Two in November 1976, she really set tongues wagging. Still inexperienced in media matters, the 'Devon Belle' revealed her favourite football team: 'I am extremely interested in Derby County. I have friends there.'

When pressed, the Wimbledon hopeful coyly elaborated, but merely succeeded in digging herself an even bigger hole: 'I have met Charlie George and Leighton James in hotels and know them quite well.' It seemed the admiration was mutual – two 'mystery Derby players' were said to have placed bets backing the 22-year-old blonde to 'win the women's singles at Wimbledon in the next five years.'

Sue Barker never did land that coveted title, but the young innocent went on to become a polished BBC television presenter. Does she still have a soft spot for the Rams? How well did she really know those two Derby forwards? She keeps us guessing – these days Sue wisely does the asking instead of the answering.

LONG MAY HE SERVE

In summer 2005 a Derby County fan became 'the most famous referee in the world' – or so the position has been described – when the celebrated Wimbledon Championships referee Alan Mills retired after 23 years in the job. Appointed as his replacement was Belper-born Rams supporter Andrew Jarrett, a former Wimbledon competitor and Great Britain Davis Cup player.

Even though he will be in charge of the tournament from 2006, Jarrett will not be allowed to sport a Rams shirt when he comes on to asses the centre court light – which is a pity because his Derby County allegiance runs deep – Jarrett achieved membership of the illustrious '92 Club' for having visited every League ground on his football travels.

A number of Rams men have fancied their chance at tennis. Alan Hinton, Darren Wassall, Darryl Powell and George Burley all wielded a useful racket – and the ace in Derby's pack was Alan Durban, one-time manager of a major indoor Tennis Centre. But none can match the Rams fan charged with delivering the toughest line in sport – 'Ladies and gentlemen, play is suspended'.

SWIM FOR IT

✪ But for a timely rescue, Derby's 1895 signing of the Liverpool outside-left **Hugh McQueen** would never have gone ahead. While training with the Merseyside club at Southport baths, he jumped off the springboard and almost drowned. Evidently the player was anxious to be one of the lads, as only after being hauled to safety did the not-so-canny Scotsman admit he couldn't swim.

✪ For many years a small knoll in the River Derwent close to Derby town centre was known as 'Goodall's Island', thus christened in the 1890s when the Rams **John Goodall**, on his way to play cricket for Derbyshire, saved a man from drowning by dragging him to safety there. No sooner had the gasping but grateful man recovered than Goodall headed off dripping wet to take the field – his second struggle in a single day.

✪ In June 1977 the former Rams striker **Francis Lee** was larking about on a fishing trip in Scotland when he fell overboard and was sucked under by the current. Witnesses said that only his sportsman's strength, determination and just a hint of natural buoyancy enabled him to avoid being included in the 'tragic deaths' section of this book.

✪ Giant Derbyshire-born swimmer **Ross Davenport**, double gold medal winner at the 2006 Commonwealth Games, counts Derby County as his greatest passion outside the pool. His ultimate reward for once giving the club worldwide TV exposure (he draped himself in a Rams towel on the starting blocks) was to take penalties against club mascot Rammie at the final game of 2005–06. Yet again Davenport struck 100 percent gold, effortlessly stroking home in double-quick time with a series of powerful kicks.

MEN OF MANY TALENTS

Many personalities connected to Derby County excelled at sports other than football. Excluding details of cricketing feats, which are noted elsewhere, here are some notable examples.

✪ Multi-talented centre-forward and captain **Frank Sugg** (1884–85) was a regular entrant at weightlifting, long-distance swimming and shot-put events. He also reached the final of the Liverpool Amateur Billiards Championship and won numerous prizes for rifle-shooting. He also played county cricket for Derbyshire.

⚽ Rams captain **John Goodall** (1889–98) was modesty personified despite excelling in almost everything he tried – 100 breaks at billiards were routine, he was a crack shot with a sporting gun, and his patient nature made him a fine fly fisherman. He was also a club champion at bowls, but his most unusual skill owed much to his Scottish upbringing – the ice-cool footballer once brushed aside all opposition to become the champion curler of England.

⚽ Glasgow-born right-winger **Jimmy Boyd** (1935–36) quickly learned to cope with bias during his time south of the border – so much so that in retirement the Scot contrived to play for England at indoor bowls.

⚽ Against the club's wishes – they believed he would become 'muscle bound' – full-back **Bert Mozley** (1946–54) was one of the first players to pursue a serious body-building regime. After emigrating to Canada in 1954, the Rams most finely-toned player won many trophies for his splendid physique.

⚽ Football people love to say 'it's a marathon not a sprint', and the Rams boss **John Gregory** took the adage a few steps further when in May 2002 he gamely ran the London Marathon in five hours, two minutes and 18 seconds. In the League marathon Derby 'hit the wall' early and were relegated in 19th place, and Gregory's own survival race also proved a struggle – he finished 26,601st.

THE SUMMER GAME

TRIED AND TESTED

Not until 1919–20 did a Football League season ever begin in August – and then only on the 30th of the month – all of which meant that pre-World War One practitioners of the 'winter game' could also become active devotees of the 'summer game' without undue overlap. For that reason many early footballers also played cricket at the higher levels, and four men with Derby County links achieved the ultimate accolade – they played for both the Rams and in a Test Match for England. These are the rare members of that noble 'double breed' which modern-day fixture lists have long-since rendered extinct:

Frank Sugg was a Rams centre-forward in their pre-League days and the scorer of the first competitive hat-trick for Derby County, in a 3–0 away win against Stafford Road on 15 November 1884. He played cricket for

Derbyshire, Yorkshire and Lancashire and his two Tests against Australia came in 1888. His passion for cricket continued into his senior years – in 1926 and 1927 he was a first-class umpire...although the players didn't always think so!

William Chatterton played inside-forward for Derby in their first Football League season and at the same time captained Derbyshire at cricket. He scored seven centuries for the county and made 48 in his one Test innings, against South Africa in Cape Town in 1892.

William Storer played 27 games for the Rams and appeared in all five forward positions. His versatility knew no bounds as he was more famous as a Derbyshire and England wicketkeeper who also captured 214 wickets for his county as a bowler. Not content with that, he set a batting record in 1896 during Derbyshire's home game with Yorkshire when he became the first professional (only amateurs had done it previously) to score two centuries in a match. The remarkable all-rounder played in six Tests against Australia and scored 12,966 runs in first-class cricket. He was uncle to the Rams player and manager Harry Storer.

Arnold Warren was both a winger and a swinger, playing a single season with the Rams in 1901–02 but gaining more lasting fame as a Derbyshire fast bowler. Between 1897 and 1920 he took 939 wickets in first-class cricket and shared in a world-record ninth-wicket partnership of 283 with Jack Chapman for Derbyshire against Warwickshire at Blackwell in 1910. In his one Test against Australia at Leeds in 1905 he took five for 57 in the first innings.

DOUBLE DERBEIANS

They have been labelled 'crickballers', 'bladder and willow' men, the 'double breed' and sometimes just 'cocky so-and-sos', but, whatever else they may be, the men who have played first-team football for Derby County and first-team cricket for Derbyshire are members of an exclusive caste – here is the roll of honour.

	With Derby	With Derbyshire
Albert Alderman	1927–34	1928–48
Ian Buxton	1959–67	1959–73
Raich Carter	1945–48	1946
William Chatterton	1884–88	1882–1902
William Cropper	1886	1882–88
Jack Davis	1905–10	1920
Percy Exham	1884	1883
Thomas Fletcher	1904–06	1906

John Goodall	1889–99	1895–96
Ian Hall	1958–62	1959–72
Stuart McMillan	1914–19	1922–24
Haydn Morley	1884–89	1891
Bob Stephenson	1962–64	1967–68
Harry Storer	1921–29	1920–36
William Storer	1891–93	1887–1905
Frank Sugg	1884	1884–86
Ray Swallow	1958–64	1959–63
Arnold Warren	1901–02	1897–1920
Levi Wright	1888	1883–1909

QUICK SINGLES

✪ On 27 April 1895 an entire Derby County team played in a Test Match – but this one was of the football variety since it was once the term for a Play-off. After finishing next to last in Division One, the Rams faced Notts County, the Second Division runners-up, to decide which side would begin the following season in Division One. The crucial decider, played at Walnut Street (later Filbert Street) in Leicester, proved one of the most pivotal and nerve-wracking games in Derby's history as they came from behind to triumph 2–1 with a goal 30 seconds from time. The famous win not only kept Derby in football's top flight but arguably secured the very survival of the cash-strapped club.

✪ Derby's Welsh international full-back **Charlie Morris** landed a plum summer job towards the end of his playing career – from 1910 to 1916 he was cricket professional to the Duke of Westminster's XI based at Eaton Hall, an immense stately pile in Cheshire.

✪ After playmaking centre-half **Ben Hall** signed for Derby in 1903, he showed his great cricket prowess in a particularly demonstrative way. Hall's party piece was to throw a cricket ball from the goal-mouth of the Normanton End of the Baseball Ground that would clear the bar of the Osmaston End goal – several reliable witnesses documented the near-impossible feat.

✪ Apart from excelling at football and baseball, the Rams striker **Steve Bloomer** might well have held his own in county cricket if only he had had the time. Just before the 1914–18 war he denied Rolls-Royce the Derby and District League title when he scored 112 not out for Ley's Works, and his form held during his wartime imprisonment in Ruhleben, near Berlin, where he set the camp batting record of 204 and once nabbed bowling figures of six for 15.

⚽ After retiring from playing football in the 1930s, the Rams high-scoring centre-forward **Harry Bedford** was said to possess 'the best pair of hands' at Derbyshire County Cricket Club, despite never having taken a single catch – indeed he never even played a game... he was the club's masseur.

⚽ The mutual respect between Derby County players and their Derbyshire cricketer counterparts was well demonstrated on two occasions, one glad and one sad. In 1936, when Derbyshire won the County Championship for the only time in their history, each member of the side was given an inscribed silver cigarette case by Derby County. Two years later, on 20 April 1938, the day of Steve Bloomer's funeral, Derbyshire cricketers left the County Ground practice nets and lined Nottingham Road in silent tribute as the eight-car cortège passed the ground where the legendary Rams striker had first learnt his trade.

⚽ **Jack Lee**, a high-scoring Rams centre-forward in the early 1950s, holds an unusual cricket record. On his debut for Leicestershire against Glamorgan in 1947 the medium-pace bowler took a wicket with his very first ball in county cricket, yet it proved the only one he ever took in the only game he ever played. Indeed Lee seemed to have a knack for doing things in ones, as although he was selected for England at football he won just a single cap before being cast aside for good, scoring one goal in a 4–1 win over Northern Ireland in October 1950.

⚽ It is difficult to imagine a Derbyshire cricket match causing a problematic fixture clash with football these days, but county cricket was once such a draw that the Rams home game against Mansfield Town on 20 August 1955 had its kick-off changed to the evening to avoid a clash with that afternoon's cricket at the County Ground. The football match was Derby's first in the Third Division North after relegation, and the club feared a dip in attendances – in the event a healthy crowd of 24,159 saw the Rams win 4–0.

⚽ Sporting all-rounder **Harry Storer**, a player with the Rams in the 1920s and their manager from 1955 to 1962, uniquely played nine matches in a County Championship-winning team while in office as a Football League manager – he appeared for Derbyshire in their triumphant 1936 season and the same year managed Coventry City to the 1935–36 Division Three South title.

☉ Records suggest that the Rams inside-forward and Derbyshire cricketer **Ian Hall** might have made a better goal 'keeper' than goal 'scorer' – playing against Warwickshire in the 1960s at Coventry, his safe hands held six catches in a single match, a significant improvement on his 1961–62 season at Derby County, his last at the club, when he registered just two goals in 12 games.

☉ **Ian Buxton**, the last player to divide his winter and summer between playing for Derby County and Derbyshire, achieved in cricket what he never managed for the Rams – a first-class hat-trick. The rare bowling feat came against Oxford University at the County Ground in 1969, but the centre-forward was unable to add the far easier football equivalent in 157 outings for the Rams.

☉ The last Derby County player to also ply his trade as a county cricketer was the centre-half **Alan Ramage**, who joined the Rams from Middlesbrough in 1980. He was forced into retirement prematurely by a knee injury and this also curtailed his cricket career – he was a fast bowler for Yorkshire from 1979–83. His luck hardly improved after that – Ramage spent some time retained 'at the pleasure of Her Majesty' after being convicted of embezzlement.

KINGS OF THE DIAMOND

☉ When Derby County secured themselves a new long-term home in 1895, they became the only football club formed from a cricket club to move from a racecourse to a baseball ground – which for good measure also staged athletics, boxing and wrestling events!

☉ The Baseball Ground name reflected that it had served the popular American game for five years already, after the Derby industrialist Sir Francis Ley introduced it to the town following a visit to the States. Ley established a National League, and the first game of baseball ever witnessed at Derby took place on what was initially called Ley's Recreation Ground on Saturday 3 May 1890 – the Derby side, smartly attired in grey and blue, beat Erdington 23–11.

- ☻ Derby were the leading 'nine' of the late-Victorian age, claiming the 1890 League title and winning the National Cup in 1895, 1897 and 1898 – their all-conquering side included Rams footballers Steve Bloomer and Jack Robinson.

- ☻ Although he probably didn't realise it, a special guest at Derby's away game against Spurs on 9 February 1935 had a particular affinity to the Rams. In the White Hart Lane stands for the 2–2 draw was the New York Yankees baseball legend Babe Ruth, who if only he had understood 'what the hell was going on' might well have become Derby County's most appropriate celebrity fan.

- ☻ When Everton's William Ralph 'Dixie' Dean scored his 353rd League goal on 2 September 1936, he broke the previous long-standing record set by Derby's **Steve Bloomer** in 1914 – although many comparisons were made, there was one curious similarity between the two men that went unnoticed. Both were highly accomplished baseball players – Bloomer starred for the pioneering Derby side of the 1890s and 40 years later, after the initial League had folded, Dean won medals with Caledonians in the revived National Baseball League.

- ☻ A number of exhibition games were played at the Baseball Ground long after its once-glittering diamond had been obliterated by a football pitch, but the final 'ball game' of any consequence took place on Saturday 22 July 1944 when a Derby County Select XI took on the United States Air Force. All the razzmatazz of the American game was replicated, with a tannoy commentary and even free chewing gum for the wide-eyed youngsters. The ball used for the final strike, inscribed with the result and players' names, now resides in the Pride Park trophy cabinet.

- ☻ On 28 June 1994 both Derby County and British sporting heritage suffered a futile loss when the unique Baseball Hotel, opened in 1895 as the first purpose-built establishment serving the needs of a sports stadium, fell to a demolition squad. The grossly premature order was given by the Rams chairman **Lionel Pickering** in order to facilitate a proposed redevelopment of the Baseball Ground – but the improvement scheme was later shelved in favour of a move to Pride Park Stadium. Although some of the Baseball Hotel fittings were incorporated into the new ground's 'Baseball Bar and Grill', the original landmark gem from the days when Derby were truly 'Kings of the Diamond' was lost forever.

GREEN BAIZE DAYS

✪ Derby's best-known celebrity fan in the 30s and 40s was the Derbyshire-born World Snooker Champion Joe Davis. The 'King of Pot', as he was innocently known, would sometimes socialise with the team, passing largely unrecognised in those pre-TV days, and the players used this to their advantage on more than one occasion. The usual drill was to accept a wager from snooker hall hustlers or to put out an all-comers challenge for a game on the club's own table at the Baseball Ground. The 'unknown' Davis would initially feign difficulty potting a simple ball, and the Rams stars would display due concern – only when someone rashly raised the stakes to 'double or quits' would the world-conquering maestro show his true colours, calmly cleaning up while the 'innocent' footballers looked on in mock amazement.

✪ On 2 March 1985 the Rams physio Gordon Guthrie was rudely given the cold shoulder by snooker star Kirk Stevens after he had stepped in to treat the player's injury. The Canadian had complained of a nagging shoulder pain prior to that day's Dulux British Open Snooker Final at Derby Assembly Rooms, but after Gordon had applied the fabled magic sponge the white-suited wonder boy wilted to a shock defeat by the South African Silvino Francisco. That was the cue for Stevens to apportion blame. Brushing aside suggestions that he had been high on cocaine, he told the press 'It was very nice of the club and Gordon to go to all that trouble, but honestly I think it just made me more aware of the injury' – Derby County remain the only football club to have lost a British Open Snooker title.

THE DERBY GAME

Over the years the saying that 'Derby is a real football town' has been regularly invoked to illustrate the locality's commitment to the Rams. However, the phrase has a much deeper historical significance than many who use it might realise, since primitive forms of football were synonymous with the town long before the modern game and Derby County Football Club were ever thought of.

✪ The official FIFA website cites Derby as the actual birthplace of British football – it suggests a form of the game was first played there in the third century AD to celebrate the locals' ousting of an unwelcome garrison of Roman soldiers stationed in the town. Although the claim is a fanciful one, celebrated football contests have certainly been staged in Derby for centuries.

⊕ Until is was finally outlawed in 1846 for being too rough, the centuries-old annual Shrovetide football game played through the streets and fields of Derby was considered the most famous in the land. It was nominally contested between the large parish of St Peter's and the minnows of All Saints, formerly known as All Hallows, whose ranks were bolstered by other parishes within the town. Although yet to be acknowledged by the *Oxford English Dictionary,* the keenly fought contest gave rise to the phrase 'local Derby' for any game between two fierce rivals.

⊕ Derby Shrovetide football had an informal 'route' which generally saw the ball 'watered' in the River Derwent before being 'banked' and pursued across open country. A traditional battling ground was the swampy mead which several hundred years later became Pride Park – so when Derby County moved there in 1997 football really did 'come home'.

⊕ A song derived from the Derby Shrovetide game is thought to be the first ever football chant bandied between rival 'fans'. The mocking taunt, dating from at least the 18th century, was sung to the tune of *Oranges and Lemons* by the children of 'rich' St Peter's Parish to their 'poor' All Hallows neighbours:

> 'Roast beef and potatoes,
> For the bells of St Peter's,
> Pig muck and carrots,
> For the bells of All Hallows.'

⊕ There is a distinct lineage between the birth of 'modern' football in Derby and the defunct ancient game. Having been denied their traditional pleasure, many a Shrovetide 'outlaw' gleefully took to the sanitised code drawn up by the newly-formed Football Association in 1863, and when Derby County were formed in 1884 the fledgling club promoted the cause of the 'new' game by shrewdly harking back to the old. On Shrove Tuesday 1885 at the County Ground they staged a 'grand association football match' between the old foes St Peter's and All Saints, and in a masterstroke of early marketing the revered 'last ever' Shrovetide ball from 1845 was put on display to promote the event. The PR ruse worked a treat – Derbeians took naturally to the new game and the rest is history – and that giant Shrovetide ball survives to this day in Derby museum, a truly iconic symbol of the 'real football town' that is Derby.

OLYMPIC GODS

Three Derby players of only modest ability boast an achievement which countless far greater stars simply cannot match – they won medals in the Olympic Games, and gold ones to boot. All were for the football events rather than athletics – **Herbert Smith** and **Horace Bailey** in London in 1908 and **Ivan Sharpe** in Stockholm in 1912.

In 1908 the Great Britain football team entered under the name United Kingdom, and they defeated Denmark 2–0 in the Olympic Final, with Bailey in goal and Smith at full-back. In 1912 the United Kingdom again met Denmark in the Final, this time winning 4–2, with Sharpe at outside-left.

The Rams winger was also no stranger to athletics for he was Sharpe by both name and nature – he won many prizes for running and when with Salford Harriers once beat off the English sprint champion. In later life he became a journalist and the long-term editor of an appropriately titled football and sports paper – *The Athletic News*.

Tewfik Abdallah, the Rams' first overseas signing, also appeared in an Olympic Games but emerged without a medal. The speedy winger, who had once played barefoot for Cairo Sporting Club, was in Egypt's football team at the Antwerp Olympics in Belgium in 1920 – they were beaten 2–1 by Italy in the first round.

REST OF THE DAY'S SPORTS NEWS

✪ Derby County seemed to be in two minds when they produced their first ever fixture card in 1884–85 – although the phrase 'Association Rules' is printed under the first-team fixtures, the back of the card shows the 'Rugby Rules'. This isn't as odd as it might first appear, for in the early days the lines between the two codes of 'football' were thinly drawn and misunderstandings were common – one early game in the Derby area ended in compromise as 15 'handlers' played against 11 'footers'.

✪ On 30 August 1897 the first athletics meeting to be arranged by Derby County was held at the Baseball Ground. The Rams players took part, and the opening event, a 100-yard sprint handicap, was won by striker **Steve Bloomer** in 11.5 seconds, ahead of full-back pairing **Joe 'Fossil' Leiper** and **Jimmy Methven**. The professional footballers' mile handicap saw centre-forward **John Boag** cross the line first in four minutes 48.5 seconds in front of a crowd of 1,500.

✪ As befits a team who played football at a baseball ground, Derby County have occasionally fulfilled fixtures at venues which became better associated with other sports. The prestigious Queen's Club in the Kensington area of London is now synonymous with tennis, but on 17 April 1897 Derby played football there against the crack amateur side Corinthians, holding the toffs to a 4–4 draw having already beaten them 6–3 at the Baseball Ground the previous December. In the same era the Rams also played Corinthians at a celebrated cricket ground – Kennington Oval – scene of the inaugural England v Australia Test match and the birthplace of The Ashes legend as well as the venue for the first FA Cup Final in 1872.

✪ Lots of Derby County players have displayed their talents on a golf course, but only one had a course named after him. **Harry Allen** played 20 games for Derby County, including the 1898–99 Cup Final, before he emigrated to Rhodesia to work on the railways. The Spondon-born former winger made quite a name for himself, becoming assistant general manager of Rhodesian Railways, vice-president of the Rhodesian FA and president of the Rhodesian amateur boxing association. He died in Bulawayo in September 1939 and is buried there, not far from the Harry Allen Golf Club.

✪ The 'modern' idea of using a football stadium to generate income from other activities is as old as the hills. On 11 May 1907, the season having just finished, the Baseball Ground hosted a full programme of boxing and wrestling events – not until Norman Hunter and **Francis Lee** slugged it out 68 years later did the ground witness such a grappling experience again. Boxing was again staged there on 9 August 1941 when the main attraction was British Empire Heavyweight Champion Len Harvey. As the *Derby Evening Telegraph* made clear, football was by then out of the question: 'The pitch resembled a hayfield, having been mown for the "Dig For Victory" campaign, and sheep grazed in the penalty areas.'

☺ Speed is important for footballers, but it isn't everything. In 1911 the Rams right-winger **Horace Wright** won a contest organised by the *Athletic News* to find the fastest man in professional football – yet when Derby won the Second Division Championship in 1911–12 Wright was selected by manager Jimmy Methven only three times.

☺ The Rams Scottish international **Douglas 'Dally' Duncan** is the only Derby player to score a hat-trick at a polo ground. He achieved the unlikely feat on 19 May 1935 in Scotland's 5–1 tour victory against a United States All Stars team at the Polo Grounds, New York. Another Derby player curiously linked to 'polo' is **Marco Gabbiadini** – in 1989 when at Sunderland his Gabbiadini Enterprises company published a 'my story' brochure, and while fishing for a title the part-Italian striker homed in on the great Venetian traveller Marco Polo, resulting in the corniest football book title of all time – *Marco Goalo*.

☺ When Derby County played their European Cup away game against Benfica in November 1972 the psychological ball skills began well before the game. **Brian Clough** and his squad arrived for their first look at the imposing Estadio da Luz stadium to find a group of locals playing rugby there – as a wayward 'ball' came Cloughie's way, he sized it up and returned a perfect kick from whence it came. Having seen their manager thus make light of the freakish 'oval' ball, the Rams players mastered the round version with total confidence, cruising into the next round after a tidy 0–0 draw.

HONOURED FEW

Try this Derby County conundrum. Ex-Rams forward William Storer did it in 1902, Steve Bloomer followed suit in 1920 and former Derby manager Harry Newbould did likewise in 1924. In turn, they were followed by fellow Rams personalities Sam Longson (1967), Brian Clough (1975) Roy McFarland (1982) and Peter Gadsby (1996).

Men connected to other football clubs occasionally do it – ex-Forest 'keeper Dennis Allsopp (1902), Billy Meredith of Manchester City (1925), the Stoke City legend Stanley Matthews (1965) and even the Everton chairman John Moores (1961). The answer? They've all thrown up in Ashbourne – or to put it more correctly, not to say delicately, they have all 'turned up' the 'matchball' to put in motion the annual Ashbourne Royal Shrovetide football game.

It is an honour to be asked to perform the most important duty associated with the revered custom, and the Rams personalities join the Dukes of Devonshire and Rutland, two Princes of Wales and a host of other worthies in having accepted the call. But one man tops the lot – the Rams 2006–07 chairman Peter Gadsby has scored a Shrovetide goal. He managed the rare feat just before midnight in the 1965 Ash Wednesday game, aged only 16, and not even the greatest Derby County strikers can match that claim to fame!

SIX – GOALKEEPERS ARE DIFFERENT...

They play 'football' with their hands, wear shirts of a different colour and sometimes sport caps. For much of a game they stand more or less still and are inclined to exchange banter with the crowd. It's even been said that they are crazy. Whether we call them goalkeepers, custodians, or goalies, the men between the sticks are certainly different. And Derby County's keepers are no exception.

SIMPLY THE WORST

Derby County followers were unusually nervous when they heard that Charlie Bunyan was to make his Rams debut away to Burnley on 8 March 1890. The 2–0 defeat that followed was not unexpected. Nor was the 3–0 loss at Everton the following week. In fact many fans had feared far worse with Bunyan in goal, for those who knew their football were fully aware that Derby County had signed the official 'worst goalkeeper in England'.

On 15 October 1887 he had been the Hyde 'keeper in the Lancashire side's first-round FA Cup tie against Preston North End. Bunyan had a bit of an off-day – Preston won 26–0. In over 50,000 FA Cup ties since, no 'keeper has conceded more in a single game, and it remains the highest score in any English competitive senior match.

There is a curious postscript to this tale of custodial incompetence. After he had played only nine games for Derby County, Bunyan was off-loaded to Chesterfield Town. In turn the Derbyshire club quickly got rid of him to Sheffield United – and he left there in 1894 without having played a game. His next club were also wise enough not to give Bunyan a first-team outing. They already knew what he was capable of – the club was Derby County. Trust the Rams to sign the dodgiest 'keeper in England twice!

NO PUDDING NO POINTS

It's perfectly sensible for an England international goalkeeper to follow a dietary regime, but Derby County's Jack Robinson took things much too far. Witness the memoirs of his teammate Jimmy Methven:

> *'Jack's motto was "No pudding, no points." If he missed his pre-match rice pudding he seemed unable to stop a shot. We once had a narrow squeak at Burnley when somehow the milky perquisite was omitted from our lunch. So Johnny Goodall set out to scour the town and returned carrying a large dish of what he called 'Burnley mixture' – quite what was in it nobody knew, but my diagnosis would be something like Quaker oats and tripe. Jack polished off the lot and we beat Burnley 3–2. He played the game of his life.'*

Despite later spells with a multitude of clubs, including a stint with Rochester in New York State, Robinson died in Derby, the place of his birth, on 28 October 1931. Few Derby County 'keepers have been as colourful as the 'pudding man'.

GOLDEN OLDIE

Horace Peter Bailey is the only Derby County goalkeeper to have won an Olympic gold medal. The Derby-born Olympian played for the Great Britain football team which beat Denmark 2–0 in the Final at the 1908 London Games.

Bailey also held another international distinction. In his five full appearances for England he conceded only three goals. Unremarkable in itself – but he watched his outfield colleagues net a whacking 35 in those same five games. No England 'keeper has ever been so bored.

It's tempting to conclude that Bailey was an all-round superstar, for his ball skills were such that he also played tennis for Derbyshire. But in fact he was selected only three times for Derby County and never finished on the winning side. The stark truth is that Bailey was one of the Rams oddest signings of all time, for he joined the club in 1910 with an unspeakable blot on his record.

Playing for Leicester Fosse in April 1909, the 'keeper had an absolute nightmare as his side were hammered 12–0 by the collective might of Nottingham Forest! What greater embarrassment can a 'keeper suffer?

Yet worse was to come, for Bailey was accused of taking bribes to throw the game. Although he was acquitted, the excuse was a corker. Bailey admitted to an investigating committee that he had still been recovering from a colleague's wedding celebrations two days previously. No wonder the Leicester reject failed to make the grade at a club with Derby's reputation – he couldn't keep pace with the drinking.

GOALKEEPERS
TURNED POACHERS

One of the most uncommon sights in football is that of a 'keeper scoring a goal. Yet a number who have stood between the posts for Derby County have achieved the topsy-turvy scoring feat at some stage in their careers.

- When **Ernald Scattergood** was elected Derby's regular penalty taker in 1912–13, the 'keeper scored three out of three using the hit and hope technique. Scattergood continued to bang them in at his next club Bradford Park Avenue, scoring five more before an unusual incident persuaded him to stand down. On Easter Saturday 1922 the South Shields 'keeper Willis Walker saved one, and Scattergood was involved in a frantic race to return to his own line – one very good reason why keepers should always 'stay at home'.

- In 41 games for Derby County **Terry Adlington** never got a single sniff of the opposition goal. But when he moved to Torquay United his luck changed. In a home FA Cup tie against Barnet in November 1963 he injured a wrist. It being the pre-substitute era, Adlington was shunted up front and banged in Torquay's final goal in their 6–2 victory.

- **Peter Shilton** played over 1,000 first-class matches but only scored once. His solitary strike was for Leicester City in a Division One game at Southampton in October 1967. Making judicious use of a following wind, he scored straight from a drop-kick in City's 5–1 win.

- The former Derby 'keeper **Mart Poom** received a hearty welcome when he returned to Pride Park as a Sunderland player in September 2003. It appeared he had obliged his old fans by letting in the Derby winner – Ian Taylor put the Rams 1–0 ahead in the final seconds of normal time. But more was to come – in the final seconds of the three minutes of added time, Poom ventured up for a corner and powered in an unstoppable header for Sunderland's equaliser. Poom received a standing ovation from both sets of fans and the *Derby Evening Telegraph* summed up the moment perfectly: 'It was real Roy of the Rovers stuff. A storyline dramatic enough to make a movie' – no wonder Sunderland fans dubbed him 'The Poominator'.

NIGHTMARE AT CHRISTMAS

It was a case of 'goodwill to the opposition' when Ken Scattergood made his Derby County goalkeeping debut on Christmas Day 1936 – the Rams were blitzed 7–0 by Everton at Goodison Park. As first outings go, it was a nightmare. But the *Derby Evening Telegraph* reporter was in forgiving mood – 'It was as great a display as any seen at Goodison Park this season' – a reference to Scattergood rather than Everton! The generous-hearted hack made the 'keeper Man of the Match and wrote that 'time and again the debutant saved the Rams from further punishment.'

Not that such seasonal disarray was anything unusual – Derby County played 39 games on Christmas Day from 1894 to 1957 and won a mere 15. Supporters were apt to blame such losses on festive 'over-indulgence,' and the *Telegraph* report of the Everton debacle did little to silence the cynics.

Readers were informed that 'Sammy Crooks pulled a muscle' and 'Dai Astley damaged a knee' – so 'both players were forced to take it easy'. Jack Barker fared even worse – 'he left the field after only 10 minutes nursing a very sore head'. Most Rams supporters quickly summed up the sorry Christmas pantomime – the Rams had been well and truly hammered.

UP FROM THE COUNTRY

A man from the Derbyshire village of Birchover caused quite a stir when he travelled to 'the big city' to attend his first ever Derby County game in the late 1940s. In local football, tradition had it that spectators took to the field at half-time for an impromptu kick-in. No one bothered to tell the wide-eyed yokel that things were different in the First Division – hot on the half-time whistle, the innocent country soul dashed onto the Baseball Ground pitch yelling 'I'll go in goal'. Three members of the constabulary removed him from his post with a salutary caution – being 'from the sticks' didn't entitle him to go between them.

SAFE HANDS

When Derby County signed Ray Middleton in 1951 they knew they had a 'keeper with a safe pair of hands. In fact, none could have been safer. During World War Two Middleton took employment as a miner and was so concerned that the arduous work might damage his most valuable assets that he took out a policy insuring his hands for £2,000.

Fortunately he had no reason to make a claim, and the canny custodian became Derby County's first-choice goalkeeper for three seasons. Middleton was an interesting character all round – the only Rams 'keeper to have been a Justice of the Peace and a town councillor.

Middleton's proudest moment was when he returned to the Baseball Ground in 1955 as 'keeper of non-League Boston United. The occasion was a second-round FA Cup tie, and the Rams were expected to run out easy winners. But Middleton's hands were as safe as ever – Derby suffered their most embarrassing defeat of all time as super-minnows Boston ran out 6–1 winners.

STRONG AS AN OX

Although wiry and slight, Ken 'The Ox' Oxford was as tough as they come. The Rams 'keeper from 1957–62 was once described by a teammate as 'not the best goalkeeper Derby County ever had, but probably the bravest – when a forward got through he would crouch down and face the music, often a full-blooded drive to the body, but not once did I see him flinch.'

It was typical of Oxford that his bravery should extend into his post-football job as a security guard with Securicor – on one near-tragic occasion in Ilkeston he became the only Derby County footballer ever to foil an armed robbery.

The fearless 'keeper continued to play for an ex-Rams XI into his 60s and sometimes turned out in Sunday League games against forwards a quarter of his age, and his unflinching style never left him. When he died in 1993 strong men wept for one of their own as they bade farewell to 'The Mighty Ox'.

BIRD OF PASSAGE

In September 1984 **John 'Budgie' Burridge** joined Derby County on loan from Wolves as cover for the injured Eric Steele – despite controversially leaving for Sheffield United after only eight games, 'Budgie' qualifies as the daftest character ever to keep goal for the Rams. He even features as the club's only entrant in a book called *Great Sporting Eccentrics*. Here are some of his qualifications.

✪ He acquired his nickname because he never stopped talking. One speciality was to give running commentary on the game – 'and what a superb save by Burridge there'. A teammate ruefully recalled his off-beat calling – 'The ball would sail over the defence and 'Budgie' would yell "KEEPERS" with great confidence. We'd relax, but a split second later he'd add "...NOT coming".'

⊕ 'Budgie' seldom landed anywhere for long. He was transferred or loaned 28 times to 26 different clubs during a career spanning almost 30 years. His career total was 771 League appearances in England and Scotland.

⊕ Burridge admitted to occasionally wearing his full kit in bed and also taking a ball with him. He was also inclined to watch *Match of the Day* while wearing kit in order to sharpen his reflexes. A friend explained 'He'd put a bowl of oranges by my chair. Every now and then I'd have to toss one unexpectedly in his direction – he got very upset if he didn't catch them all'.

⊕ He modelled himself on **Peter Shilton**, particularly regarding fitness. His acrobatic pre-match warm-up could be an entertainment in itself. He said of his regime – 'For years on end I was the hardest trainer in British football. I ate rice and fruit and listened to self-hypnosis tapes. They all said I was a bird-brain but now everybody's at it. Sports psychology they call it.'

Burridge was booked on his Rams debut at Reading for 'carrying the ball away at a throw-in'. Despite only three losses with the madcap 'keeper between the sticks, manager Arthur Cox wasn't too distressed when his 'Budgie' took sudden flight.

HEAD SHAKERS

Impeccable timing and sound judgement were **Peter Shilton**'s greatest assets. Although allegedly 'past his best' when he joined Derby from Southampton in 1987, the world-renowned England 'keeper always came for the ball at exactly the right moment and rarely made silly errors. Unfortunately that same good judgement was inclined to entirely desert him off the field.

⊕ On Tuesday 18 April 1989, three days after helping Derby win 2–0 at Manchester United, Shilton's racehorse Between the Sticks won the two o'clock at Newmarket at the rank outsider's price of 33–1. But its famous owner took not a single penny from the bookies. Intending to lay a lucrative bet at the course, Shilton arrived a fraction too late to back his own winner. Well-meaning sympathisers were treated to the bark of his favourite catchphrase – 'Away, away' – four days later Shilton kept another clean sheet but was still shaking his head at the only 'keeper's error of his whole career that he didn't try to blame his defenders for.

☺ Shilton's biggest error of judgement occurred in a quiet lane near Nottingham racecourse. Late one night in 1980 an irate husband discovered his wife in a state of undress in the back of Shilton's Jaguar. The police were called, but Shilton attempted a hasty escape and wrapped the car around a lamp-post. He was discovered to be well over the drink-driving limit and was banned from driving for 15 months and fined £350. Fans up and down the country had a field day as 'Does your missus know you're here?' became a favourite chant behind the Shilton goal.

☺ Nor was 'Shilts' the quickest off the mark in the verbal department. His bloopers included this one: 'If you stand still there's only one way to go, and that's backwards'. But his most uninspiring piece of rhetoric came ahead of a crucial World Cup game: 'You've got to believe that you're going to win, and I honestly believe England will win the World Cup – until the final whistle blows and we're knocked out.'

☺ It proved a prophetic speech, but not one that should detract from Shilton's truly amazing career. The most famous 'keeper to play for the Rams turned out in 1,390 first-class matches all told and made a record 1,005 League appearances, of which 175 were in a Derby County jersey. He made his last ever appearance in a Rams shirt in the Ted McMinn Benefit Match at Pride Park on 1 May 2006 – then aged 56, 'Shilts' pulled off one clawing save and made sure to keep a clean sheet by leaving the field midway through the first half with a hamstring strain.

CHERRY KNOCKING

Steve Cherry played 90 games for Derby County. Fans voted him Player of the Year in 1982–83. Yet the Nottingham-born 'keeper is best-remembered for a single costly error in the following season. For such was the backdrop to the match dubbed 'Cherry's Game' that his momentary misjudgement plunged Derby County devotees into the darkest gloom that many had ever known.

The occasion was a sixth-round FA Cup replay against Plymouth Argyle on Wednesday 14 March 1984. The initial tie at Home Park had ended 0–0, ironically thanks to a wonder performance from Cherry. Now Derby had to finish off their Third Division opponents. The Baseball Ground crowd of 27,000 expected nothing less.

Yet the circumstances were surreal. Manager Peter Taylor had pulled off a Cup miracle, for Derby occupied a relegation place in the Second Division and had won only once in their last 11 League games. The club's debts were so serious that it faced the genuine spectre of bankruptcy. At a High Court hearing on Monday 12 March the Rams delegation were sent away with a clear message that time was running out. Derby County faced the real possibility of oblivion.

The match two days later produced but a single goal. In the 18th minute Plymouth's Andy Rogers took an in-swinging corner. The ball eluded Cherry's flapping grasp and flew straight into the net. Before the game closed, news filtered through to the crowd that media tycoon Robert Maxwell had withdrawn his proposed rescue package. Many Rams fans made their way home genuinely believing they may have witnessed the club's last ever game.

On the darkest night in Derby County history, pubs became the favoured place of refuge, and the unfortunate Steve Cherry became the universal scapegoat. He left the club for good after only nine more appearances.

Derby later survived their financial crisis, but in the interim the supporters fell back on their legendary sense of humour. A story circulated that a Spondon man had entered his local straight after the Plymouth game and gloomily ordered a Babycham for his girlfriend – without the cherry. It was probably true.

BRUISING TACKLE

Derby's Estonian international Mart Poom picked up an unusual injury in July 2000 when he agreed to play as a 'ringer' for Flora Amateurs in a charity match in Tallinn. Despite the imminent start of pre-season training back in Derby, the giant 'keeper risked the outing without seeking permission from manager Jim Smith. It proved to be a particularly painful decision.

The ultimate culprits were the rock group Iron Maiden, who had arranged the game ahead of their sell-out gig in the Estonian capital. As several other Estonian internationals played for the local side, the result was hardly a surprise – Flora Amateurs 7 Old Maidonians 1 – so for light relief Poom ventured into attack late in the game. That was his downfall – he was 'badly caught' by Maiden's lunatic drummer Nicky McBrain.

One newspaper reported that the Rams 'keeper was 'taken to hospital with concussion' and another said he had 'a suspected fracture of the skull'. Only the *Observer* chose not to mince words: 'Whilst playing as a striker in a charity match, Derby's Estonian 'keeper was involved in an awkward collision and badly bruised his penis.'

Nursing the most sensitive injury in Rams' history, Poom sheepishly returned from his 'holiday' to face Jim Smith and explain his funny walk. The comments of his Derby County teammates can only be guessed at.

THEIRS FOR KEEPS

Beginning in 1968–69, supporters voted annually to elect their Player of the Year. The honour now known as the Jack Stamps award is greatly prized by the winners. In the 38 seasons up to 2005–06 the trophy went 20 times to defenders, nine times to strikers, and five times to midfield men. But on only four occasions was the award granted to a goalkeeper. This is the keepers' roll of honour.

- **1980–81 Roger Jones** – The 'forgotten 'keeper' arrived from Stoke City in the summer of 1980. He was ever present in 46 League and Cup games in an outstanding first season in which Derby finished sixth in Division Two.

- **1982–83 Steve Cherry** – The former Derby County apprentice replaced Yakka Banovic after Derby had won only one of their first 11 games and appeared to be prime relegation candidates. But Cherry dug in for the rest of the season and nine more victories saw Derby finish 13th in Division Two.

- **1993–94 Martin Taylor** – Reporter Gerald Mortimer perfectly summed up the 'keeper's ever-present season: 'He carried his composure, courage and excellent handling with him throughout.' Derby finished sixth in Division One and were only denied promotion to the Premiership after a Play-off defeat against Leicester City.

- **1999–2000 Mart Poom** – The sheer presence of the 6ft 4in Estonian international was an inspiration when Derby needed it most. Despite finishing 16th in the Premiership and only five points clear of relegation, supporters recognised that Poom's supreme confidence and agility might well have saved a struggling side from the drop.

CELEBRATED BENDERS

In more innocent times it was quite possible to label a goalkeeper 'a bender' without causing too much offence – it simply implied that he spent rather too much time stooping to pick the ball from his net. Here are 10 games in which hapless Derby 'keepers became the butt of the crowd's humour by conceding seven goals or more.

Year	Competition	Result	Goalkeeper
1890	FA Cup first round	Everton 11 Derby 2	Enos Bromage
1891	League Division One	Blackburn 8 Derby 0	David Haddow
1894	League Division One	Sunderland 8 Derby 0	Jack Robinson
1937	League Division One	Stoke City 8 Derby 1	Ken Scattergood
1884	FA Cup first round	Derby 0 Walsall Town 7	Len Gillett
1958	League Division Two	Swansea Town 7 Derby 0	Ken Oxford
1889	League Division One	Aston Villa 7 Derby 1	Enos Bromage
1959	League Division Two	Derby 1 Middlesbrough 7	Ken Oxford
1991	League Division One	Derby 1 Liverpool 7	Peter Shilton
1890	League Division One	Everton 7 Derby 0	David Haddow

The 11–2 Cup defeat away to Everton (played at their then ground Anfield!) remains Derby's heaviest of all time – and that after the Rams had led 2–1. Haddow and Robinson both share the shame of the heaviest League defeats (8–0 both away), while the club's worst home League loss is 7–1. That occurred three times in all, but it won't please Peter Shilton that he presided over the most recent.

Overall things look decidedly bad for Enos Bromage and Ken Oxford, but poor David Haddow must be awarded the 'All-time Biggest Bender' title – in his 16 League appearances for the Rams he picked the ball from the net 69 times!

WHO'S IN TODAY?

In 1944–45 Derby County won both the Football League North and Midland Cup despite wartime uncertainty forcing them to field no less than 10 goalkeepers in the season. To say they were a mixed bunch is no exaggeration – two were guests who went on to keep goal for England – Bert Williams and Bernard Streten – one was trainee teacher Alick Grant and another was the former Rams defender Jack Nicholas, pressed into action during a crisis. Yet another loan player invariably appeared in the programme as Savage (Queen of the South) – in his book *Are the Fixtures Out?* the *Derby Evening*

Telegraph reporter Gerald Mortimer confessed that as a small boy ignorant of Scottish club names he had innocently assumed that the brackets contained Reg Savage's nickname!

BEATEN MEN

Some legendary goalkeepers have endured nightmare games against Derby. One of the worst experiences befell Manchester City's German international Bert Trautmann on 3 December 1949. The former Prisoner of War had a torrid time as Derby recorded their biggest peacetime win since 1934 – City were hammered 7–0 at the Baseball Ground. Here are a famous Englishman, Irishman and Scotsman to keep Trautmann company.

☺ The legendary England international Gordon Banks visited Derby with Stoke City on 11 September 1971. **Colin Todd, Archie Gemmill, John O'Hare** and **Alan Hinton** beat the 'world's greatest 'keeper' once each to give the Rams a famous 4–0 win.

☺ The Tottenham Hotspur and Northern Ireland goalkeeper Pat Jennings had seven years bad luck against Derby County. On 20 September 1969 the Rams beat Spurs 5–0 before a Baseball Ground crowd of 41,826 – a home record. On 7 February 1973 Jennings again kept goal when Derby won 5–3 after extra-time in a famous FA Cup tie at White Hart Lane, **Roger Davies** scoring a hat-trick. When Spurs visited the Baseball Ground on 16 October 1976, makeshift striker **Bruce Rioch** scored four in Derby's astonishing 8–2 win. In three games Jennings had conceded a nightmare 18 goals – no star 'keeper has ever suffered so badly at the hands of the Rams.

☺ On 25 November 1972 Arsenal's Scotland international Bob Wilson looked uncomfortable throughout as Derby stuck five past him at the Baseball Ground without reply. At one point Wilson, returning after a long lay-off due to injury, seemed to be blaming shooting pains in his back, but the real shooting pains that day were the Rams five marksmen – **Roy McFarland, John McGovern, Kevin Hector, Alan Hinton** and **Roger Davies**. It has been said that Chesterfield-born Wilson slipped through the hands of Derby's scouts – all fans who saw that day's performance were mighty glad he did.

ON AND OFF

Liverpool's visit to the Baseball Ground on 19 October 1957 looks unremarkable in the record books – a 2–1 win for Derby. But the comings and goings in goal were something to behold. The Reds started with their Scottish international 'keeper Tommy Younger, who was beaten by Dennis Woodhead in the 24th minute. However, four minutes before half-time Younger sustained a back injury and retired to the dressing room. That reduced Liverpool to 10 men (no substitutes then), so outfield player Ronnie Moran, later a legendary member of the Reds backroom staff, went in goal.

When the second half began Tommy Younger was fit enough to try his luck at centre-forward, but in attempting a shot he again injured his back and retired to the dressing room. Soon afterwards Liverpool's 10 men equalised. Five minutes from time though George Darwin put Derby 2–1 ahead. That was the signal for Tommy Younger to again come back on and this time resume his place in goal as Liverpool pushed unsuccessfully for an equaliser. At the final whistle, Younger must have wondered whether he was coming or going. During the course of the game he had entered or left the field of play six times in all and had two spells in goal and one at centre-forward.

BETTER LATE THAN NEVER

When a 'keeper comes late it usually spells trouble. But the tardy arrival of Roger Jones was well worth waiting for. In a *Football Special* in April 1968 the reporter George Edwards revealed the rumour that Jones was expected to join Derby from Bournemouth. The 'keeper did indeed sign for the club and his first season with the Rams earned him the Player of the Year award. But Edwards could hardly say 'I told you so' – Roger Jones was signed from Stoke City in July 1980…12 years after the rumour-mill had predicted it!

THUMBS UP

Goalkeeper Colin Boulton has a proud place in the Derby County record books. He played in all 84 games of the club's two Championship-winning seasons – 1971–72 and 1974–75 – and is the only player to achieve that feat. But that isn't his most unusual claim to fame. Boulton was named in the Derby County Reserves side which lost 8–0 at Leeds United on 22 October 1966 – but he still left Elland Road claiming to have kept a clean sheet. In fact Boulton was spot on – he had travelled to Leeds nursing an injured thumb but was considered such a talented outfield player that he was named substitute for the day.

NERVOUS WRECK

The most nervous goalkeeper in Derby County's history was undoubtedly the England international Reg Matthews (1961–67). Although blessed with lightning reflexes, great agility and immense courage at his peak, he was often beset with severe anxiety prior to a game, so much so that his first manager Harry Storer turned a blind eye to Matthews's habit of hiding in a toilet cubicle right up to kick-off – Storer was happy to set aside club rules so that his 'keeper could enjoy a calming smoke. Nor did Matthews care for the 'unknown' – despite his bravery on the field he had a fear of ghosts, and once when on a training visit to Bisham Abbey – reputedly one of the most haunted houses in Britain – the otherwise fearless 'keeper flatly refused to enter the building. Fortunately his nerves held up better on the field – Matthews played 246 times for Derby before eventually giving way to Les Green.

DROPPED FOR GOOD

When it comes to finger-pointing there is no more blatant gesture in football than a goalkeeper being dropped – even the word itself seems to mock the victim. A number of Rams 'keepers have met with particularly sorry ends, some wholly unjustified, from which there was no return – here are some who suffered the fate.

- ☺ On 4 February 1948 Derby found themselves with only one fit goalkeeper for the crucial fifth-round FA Cup tie at Middlesbrough. He was 21-year-old **Frank Payne**, whose only previous experience was eight reserve games. But the young debutant performed so heroically in the Rams 2–1 win that the game became known as 'Frank Payne's match' – an aptly 'singular' description as it turned out. Derby quickly signed a more experienced 'keeper and Payne – the original one-game wonder – was never selected again.

- ☺ **Les Green** was small and stocky but a giant presence in Brian Clough's legendary side of the late 1960s. From his Rams debut on 10 August 1968 he made 129 consecutive League and Cup appearances before he was dropped after a calamitous display in a 4–4 draw at home to Manchester United on Boxing Day 1970. No Derby player has suffered a more decisive fall from grace after such an impressive run – it was the last Football League game Les Green ever played and a broken leg in 1973 ended his playing days for good.

✪ **Mark Wallington** performed heroically in the away game at Ipswich Town on 4 April 1987. Despite breaking a finger in the second half, he bravely carried on to the end of the game as Derby gained a crucial 2–0 win. Eric Steele deputised until the end of the season, and by the time Wallington had recovered Peter Shilton had been signed. So Wallington's reward for beating the pain barrier was that he never played for Derby again.

✪ Although he kept a clean sheet in Derby's 2–0 win at Sheffield United, **Steve Sutton** was one unhappy man on 7 October 1995. He suffered the ultimate humiliation for a goalkeeper of being substituted at half-time, despite not being injured – manager Jim Smith brought Russell Hoult on in his place. Sutton played 95 games for the Rams and the mystery substitution at Bramall Lane marked his last game for the club.

MAN MOUNTAIN

All goalkeepers try to 'look big', but some find it easier than others. One such was Harry Maskrey whose reach between fingertips with arms outstretched was 6ft 7in. His impressive physique helped him into the Grenadier Guards during World War One, and he paraded the Rams goal 222 times between 1902 and 1920 and also kept wicket for Derbyshire on occasions. He had an appropriate end for a 'keeper – having spent so much time under the bar he died behind the bar, at his pub, the New Inn, in Derby in 1927. The gentle giant was sadly missed, and no Rams goalkeeper has ever had a more appropriate nickname – it was 'Big Mass'.

SAVE OF THE SEASON

Most goalkeepers are said to have made the save of the season at some time or another, but only one Derby County player has earned the accolade officially. Les Green won the BBC *Match of the Day* Save of the Season award for a tremendous flying effort against Chelsea at Stamford Bridge on 11 October 1969.

SPOTLESS SHEETS

In the 65th minute of the First Division match against Chelsea at the Baseball Ground, on 23 October 1948, the Rams goalkeeper Bill Townsend had an unfamiliar experience – he was beaten. The goal by Chelsea's John McInnes in Derby's 2–1 win brought to an end a run of 458 minutes in which Derby had kept their goal intact. The last time Townsend had been beaten was at 4pm on 18 September against Wolves, the equivalent of more than five games without conceding. Townsend played 93 times for the Rams, but never again did he have such a remarkable run of spotless sheets.

I'll GO IN

Derby County have links with a number of outfield players who have found themselves either willingly or reluctantly going in goal. Here are a few of them.

☻ The Rams full-back **Charlie Morris** is the only outfield player to have deputised in goal in both an FA Cup Final and an international. He took over from the injured **Jack Fryer** in Derby's disastrous 6–0 defeat by Bury in 1903 and on 16 March 1908 filled in for part of the game at Wrexham when Wales faced England. There was a curious consistency in the margin of defeat as the disgruntled Welsh crowd saw their side crushed 7–1.

☻ On 16 September 1944 a chapter of accidents led to the Derby full-back and temporary manager **Jack Nicholas** playing in goal at Barnsley for the whole game, one of only three outfield Rams players (along with John Goodall and Arthur Latham) to suffer that fate. First-choice 'keeper **Frank Boulton** was stranded in Birmingham after missing a train connection, so the reserve 'keeper Vanham was called for – but he arrived at Derby Bus Station moments after the team coach had left. Stand-in Nicholas performed admirably despite Derby's 2–0 defeat.

✪ Emergency 'keepers generally finish on the losing side, but the Rams forward **Frank Broome** is an exception. In a home FA Cup replay against Chelsea on 29 January 1947 he was called into action for all but five minutes of the entire game plus extra-time. Derby won 1–0, but Broome's clean sheet went to waste. When he reverted to left-wing in the next round, Derby lost 1–0 at Liverpool.

✪ When the rugged defender **David Webb** arrived at Derby in 1978, he already had a history of goalkeeping exploits. In a crisis he had been selected to play in goal for Chelsea at home to Ipswich Town on 27 December 1971 and began the game by saying a mock prayer in front of the fans – the gesture worked as he kept Ipswich at bay for the entire game, and Chelsea ran out 2–0 winners.

✪ The Rams centre-forward **Colin Chesters** scored the same number of goals for Derby as he made appearances in goal for Crewe – precisely one. He was picked in goal for the Alex in April 1982 in an emergency following injury to Ken Mulhearn.

✪ On 20 April 1991 Derby were relegated from Division One after a sorry defeat at Manchester City, but the result alone failed to tell the full story. The City striker Niall Quinn put his team ahead after 23 minutes before Derby were thrown a lifeline 12 minutes later when City 'keeper Tony Coton conceded a penalty and was sent off. **Dean Saunders**'s spot-kick was saved by Quinn, who had donned the gloves with apparent relish. The Irish international's 'score and save' feat is believed to be unique, and a deflated and clueless Rams team were defeated 2–1 by the gallant 10 men.

✪ It was a tale of two Pauls on 6 September 1992. Derby led Bristol City 2–0 at home when the Rams 'keeper **Steve Sutton** was sent off for a rugby tackle in the box. Midfielder Paul Williams took over in goal and failed to save the resulting penalty before letting in three more in the second half. Despite a **Paul Simpson** hat-trick and some fine **Paul Williams** saves, Derby were beaten 4–3.

THAT'S MY BOY

On Friday 30 September 2005 Derby County became embroiled in one of their best ever bizarre football firsts when the father of the Rams young goalkeeper Lee Camp rang a local radio station to deliver a five minute rant on air in defence of his 'badly treated' son. Mick Camp had just heard that Lee was to be replaced in the next day's game at home to Leicester City...by Derby's 42-year-old goalkeeping coach Kevin Poole.

Thousands of Radio Derby listeners were taken aback as Camp senior accused Poole of being a useless coach and said the Rams manager Phil Brown had 'lost the plot'. He also laid into defender Andrew Davies, whom he accused of never accepting responsibility for his own mistakes and 'always blaming my Lee'. Even by Derby County standards it was an astonishing outburst, the sort frequently delivered by an outraged supporter but never before by a player's father.

Although the embarrassed Camp junior issued a swift apology on behalf of his father, it seemed for a time that the 'keeper's Rams career might be in jeopardy, but after Brown left the club before the season's end and Poole left during the close season Camp again regained a regular place. Meanwhile a new catchphrase caught on around Derby, mischievously invoked for those 'embarrassing parent' moments – 'Lee Camp's Dad' – they say 'you couldn't make it up'...with Derby County there's no need to.

SEVEN – HALF-TIME REFRESHMENTS...

UNSAVOURY SNACK

At the end of his first season as Derby manager, Brian Clough wrote to all season-ticket holders promising 'improved results' and 'better catering'. The first was delivered with a flourish, the second less so – indeed culinary standards appeared to hit an all-time low during Clough's last full season at the club.

On 18 November 1972, following a reserve game against Blackpool, a group of youths spotted what they thought was a severed head in a plastic bag in one of the refreshment kiosks – although they at first shrugged it off as impossible, they gained access to the ground later for a second look. After peering into the darkened kiosk through its shutters and catching a glimpse of something 'lumpy and fleshy white' they became convinced of their grisly find. The police were called and raced to the ground as club staff were scrambled to face the worst. When the kiosk was opened up, there, sure enough, was the bulging bag with its unsavoury contents – a large packet of bread rolls which had failed to tempt the knowing Baseball Ground gourmets...put by for the next game a week later!

FOOD FOR THOUGHT

When the Bosnian international defender Muhamed 'Mo' Konjic joined Derby County from Coventry in May 2004, few supporters were fully aware of the tough time he had experienced earlier in his career.

When the Balkan Civil War erupted in 1992 Konjic had to fight for his country. In 1993 he was permitted to leave his club in Sarajevo when the city was under siege and was transferred to NK Zagreb in Croatia. The fee was an unusual one – a consignment of food. 'There was no point paying cash,' said Konjic. 'Money meant nothing because there wasn't anything to buy.'

To get to Zagreb he had to flee through the mountains, but his car plunged down a ravine and he broke both arms. Two weeks later Konjic cut off the plasters and declared himself fit. He played in great pain for weeks and explained – 'I was paid £100 a match. I had to play to be able to send home food to my family.'

Konjic was plagued by injury at Derby. A long-term knee problem, stomach strain, a broken nose and double vision all tested his resolve. In one game he played in a protective face mask and even suffered what the club described as 'a gardening injury' – slicing off part of a finger with his lawnmower.

Yet Konjic kept smiling through it all, even though on the rare occasions he did play his form might best be described as mixed. Many supporters levelled criticism at the big-hearted defender – some observed that he seemed 'happy just to be playing'. Only his Bosnian countrymen fully understood why.

DRESSED FOR THE OCCASION

There have been few cheerier players than Derby's late-80s winger Nigel Callaghan. On the pitch he played with freedom; off it he knew how to relax. His Saturday nights were generally spent performing DJ duties in a Derby nightclub. The spiky-haired lad with the toothy grin was a carefree soul at heart. Except when it came to pre-match ritual, for Callaghan once told readers of *Shoot* magazine that he had a peculiar superstition. As quirky confessions go, this one sounds fishier than most – 'I always eat crab on a Friday night'.

The unusual creature comfort seemed to do the trick. Not once did the crab affect his style – despite the Baseball Ground pitch often resembling mud flats, Callaghan moved speedily forwards rather than slowly sideways. 'Super Cally' played 100 games for the Rams – as befits a man with such a peculiar fetish, he will always be remembered as a genuinely nippy winger.

MORE PINTS THAN POINTS

When new manager Phil Brown arrived at Derby County in June 2005, it was impossible not to notice one thing – the appropriately-named new arrival had the deepest tan in Derby County history.

This was quickly seized upon by season-ticket holder and brewer of the Derby Brewing Company Trevor Harris, who launched a new beer named 'Golden Brown' dedicated to the Rams boss. All the expected quips were soon doing the rounds – the *Evening Telegraph* hoped it heralded 'a new golden era for the club', but as the team slipped close to the relegation zone during Brown's tenure the drinkers of Derby had their own take on the splendid ale.

Most agreed it was 'going down' well and declared themselves ever more 'ready for a drop' as the season progressed. There were also uncharitable comments about 'dregs' and 'short measures'. As his side continued to struggle in his first season, Phil Brown was sacked in January 2006. Quite a few glasses were raised in Derby that night, and Brown was said to be very bitter about the whole affair.

But 'Golden Brown' was not the first beer linked to the Rams. In the club's 1984–85 centenary season their main sponsor Bass Worthington produced a limited edition 'Celebration Ale' in half pint bottles, and in April 1996 the Brunswick Brewing Company served up 'Rams Return' to celebrate the club's promotion to the Premiership. The collectors' dilemma of whether or not to drink the contents was one to which cunning memorabilia expert Andy Ellis had a ready solution – 'My advice is to buy two but only drink one – that way you can't lose.'

THEY ATE ALL THE PIES

Standards of fitness in football have never been higher than they are today, but there was a time when players who were 'carrying a bit' routinely made the line up – indeed some were positive stars. Here is a rotundity of Rams who all struggled to keep in trim at some time during their careers and who by today's yardstick, irrespective of their ability, would surely have endured spells on the sidelines until they shed a few pounds.

Alan Hinton (1967–76)
Dave Mackay (1968–71)
Francis Lee (1974–76)
Steve Buckley (1978–86)
Kenny Burns (1982–84)
John Robertson (1983–85)
Andy Garner (1983–88)
Mickey Lewis (1984–88)
Marco Gabbiadini (1991–97)
Giorgi Kinkladze (1999–2003)

Hinton was eternally 'hippy', Mackay 'gutsy' in more ways than one and Francis Lee simply the greatest 'all-rounder' ever to pull on a Rams shirt…sometimes with enormous difficulty. A Manchester City website once described him as 'a porky David Soul', which for those who remember television's *Starsky and Hutch* should strike a resonant chord. Yet all three men were huge stars and larger-than-life characters – Mackay led Derby to a celebrated promotion, and both Hinton and Lee won Championship medals. As for Burns and Robertson (the latter was variously described by Brian Clough as a 'dumpy little bugger' and a 'fat unshaven tramp'), the portly pair won the European Cup with Forest. Therein lies the triumph of class over mass.

Moving through the years, the chunky Gabbiadini was affectionately dubbed 'The Pie Man' by supporters, but there was little affection in the reception given to Paul Williams when the defender returned to Derby as a slightly heavier Coventry player on 16 December 2000. After continually throwing his weight around, he was subjected to ribald chanting from a 3,000-strong section of the Pride Park crowd – they began with 'Who ate all the pies?' But after Williams crudely crocked Stefano Eranio and was booked, this progressed to 'You fat bastard'. The police misheard the chant and threatened prosecutions and even jail for the 'racist taunt', but when they were alerted to the truth they refused to drop the case and instead warned fans that 'personal abuse of this nature is simply not acceptable'. The story made the national press as Derby County supporters secured their place as the first in the world chastised for 'fattism'!

SPUD-U-DON'T-LIKE

According to a story by Steve Bloomer in the *Derbyshire Football Express,* the restaurant at Manchester's Victoria Station was once the scene of the most unwise pre-match meal of all time. The sickening incident occurred in 1903–04 before a game at Bury and concerned the Rams Irish international winger Jack 'Toby' Mercer. It seems the outside-right was rather fond of potatoes, and he persuaded the Derby trainer to allow him to indulge ahead of the game – after he had instructed the waiter to 'bring me some murphies with their jackets on', two giant baked spuds duly arrived at the table and were polished off by Mercer.

Bloomer concluded the yarn thus – 'Although the lunch was two and a half hours before the game, Jack was a sick man after twenty minutes play – I remember receiving the ball and looking round for him, but there he was on his hands and knees on the wing being very, very ill.'

PROBABLY THE BEST GOALKEEPER IN THE WORLD

In the run-up to the 2006 World Cup the long-retired Rams goalkeeper Peter Shilton pulled on his jersey one more time in earnest for a team of veteran England internationals (average age 51) led by their white-haired manager Bobby Robson.

Legends including Bobby and Jack Charlton, Alan Ball, Chris Waddle and Peter Beardsley turned out in the surreal game which was filmed as part of a £10.5 million Saatchi and Saatchi advertising campaign for Carlsberg lager. The hefty but still skilful XI were shown thoroughly outwitting a much younger amateur pub team before popping off to the local – 'The Old Lion' – for a celebratory pint of lager. The award-winning advert began with a sleepy-headed Shilton crawling out of bed and ended with a neat trademark tagline – 'Carlsberg don't do pub teams, but if they did they'd probably be the best pub team in the world.'

Shilton isn't the only ex-Ram to take the TV shilling for promoting consumables. In 1991 his England and Derby teammate Mark Wright bade the country to 'work, rest and play with a Mars bar', but neither player had as big an appetite for promotion as Brian Clough. In 1989 the former Rams manager threw his not inconsiderable weight behind a Shredded Wheat campaign in which the great man suggested that no player would get in his team 'unless he can eat three'!

BREW XI

Many in football have taken advantage of their 'celebrity' by entering the licensed trade, some while still playing or managing. Here is an XI of Derby County personalities who were all mine host locally at some time or another.

Alas, some of the hostelries, like their landlords, stopped serving many years ago.

Harry Maskrey	– The New Inn, Derby
John Goodall	– The Station Inn, Derby
Stuart McMillan	– The Nag's Head, Mickleover
George Davis	– The Plough Inn, Alfreton
Tom Crilly	– The Hilton Arms, Derby
Billy Hughes	– The Rising Sun, Derby
Eric Steele	– The Hollybush Inn, Breedon-on-the-Hill
George Thornewell	– The White Hart, Duffield

Kevin Hector	– The Staff of Life, Ticknall
Roger Davies	– The Cock Inn, Hanbury
David Nish	– The Turk's Head, Donisthorpe
Des Anderson	– The Dog, Burton upon Trent

QUICK BITES

✧ In the late 1890s the club joker **Jack** Cox once let the Rams trainer **Harry Dakin** massage his 'injured' thigh for close to half an hour before casually telling him it was the other leg that required treatment. Dakin said little but instead rubbed in a very liberal and rather 'careless' application of a proprietary lotion called 'Chilla-paste' which relied on its key ingredient for its 'heating effect'…the Mexican chilli pepper. Full-back Cox was still suffering after-burn to his thigh and 'intimate areas' several days later, and never again did he take a rise out of the po-faced Dakin.

✧ While serving with the Northumberland Fusiliers in World War One, the former Rams centre-half **Sandy McAllister** met an unfortunate end. Having somehow managed to avoid being shot, gassed or blown to pieces, he endured a sickening death from food poisoning.

✧ Today's style-conscious players might well nominate sushi or fresh pasta as their preferred diet, but in less glitzy days footballers actually told the truth. In a survey for *Shoot* magazine in the 1970s the Rams Welsh international **Terry Hennessey** innocently revealed his favourite meal as 'steak, mushrooms, mashed potatoes and braised celery.' While celery retains a bizarre place in football's lexicon through its cult status at Chelsea (don't even ask!), Hennessey remains the only professional footballer on record ever to have used the word 'braised' during an interview.

✧ A mind-numbing quote from Rams captain **John Goodall** in 1897 when asked about diet – 'While potatoes and veg are not the best food for a player, they should not be strictly avoided if he likes them.' Over 70 years later Hennessey was the living proof.

✧ The one-time Rams boss **Peter Taylor** had an eccentric penchant for references to the 'Pork Butchers' XI', but had he been at the club during **Bert Mann**'s time the joke might have ended up on Taylor. After Mann retired as a player in 1933, the former left-winger actually became a pork butcher and in 1958 was elected president of the Derby and District Master Butchers' Association!

⚽ After Derby suffered relegation to the Third Division North in 1954–55, a supporter who had known better times reflected ruefully on the club's sorry demise – 'It was the scrap yard of the Football League and for us a drastic change in diet…like going from caviar to crisps, and broken crisps at that.'

⚽ When the results of other club's outstanding games rendered Derby County the 1971–72 League Champions, most of the Rams players were enjoying a holiday in Mallorca, but **Roy McFarland** and **Colin Todd** were at home about to report for England duty. This is how McFarland described the pair's wild celebration – 'On the way to join the squad we heard on Toddy's car radio that Leeds had lost at Wolves and Liverpool had drawn with Arsenal, so we knew we were champions. But when we arrived in London some of the Leeds and Liverpool lads were there too, so there were few congratulations, and we decided to tone it down a bit. Toddy and I celebrated becoming champions with tea and biscuits.'

OVER THE BAR

⚽ After the Scotsman **Jimmy Methven** joined Derby County in 1891 he spent a record 31 years at the club as a player and manager. But he would never have joined them at all if not for a fondness of what he liked to call 'Scottish water'. He was initially set to join Burton Swifts, but when his wife Agnes discovered the contract included a hotel managership she absolutely forbade him to take the job, and Burton's loss became Derby's considerable gain.

⚽ The Derby County archives record that striker **Steve Bloomer** had a thirst for something else besides goals. The club's minute book for 27 November 1899 states – 'Bloomer was reported for insobriety on 22 November 1899 and had absented himself from training. Fined 5 shillings.' The minutes of 8 August 1900 noted a similar but more extreme offence for which he was fined 10 shillings, and the hat-trick was completed in the minutes of 30 August 1900 when Bloomer was this time hit with a fine of £1. The season began only two days later and within a fortnight the Rams incorrigible 'bad boy' was at it again and had been fined a further £1 – yet he proceeded to notch 16 goals in the first 15 games and finished the season with 24 League goals in 27 appearances. Also that year, Bloomer scored four times in a game against Wales to become the first player to score a hat-trick for England in two different centuries. All of which suggests that genius often treads a wayward path and that some players can take a few beers in their confident stride.

✪ On Saturday 2 September 1939 the Angler's Arms in Spondon was the scene of a sad little cameo in Derby County history when all the players gathered there after that day's 1–0 home win over Aston Villa. Never did a Rams drinking school appear more sombre, because they knew the Villa game was the last before the League programme was suspended due to war. Effectively, the players were out of work and had no idea what the future held – those last few drinks together had to sustain team spirit for a whole seven years, for the next Football League game 'proper' was on 31 August 1946...when only four of the same men played.

✪ When the Rams fit young boss **Brian Clough** won the Bell's Whisky Manager of the Month Award in August 1969 his prize of a giant bottle of Scotch was not considered ironic. After he underwent a life-saving liver transplant in January 2003, Clough spoke frankly of his problems – 'Yes drink did cloud my judgement, definitely, and as for walking on water, which I did on the River Trent and Derwent for years you know, I'm aware that most people will be saying I should have taken more of it with my drinks, and they're absolutely right.' But Clough was not the first Derby manager with a weakness for the malt – intimates of **Stuart McMillan** said he drank a bottle of whisky every day and had a curious nose-twitch for his trouble...but he still won the Cup for Derby in 1946.

✪ **Steve Bloomer** spent the last two years of his life living in the Great Northern Inn on Junction Street, in Derby's Rowditch area. His daughter Doris ran the establishment with her husband Cyril Richards, and Derby's greatest player died there on the morning of Saturday 16 April 1938, aged 64, a few hours before the Rams beat Liverpool 4–1 at the Baseball Ground.

✪ A public house was to blame for the shock decision of the Derby County star **Peter Doherty** to leave the club in December 1946. The flame-haired Irishman was determined to take over the Arboretum Hotel, not far from the Baseball Ground, but the Derby directors flatly refused him permission for fear it would affect his game. A proud Doherty reacted accordingly – 'If they thought that, then they didn't know me. I had no option but to leave, though it almost broke my heart because I loved Derby.'

❂ In November 1972 Rams fan Cec Winfield, landlord of the Elm Tree in Nottingham, left home at 5.30am for Derby's away game against Benfica in the European Cup. It seems he may have been given a good send off the night before because he completely forgot to put his shoes on and flew all the way to Lisbon in his slippers.

❂ Countless Rams players have run pubs, but only one has had one named in his honour. It happened by chance in 1998 when the owners of a national chain of premises all called 'Jack Stamps' decided to open up in Derby Market Place. When they were told that the Rams 1946 Cup Final hero was called **Jackie Stamps** the chain owners agreed to call the Derby premises by the revised name and Stamps's portrait in his Rams kit was painted on the pub sign. Alas Jackie was dropped in 2001 and the premises re-opened as an Australian theme bar called Walkabout! One other Rams player also had his portrait on an inn sign, albeit sporting Arsenal colours. For many years from the 1970s, even after he had signed for Derby, a striking image of a white-booted **Charlie George** adorned The Gunners public house close to Highbury Stadium.

❂ The only Derby County player to publicly acknowledge a drink problem while still playing for the club was midfielder **Adam Murray**. After he returned to Derby early following a loan spell with Kidderminster Harriers in 2003, the reason was initially given as 'exhaustion', but the 22-year-old was soon admitted to the famous Priory Clinic where he was treated for 'alcohol abuse' before being released by the Rams and joining Solihull Borough.

❂ In his 2005 autobiography the former Rams star **Charlie George** pulled no punches in talking about the 'work hard play hard' ethos of Derby's 1974–75 Championship-winning side – 'The drink culture I left behind in London was just as much a part of my life in Derby. We had some phenomenal players and some drinkers to match – our sessions at the Midland Hotel were legendary. And Derby people in general too – they drank, they gambled, they liked a joke and they loved their football...my sort of folk.'

FIT FOR A KING

✪ On 1 October 1934 Derby County Football Club held a grand dinner at the town's drill hall to celebrate the club's 50th anniversary. Players from the 1884 side and every era beyond enjoyed a full menu – it began with fresh lobster followed by a choice of fricassee of chicken, roast turkey, roast duckling and cherry sauce, York ham, ox tongue, galantine of veal or grouse pie with Russian and tomato salads, then ices, trifle, meringues and cream, chartreuse of fruits, stilton, cheese and coffee, wines, liqueurs, whiskies and brandy – just a modest affair then...no wonder the club had difficulty balancing the books!

✪ On 27 September 1984 Derby County held their centenary celebration dinner at the Novotel in Sandiacre. Again many personalities from the club's past made great efforts to be there, but one man who had fallen out with the club sent a brief letter addressed to Derby's board of directors and typed on Nottingham Forest notepaper – 'Unfortunately I will not be able to accept as I have already agreed to attend the official opening of the Junction 28 Exclusive Leisure Complex at the Swallow Hotel on that evening' – not one of Brian Clough's better moments, to be fair.

✪ At the same above banquet a telegram from Queen Elizabeth II was solemnly read out in which Her Majesty offered Derby County Football Club her sincere congratulations on reaching its 100th birthday. Almost 20 years later, when the Baseball Ground was being cleared pending demolition, the 'cherished' artefact was found by accident, stuffed in a box of discarded papers in a storeroom behind the gents' toilets underneath C-Stand. Only the keen eye of the enthusiast who discovered it saved the historic message for posterity, and it is now kept at Pride Park...well away from the gents.

EIGHT – ARTS AND ENTERTAINMENT...

Games are described as 'dramas', players are 'stars', grounds have been dubbed 'theatres' and goals 'sheer poetry'. It seems football has become a performance art in itself, and its links with the worlds of television, radio, music, literature, cinema and the arts in general are inescapable. Derby County are a down to earth club and their place in that rarefied world is a small one – but the following pieces of Rams-related trivia are all linked in some way with the arts and entertainment.

ALL IN THE GAME

For one sublime season in the 1970s Derby County were the reigning 'most skilful side in British football'. At least as far as television was concerned. On Sunday 28 July 1974 the Rams took part in a brand new skills contest named *All in the Game,* which was televised for ITV's *World of Sport.* It was devised by Bristol City's go-ahead young manager Alan Dicks and filmed at their Ashton Gate ground.

Derby's reserve-team coach Colin Murphy took charge of the six Rams players who represented the club. They saw off Chelsea, Wolves and Bristol City before meeting Norwich in the grand final. Although Derby's team included such notable talents as Graham Moseley, Donald O'Riordan and Jeff King, that in itself might not have been enough to secure the trophy. But the Rams had a secret weapon – veteran winger Alan Hinton.

A bewildering array of cones, hoops and dummy walls proved no obstacle to the consummate artistry of 'Gladys', and the Derby side took the title in style. As the *World of Sport* anchor man Dickie Davies presented the team with the trophy, Rams supporters must have wondered how much better it could get, but they soon had the answer – a lot better. Nine months after their *All in the Game* triumph, the official 'most skilful side in British football' were crowned 1974–75 League champions.

SHORT AND SWEET

The shortest verse penned in honour of a Derby County personality is the three-line *Cloughie* written by poet Parry Maguire shortly after Brian Clough's death in September 2004. Although it comprises a mere 14 words, admirers of Derby County's most celebrated manager would consider no more needs be said.

> Tell Heaven's XI to get their
> Boots and shirts on
> The manager's just arrived...

MUSICAL TRIBUTES

Despite the dubious quality of some of the offerings, most football personalities would consider it flattering to have a tribute record or CD made in their honour.

One of the most affectionate was *I Wish I Could Play Like Charlie George*, released in 1980 by The Strikers and Selston Bagthorpe Primary School Choir. Although the cute ditty features on the CD *The Rams Songs,* it isn't quite the tribute to the talented Derby striker that supporters might think.

It was originally written in honour of George Best, but on the day the band had arranged to record it the wayward genius was imprisoned for a drink-related offence. Feeling uneasy about asking a primary school class to sing the praises of a drunken jailbird, the band hastily thought of a name that sounded the same – thus it was that Charlie George served as a last-minute substitute.

George scores a neat hat-trick as he is also honoured by at least two more songs. Here's a top 10 of releases either about or by personalities connected with Derby County.

Title	Artist
Steve Bloomer's Watching	Robert Lindsay and the Pride Park Posse
I wish I could play like Charlie George	The Strikers and Selston Bagthorpe Primary School Choir
Roy McFarland	Rockin Johnny Austin
Brian (Brian Clough)	Fat and Frantic
The Charlie George Calypso	Stephen North and the Flat Back Four

Gio (Giorgi Kinkladze)	Kevin Phoenix
You can't win 'em all	Brian Clough, Peter Taylor and Stuart Webb with J.J. Barrie
Singing the Blues	Terry Curran (Rams 1970s winger)
Paulo Wanchope	Alfie
Charlie George	Halftime Oranges

A number of other Derby players also grabbed the mike in moments of madness. Despite being born in Edinburgh, Dave Mackay recorded *I belong to Glasgow* with his Spurs colleague Alan Gilzean, Francis Lee sang *Sugar Sugar* with Bobby Moore, and Peter Shilton strangled *Side by Side* in a cringeworthy duet with his England goalkeeping colleague Ray Clemence.

Lest the out-of-tune trio should wish to quietly forget their moments of shame, there is bad news. All three have been re-released on CD compilations!

THE PHANTOM DARNER

The most famous goal scored by any player connected to Derby County is the one by Archie Gemmill for Scotland against Holland in the 1978 World Cup in Argentina. It was nominated by FIFA as one of the top 10 in World Cup history.

It came in the 68th minute of Scotland's 3–2 victory. Gemmill weaved his way into the box on the right and left three Dutch players for dead before curling a shot over the 'keeper. Scotland departed the World Cup despite the win, but the goal itself entered the nation's folklore. This dialect verse by the Scottish poet Alastair Mackie immortalised the moment.

> It's nae o Argentina that I mind
> Nor Brazil, passin their triangles neat.
> Na, it's o Archie Gemmill's feet streekin
> A pattern on the edge o the box.
> His skeely needle threaded the ba past
> Three men, their legs fooled by the phantom darner.
> It was a baldy-headed goblin scored the goal.
> His shot, a rainbow, arches ower his name.

Nor was that the end of it. In 1996 the goal became one of only a handful to appear in a feature film when it was shown in the movie *Trainspotting* – the scorer admitted to being thoroughly embarrassed that the graphic script and images compared the sublime moment to both a heroin high and a sexual climax.

And there was more to come. In 2000 the goal was voted 'Best-ever by a Scottish footballer' and a year later the choreographer Andy Howitt turned it into a piece of modern dance – it featured as the centrepiece of his ballet *The Nutmeg Suite*.

What did the down-to-earth Gemmill think of the hype? He was by then working as overseas scout for Derby County under Jim Smith and gave a diplomatic answer when interviewed: 'I find it strange that a single goal should create such a fuss after so many years, and to be honest I don't really understand it. It's weird to see a bunch of dancers doing my clenched fist salute to music – but of course it's very flattering.'

While Scotland fans were able to see Gemmill play only occasionally, others were more privileged. The 'Phantom Darner' played 404 games for Derby County in two separate spells between 1970 and 1984 and scored 33 goals.

FOREST OWN-GOAL

In the late 19th and early 20th centuries it was quite common for supporters or enterprising printers to publish verse after a big game victory, but Nottingham Forest couldn't wait. On the occasion of their FA Cup tie at Derby on 6 March 1909, they went to print before the result was known.

> Dear old pals, right glad we are to greet you
> Friends we have been before and friends we will remain
> If fortune favours us and we should beat you
> We will wish you luck next time you try again.

A Baseball Ground crowd of 16,000 saw Derby County win the game 3–0 through a hat-trick by Alf 'Snobby' Bentley. Forest tried their luck on many more occasions after that, but it was 1959 when they finally lifted the FA Cup again, 50 years after that ignoble loss to the redoubtable Rams.

THE RAMMIES

Most football reports are quickly forgotten, but occasionally a resurfacing phrase or passage confirms that the best football wordsmiths can turn their job into a real art. If there was such an award as a Rammie for erudite Derby County prose, these examples might well form a 'Top Five' shortlist.

☙ Author **Alfred Gibson** describes the Rams and England striker Steve Bloomer in *Association Football and the Men Who Made It* – 1905: 'He is a strange compound of the philosopher and the stoic, giving the spectator the impression of being unnaturally calm, even disinterested, as he stands, hand on hip, aloof from the game. But out of the corner of his eye he is watching and his brain is formulating a plan – and when the supreme moment comes he pounces on the ball like a greyhound, darts past his opponents and swerves towards open ground. Before the defence know what has happened the ball is in the net. He is a man of action, a living force, a strong, relentless, destroying angel.'

☙ Cricket correspondent and passionate closet football fan **John Arlott** on a former Rams forward playing for Reading in the 1930s: 'Arthur Bacon was a tall man from Derby County with a shaving brush tuft of hair growing out of a shallow forehead above a mighty jaw. His chest was like a drum, his thighs hugely tapering, and he had two shooting feet which he threw at footballs as if to burst them.'

☙ **George Edwards** of the *Derby Evening Telegraph* strikes a wistful note in charting the Rams destruction of Manchester United in 1970: 'While Dave Mackay sauntered imperiously through the game for the Rams, the saddest sight of all was that of the all-time great Bobby Charlton feebly trying to impose himself.'

☙ **Gerald Mortimer** of the *Derby Evening Telegraph* assesses a posturing official: 'Mr Reynolds refereed the game in a blithe cocoon of self congratulation.'

☙ **Stuart Hall**'s lyrical radio report of Derby 3 Liverpool 2 on 13 March 1999: 'A record audience leaned forward like a string section under Bernstein's baton.'

FLAWED GENIUS

Few men in Derby County history can have played with more calm assurance than the Republic of Ireland international Paul McGrath. In 1996–97, Derby's first season in the Premiership, the gifted defender made 25 near-flawless appearances. Yet beneath it all he was often deeply troubled by life off the field and clashed with authority on many occasions. This poem by Parry Maguire will stand the test of time as a fine epitaph to an enigmatic personality.

> The old knees
> with their battle-weary scars
> That spoke so many grand stories
> The voice gentle as velvet
> Yet not always so secure
> and the rogue's heart
> that took to wandering
> with a smile
> with a shrug
> carried the patience of saints
> and earned the love
> of those who saw the man
> and forgave the flaw.

ENGLAND EXPECTS

Steve Bloomer was voted Derby's best-ever player in a 2005 poll. But a hundred years earlier the prolific striker was regarded not only as the best in Derby but indeed in the whole of England – and by natural extension that made Bloomer the finest footballer in the world at that stage of the game's development.

The following lines of verse are taken from Bloomer's biography *Football's First Superstar*. They sum up exactly how important he was to the England cause.

> Bloomer is picked, and we shall watch some more
> His carving swoop adown the field,
> Amid old enemies who yield
> Room for his fleeting passage, to the roar
> Of multitudes enraptured, who acclaim
> Their country's hero bearing down on goal,
> Instant of foot, deliberate of soul......
> All's well with England; 'Steve' is on his game.

CHARLIE'S ART

Few would deny that Charlie George was an artist among footballers. But not all of his admirers are aware that the gifted Derby striker was also a footballer among artists.

Sarah Lucas first painted Charlie in her teens in the 70s. Charlie moved on and so did the girl. Thirty years later Sarah Lucas had become one of Britain's most acclaimed contemporary artists. Yet despite counting celebrities like Damien Hirst and Tracey Emin among her arty friends, she never forgot the man who once scored a hat-trick for Derby County against Real Madrid.

Her much vaunted installation of 2002 was titled *Charlie George*. Self-consciously controversial, not unlike the man himself, the exhibition featured abstract renditions of the player in the form of porcelain toilet bowls. The contraptions dangled from a ceiling in the company of a black and white painted bidet entitled *Susan Farge* – a dubious 'tribute' to the footballer's wife.

And so it went on. Charlie's facsimile autograph adorned a series of urinals and his portrait graced the cover of a limited edition LP specially cut to celebrate the event. Even the most avid collector of Rams memorabilia might hesitate to add that particular 'footballer's record' to their haul – a copy for sale in a London art gallery in 2006 carried a cool price tag of £1,000.

The reaction of a down-to-earth bloke like George to this homage in art can only be imagined, but the *cognoscenti* of the art world stroked their chins and purred admiring words like 'wonderful', 'uncanny' and 'sublime vision'.

Somebody should have told them that the much shrewder critics who watched a genius at work at Derby in the mid-70s had beaten them to it by three decades. Charlie George remains the most artistic player in Derby County history.

DREAM MOVE

The most unusual transfer in Derby's history existed purely in the realms of fantasy. When Dean Sturridge banged in 20 League goals in 1995–96 other clubs began to take notice. When he again finished as the Rams leading scorer the next season – Derby's first in the Premiership – figures of his worth began to circulate. By July 1997 his price tag was being widely touted as £7 million.

Derby began to believe the hype – a bid of £4 million from Middlesbrough was brusquely rejected by the Rams chairman Lionel Pickering as 'well off the mark.' Sturridge believed it too – after rejecting a £10,000-a-week contract extension he finally got his dream move in March 1998 at a cool fee of £5 million.

But this was no ordinary transfer – the deal was a fictional one which took Sturridge to Harchester United, a Premiership club whose sole domain was the one created by Sky TV for their new soap opera *Dream Team*. Sturridge had been so desperate for the 'big move' that he had agreed a contract to appear as himself in the glossy serial.

Being detached from reality suited the striker perfectly – he scored the goals that helped Harchester avoid relegation before the scriptwriters had him sold back to Derby to resume his career at Pride Park. But this was one occasion when life failed to imitate art – during his spell on screen Sturridge's real-life form for the Rams dipped as he became more and more injury prone and with it so did his value. In the absence of a wondrous scribe the prospects of a genuine dream move grew slimmer with each lingering month. No clubs of genuine quality showed any interest, and Derby eventually sold the ex-Harchester man to Leicester City in January 2001 – for the nightmare price of £350,000!

BIG SCREEN MOMENTS

☻ Although contemporary reports state that an Edison kinematograph captured moving pictures of the 1899 FA Cup Final between Derby and Sheffield United, the film remains tantalisingly undiscovered. So the earliest known footage of Derby County is the newsreel of the fourth-round FA Cup tie at Newcastle United on 13 March 1911. Failing their screen test miserably, the Rams suffered a resounding 4–0 defeat. Their captain that day also fluffed his lines hopelessly – the only known film of **Steve Bloomer** in action shows him meekly pass the ball to the opposition immediately following the kick-off.

☻ The Newcastle United wing-half **Ralph Hann** joined Derby County in unusual circumstances. In March 1932 he was watching a film in a cinema when a message was flashed on screen asking him to report to St James' Park. Waiting for him there was the Derby County manager George Jobey. Hann promptly signed for the Rams and made 120 appearances before becoming the club's trainer in the 50s and 60s. He never did see the end of that film.

☻ The Rams enjoyed an unexpected cameo role in the 1969 comedy film *Some Will Some Won't* in a scene where the Derbyshire-born actor Arthur Lowe (Captain Mainwaring in *Dad's Army*) selects Crystal Palace v Derby County as a draw on his pools coupon. The director was evidently no football fan, for that season's promotion-winners were hardly a good bet to uphold the filmic 'continuity' – by the time the movie was released, goals from **Roy McFarland** and **Willie Carlin** had seen Derby win at Selhurst Park by two goals to one.

✪ When he was a player at Ipswich Town, the Derby County manager **George Burley** declined a chance to appear with Sylvester Stallone and Michael Caine in the 1981 film *Escape to Victory*. In a *Sunday Times* interview Burley explained – 'I was with the Scotland squad in Hungary and the film was being shot there. I was asked to stay but said no because I wanted to get back home to see my wife.' Several Ipswich players did feature in the football-related war film, among them Repton-born Russell Osman whose father Rex played for Derby in the 50s.

✪ The Derby and England goalkeeper **Peter Shilton** starred as himself in the 1987 movie *Hero*. Central to the dramatised story – that of the 1986 World Cup in Mexico – was the infamous 'Hand of God' goal fisted past Shilton by Argentina's Diego Maradona, which effectively eliminated England from the competition. The 'keeper's apoplectic reaction to the illegal strike required no acting – but playing to a studio camera proved a far greater challenge. Derby County's sole film actor is still waiting for a call from Hollywood.

✪ Rarely does a real-life goal appear in a movie, but a wonder strike by Derby's Welsh International **Dean Saunders** did. It features in the 1996 film *Fever Pitch,* which centres on Arsenal's 1988–89 Championship-winning season. It was Saunders's goal in Derby's unexpected 2–1 win at Highbury in May 1989 that looked to have robbed the Gunners of the title. Arsenal finally did clinch it at Liverpool in the last second of an incredible game which formed the climax to the film. But for the Saunders goal, the movie might never have been made.

THE ENTERTAINERS

A number of Derby County players have been adept at a performing art other than football. Here are the most entertaining men in the club's history.

✪ After retiring from the game, defender **Archie Goodall** (1889–1902) toured the music halls and theatres of Europe and America presenting his own strong-man act. His party piece was 'The Hoop', first presented in

1909 at the Grand Theatre in Derby. Goodall wore 'magic boots' to walk around the inner circumference of the giant steel wheel, pausing while upside-down to suspend two female assistants using only his teeth. By the time he revisited Derby in 1917 the girls had been replaced by three acrobats swinging from a trapeze. Archie Goodall is undeniably Derby's strongest defender of all time!

* Some would say Derby County provided **Jack Kifford** (1898–99) with the perfect training for a second career. When the Rams full-back retired from football in 1909, he joined the celebrated Fred Karno's Troupe, a touring circus and theatre act whose trademark was creating total chaos out of perfect order. Kifford's career fared less well than that of two of his young Karno colleagues – Charlie Chaplin and Stan Laurel – and the madcap antics seem to have taken their toll. Kifford died aged 43 in 1921 near Glasgow...in The Paisley Asylum for the General Paralysis of the Insane.

* It was a pity **Arthur Armstrong** (1906–07) scored only one goal for Derby County because he might well have developed a spectacular line in celebrations. The bouncy right-winger spent just one season with the Rams but prior to joining the club had toured for three seasons as an acrobat with Sanger's Circus.

* Prior to joining Derby in 1926, left-winger **Georgie Mee** had been a vocalist and entertainer. On one occasion he used his stage experience to dramatic effect when on a Friday evening in Sunderland in the late 1920s the Derby players followed their eve-of-the-match tradition by attending a show. The acts were so feeble that Mee jumped onto the stage, grabbed the microphone and proceeded to astonish the audience with a polished routine of his own. The man of many talents was also a leading light in Derby Operatic Society and his conjuring skills earned him membership of the Magic Circle. George 'Shortie' Mee played 155 games for Derby and scored 15 goals.

* When **Christian Dailly** joined Derby for £1 million from Dundee United in 1996 he definitely brought new talent to the dressing room. The 'defender with attitude' later assumed the role of lead singer and guitarist in a rock group called Hooligan, a name subsequently changed to the less controversial South Playground. Even when Dailly became captain of Scotland, he still harboured dreams of a second career and remains the only Derby County player to seriously declare 'I want to be a rock star.'

VINTAGE CLASSICS

Many personalities connected with Derby County have either written their autobiography or been the subject of a biography. Here is a round dozen of vintage classics charting the lives of men who played for the Rams prior to 1960.

Revd Llewellyn Henry Gwynne (1888)	*Pastor on the Nile*, 1960
John Goodall (1889–98)	*Association Football*, 1898
Steve Bloomer (1892–1905, 1910–13)	*The Story of Football's First Superstar*, 1999
Ivan Sharpe (1911–12)	*40 Years in Football*, 1952
Frank Buckley (1911–13)	*The Major*, 2006
Hughie Gallacher (1934–35)	*The Hughie Gallacher Story*, 1989
Billy Steel (1938)	*Scotland's Little Maestro*, 2003
Peter Doherty (1945–46)	*Spotlight on Football*, 1948
Raich Carter (1945–47)	*Footballer's Progress*, 1950
Tim Ward (1937–50)	*Armed With a Football*, 1994
Bert Mozley (1946–54)	*When Football was Fun*, 1999
Stuart Imlach (1954)	*My Father and other working class Football Heroes*, 2005

BATED BREATH

Even the greatest suspense thriller might fail to match the hottest Derby County title of all time. The internet bookseller Amazon lists its price as £15.99 but warns potential readers that 'availability is limited'. No shop seems able to track one down. Even the British Library, which stated the book's year of publication as 1998 and gave it an ISBN of 1859830676, has given up their quest for a copy.

There is absolutely no doubt that *My Derby County Years* by former Rams secretary and director Stuart Webb is the scarcest and hardest to find volume connected with the club…for the simple reason that the book doesn't exist.

The potential blockbuster was 'withdrawn on legal advice' prior to publication. A spokesman for the publisher confirmed – 'It was a red-hot read, sizzling in fact, but far too hot to handle. Some of the revelations were absolute mustard even by Derby County standards – but we just couldn't risk being sued.'

Many men (and quite possibly women) heaved a huge sigh of relief when the plug was pulled on the forthcoming title at the eleventh hour – they were safe in the knowledge that their identities and the revelations surrounding them would remain secret forever......unless, that is, the publisher changes their mind!

LITERARY CURIOSITIES

☺ There is no more unusual book associated with Derby County than the one penned by Llewellyn Henry Gwynne in 1924. By then the footballing cleric had travelled a long way since turning out as the Rams centre-forward in 1888 – and that means literally. None but the most assiduous Derby County bibliophile would dream of adding the blockbusting title to their collection – *The Romance of Christian Missions in North and Central Africa*.

☺ **Steve Bloomer** is the only Rams player to figure prominently in a work of fiction. The celebrated humorist and novelist P.G. Wodehouse honoured the Derby and England striker in his short story *The goalkeeper and plutocrat*, which was first published in the January 1912 edition of *Strand Magazine* and later included in Wodehouse's 1914 book *The Man Upstairs*. The amusing yarn concerns two obsessive collectors named Rackstraw and Dodson who vie for possession of 'the most coveted item of sporting memorabilia known to mankind' – the pair of boots in which Bloomer first played for England.

☺ In 1981 Penny Watson belied the 'dumb blonde' stereotype by becoming the first footballer's wife to go into print. Her husband was the England centre-back **Dave Watson**, who played 39 times for Derby County in the 1984–85 season. The book is both a biography of the player and a rare insight into that much-maligned breed of 'footballers' wives'. Penny was unable to resist a nod in the direction of Sherlock Holmes – she called the book *My Dear Watson*.

☺ Watching Derby County can be a murderous experience, but thriller-writer Frank Palmer took matters a step further in his 1998 novel *Final Score*. While the Baseball Ground features in a fond reminiscence by one of his characters, Derby's Pride Park Stadium becomes a running location in a grisly tale of murder and retribution – and that doesn't mean a boardroom struggle. The book also features Derby County's Irish international Robbie Hill, who remains conspicuously absent from the club's official *Who's Who*.

✪ When the Canadian international striker **Paul Peschisolido** signed for Derby in March 2004 he must have prayed that none of his new colleagues were familiar with the literary *oeuvre* of his wife Karren Brady. *Brady Plays the Blues* (1995) charted her early days at Birmingham City as the first ever female managing director of an English football club – but it also gave a girlishly romantic account of how she had been wooed and wed by her 'wonderful husband'. Worse still, Karren had later written two novels promoted as 'sizzling football bonkbusters' – *United* (1997) and *Trophy Wives* (1998) – and one reviewer dared to articulate the thought that might have occurred to readers: 'One wonders if the over-the-top sex scenes in Brady's novels are based on the writer's own marital experience. If so her footballer husband must be cringing in his boots – they were as ludicrous as they were laughable.'

MODERN CLASSICS

Although many Derby County greats have yet to lay bare their souls in print, a full Rams-related library still extends to many volumes. Here is a shelf full of books either by or about personalities connected to the club post-1960, and each was written after they became associated with the Rams.

Brian Clough	– manager 1967–73	*Cloughie: Walking on Water* (2002)
Dave Mackay	– defender 1968–70 & manager 1973–76	*The Real Mackay* (2004)
Archie Gemmill	– midfielder 1970–77 & 1982–83	*Both sides of the Border* (2005)
Charlie George	– striker 1975–78, 1981	*Charlie George – My Story* (2005)
Peter Taylor	– asst manager 1967–73 & manager 1982–84	*With Clough by Taylor* (1980)
Tommy Docherty	– manager 1977–79	*Call the Doc* (1981)
Robert Maxwell	– owner 1983–91	*Maxwell's Fall – The appalling legacy of a Corrupt Man* (1992)
Mickey Thomas	– midfielder 1985	*Wild at Heart* (1997)
Frank Stapleton	– striker 1988	*Frankly Speaking* (1991)
Peter Shilton	– goalkeeper 1987–91	*Peter Shilton: My Autobiography* (2004)
John Harkes	– midfielder 1993–95	*Captain for Life* (1999)

Jim Smith — manager 1995–2001 *It's Only a Game* (2000)
John Gregory — midfielder 1985–87 *The Boss* (2000)
                     & manager 2002–03

A number of other players penned their autobiography prior to arriving at Derby. These include Francis Lee (*Soccer Round the World* – 1970), Kevin Ratcliffe (*The Blues and I* – 1988), Paul McGrath (*Ooh Aah Paul McGrath* – 1994) and Rob Lee (*Come in number 37* – 2000).

The list suggests that midfielders are more literary than goalkeepers, defenders and strikers, but not as willing to go into print as managers – Brian Clough tops the overall charts with at least a dozen titles carrying his name.

Potential Derby bestsellers yet to be written include *The King* (Kevin Hector), *Roy Mac* (Roy McFarland), *Lionel* (Pickering), *Igor Igor* (Stimac) and *One Graham Richards*. The least appropriate title was published in 1978 when its author Tommy Docherty was manager at Derby – *The ABC of Soccer Sense: Strategy and Tactics Today* remained a closed book even to the writer himself.

ROUTE ONE FOOTBALL

Some wins are so much part of a football club's folklore that they should never be forgotten – one such is the 1970–71 televised game between Derby County and Crystal Palace which ended in a glorious 4–2 triumph for the Rams. But despite the famous victory earning them a handsome trophy, this proud moment has been gravely omitted from the club's official history books. That's because it occurred in the final of the BBC TV general knowledge quiz show *Quiz Ball*. Here for posterity is a celebration of that gloriously trivial occasion.

The series began in 1966–67 hosted by David Vine. Arsenal (captained by former Rams youth player Bertie Mee), West Bromwich Albion and Celtic (twice) all won the title before the cerebral Rams entered for the first and only time in 1970–71 – Stuart Hall was by then referee.

The concept matched the contestants – on the whole it was simple. Each team comprised three members of the club and one celebrity guest. The team correctly answering a starter question was obliged to choose one of four 'routes' to goal – 4 easy questions, 3 medium, 2 difficult or 1 hard – the latter being the instant 'route one' way to score from which the now popular term of derision originated. The opposition were allowed a 'tackle' to regain possession except on route one – but a wrong answer to a tackle question resulted in an automatic own-goal. Progress downfield was shown on a primitive pitch with the aid of illuminated bulbs. High-tech it certainly wasn't, but the show's ratings were high – 'talking footballers' were a rare breed at that time when 'sick as a parrot', 'over the moon', 'I just hit it Brian' and 'early doors' were all some players could muster.

Eight teams took part – Derby's starting side for the first-round tie against Cowdenbeath were Alan Durban, Alan Hinton, Roy McFarland and guest Bob Arnold – who played Tom Forrest in the radio serial *The Archers*. The Rams progressed but not without some dodgy finishing – faced with the question 'What sport is governed by the Queensbury Rules?' Alan Hinton panicked in front of goal and gave the immortal answer 'cards' instead of boxing. Hinton later suffered the most humiliating fate ever to befall a Derby County footballer – he was dropped from the *Quiz Ball* line up.

John O'Hare stepped in as Derby next beat Tottenham Hotspur 3–1 despite the intelligent play of comedian Peter Cook threatening to carry the day for Spurs. That left only the final, and Derby romped home as fine goals from Durban (2), O'Hare and Arnold clinched the 4–2 victory for the brainiest side in Britain.

Arnold's goal made him the only player known as 'Forrest' to score for Derby, and trivia buffs ought also to know that three more Rams figures competed for rival sides during the series – Francis Lee (Manchester City), David Webb (Chelsea) and the former West Bromwich Albion manager Jimmy Hagan, who played for Derby in the 30s. As for the goals conceded by Derby in the surreal final, both were tucked away by Palace's guest – the precious Richard Wattis – who remains the only character actor ever to score a brace against the Rams. What more can possibly be said? The *Quiz Ball* research files are now officially closed.

RAMS ON THE BOX

✪ Some Rams fans swear to have watched the 1946 FA Cup Final live on TV. However, it is a 'false memory' for most – Derby's 4–1 win over Charlton Athletic was shown extensively as a Pathé newsreel in cinemas but was never broadcast live in the Midlands television region. Only a few privileged viewers in London could truly make the claim – parts of the game were shown as an experimental transmission for those with state-of-the-art equipment.

☺ Derby's first appearance on national television was their first-round FA Cup tie against Bradford City on 17 November 1956. Brief extracts of the Rams 2–1 home win were shown on BBC's *Sports Special* – then such a novelty that it was mentioned in the match reports. **Dennis Woodhead** played to the cameras with a stunning left-footed goal, but the ever-artful **Tommy Powell** stole the show by scoring the second goal direct from a corner.

☺ It wasn't until 1964 that the BBC were permitted to show extracts of League games. The first ever *Match of the Day* was broadcast on BBC Two on Saturday 22 August 1964 – it showed Liverpool beating Arsenal 3–2 at Anfield in front of 40,000 – but only 20,000 tuned in to watch the highlights! Second Division Derby County at last made their *MOTD* debut on 10 April 1965 when **Alan Durban** scored both Derby goals in their 2–2 draw at Northampton Town.

☺ The first Derby County game broadcast live in its entirety on British television was the first leg of the European Cup semi-final against Juventus in Turin on 11 April 1973. Much of Derbyshire tuned in to BBC One to see the Rams lose a controversial game 3–1 – two weeks later the second leg finished 0–0 at the Baseball Ground and Derby were out of Europe.

☺ Derby County's third-round FA Cup tie against Everton on 3 January 1976 was watched live on television by a pretty cool audience. Commentators from Norway, Sweden and Denmark were at the Baseball Ground, while a hard-up Finn cheated shamelessly by broadcasting from a Helsinki studio. The Rams 2–1 win courtesy of a Charlie George double was viewed live by 6 million fans in Scandinavia, while they endured an enforced winter fixture break. Many Rams games shown only as highlights on ITV's *Star Soccer* were broadcast live there – Derby County's huge fan base in Scandinavia remains loyal to this day.

☺ Derby's first live League appearance on British television was their home game against Chelsea on 22 November 1987. Goals from **Steve Cross** and **John Gregory** sealed a 2–0 win, and Peter Shilton made his 1,000th competitive appearance in club football.

TELLY TRIVIA

✪ Derby's 2–1 home FA Cup victory over Everton on 3 January 1976 was the scene of an unusual presentation by Ilkeston Junior Rams. The proud recipients – Derby director Trevor East and his fellow TV presenter Chris Tarrant – were stars in the cult children's programme *Tiswas* (Today Is Saturday, Watch And Smile). In keeping with the show's anarchic character, the unforgettable gift was a giant custard pie! In the mid-1970s East used to run on to the show yelling 'Rioch, Rioch' every week.

✪ Derby-born actor and Rams fan the late Kevin Lloyd, best known for his role as Detective Constable Alfred 'Tosh' Lines in the ITV police drama *The Bill*, once insisted on having a script partially re-written to include a speech about Derby's 1971–72 Championship winners.

✪ On 18 February 1981 the entire Derby County first team appeared on *This Is Your Life* to honour fan and director Tim Brooke-Taylor. The Buxton-born comic actor rarely missed an opportunity to promote his club on TV – in the 1970s comedy show *The Goodies* he wore a Rams shirt and gave pride of place to a Derby County teddy bear. Nor did his eye for 'product placement' fade – in November 2002 he became the first person to appear on *Countdown* wearing a Derby County tie!

✪ Derby's 0–0 draw at home to Bristol Rovers on 23 March 1985 was notable for only one thing – the matchday mascot. The team were led out by 35-year-old Simon Groom, a presenter on BBC's *Blue Peter* programme. Born on a farm in Dethick, Derbyshire, the celebrity Rams fan had spent time training with the players and meeting supporters for a special feature which aired on *Blue Peter* on 15 April 1985. Groom remains the oldest Derby County mascot on record.

✪ On 9 November 1985 the special guests at Derby's home game with Lincoln City were the cast of the children's drama series *Murphy's Mob* accompanied by a racehorse of that name. Early episodes of the series, concerning the fortunes of third Division Dunmore United, were filmed at Watford's Vicarage Road – but the Baseball Ground later became their home since it was closer to the Central TV studios. The cast and horse proved lucky mascots – goals from Hindmarch (2), Micklewhite (2), Chandler, Davison and Garner gave Derby a 7–0 win.

✪ Several personalities connected to Derby County have been the subject of

This Is Your Life. They include players **Peter Shilton** (1981) and **Francis Lee** (1994), chairman **Robert Maxwell** (1988) and celebrity supporters Robert Lindsay and Kevin Lloyd, both presented with the famous Red Book in 1992. **Brian Clough** was high on the 'wanted' list, but television executives shied away from confronting the unpredictable manager for fear he would refuse to participate.

☻ Derby County and their travelling fans have a permanent claim to fame as fleeting television extras. At the Rams game against Coventry City at the Ricoh Arena on 21 January 2006 scenes were shot for the Channel Four drama *All in the Game* starring Ray Winstone, which aired on 11 May 2006. The match itself also proved 'dramatic' for the Rams, mingling farce, tragedy and slapstick in equal measure as they tumbled to a disastrous 6–1 defeat.

FANCY THAT

It is difficult to imagine a modern-day Derby County squad rallying to the cause in the way once adopted by the early players. When the club found themselves in dire financial straits during the 1893–94 season the team agreed to play a game in fancy dress. The match took place at the County Ground on 31 January 1894 against a side comprising members of the Grand Theatre's *Babes in the Wood* pantomime cast. The oddest Derby County line up of all time included future manager Jimmy Methven (dressed as a negro) and England internationals John Goodall (Bold Bad Baron) and Jack Robinson (Fat Policeman). Even so, there is a suspicion that the idea was beyond the dignity of at least one star player – Steve Bloomer, due to appear as a convict, dropped out through a very convenient 'illness'.

LASTING TRIBUTE

At a poignant memorial service for Brian Clough held at Pride Park Stadium on 21 October 2004, the following poem by David Prouse was read by Clough's widow Barbara to the 15,000 who had gathered to pay a final tribute to the former Rams manager.

What made him so endearing is elusive to explain,
This tyrant in a sweatshirt barking orders in the rain.
Today he offered vitriol, tomorrow marzipan,
A paradox, a puzzle but a diamond of a man.

When the Gods apportioned modesty, one youngster wasn't there,
He was in the queue marked confidence, receiving twice his share.
With two good feet beneath him he considered it enough,
And so was born the character we know as Brian Clough.

Young Cloughie did things his way, for no one showed him how,
Emerging from the backstreets like a blossom on a bow.
Becoming proud and peerless as a hero of his time,
And then, one tackle later, down and out at twenty-nine.

Where others might have wilted or nestled in their grief,
Cloughie found salvation in his cocky self belief.
Come set-back or adversity, a man is still a man,
So it was, as one dream ended, that another one began.

Reality was Hartlepool, the lowest of them all,
In the Fourth Division basement with their backs against the wall.
All patchwork roofs and puddles and frostbite in the shade,
It was hard and it was humbling, but the boy would learn his trade.

Along came Peter Taylor and the dugout was complete,
Two canny minds would meet and merge to share the judgement seat.
Two mop and bucket soldiers to pound a broken drum,
But the cavalry would gather and the glory days would come.

For Cloughie had a quality no training could provide,
The gift of lending common men the jauntiness of stride.
Players tapped abilities they didn't know were there,
And good ones climbed to greatness on a goading and a glare.

Cloughie's team played football in the manner meant to be,
A joy for those who wore his shirt and those who came to see.
No arguments, no ego trips, no stars to shine alone,
As Cloughie scolded, Cloughie scowled, and loved them as his own.

For behind the bullish phrases, all the arrogance and pride,
There beat a kindly human heart, as deep as it was wide.
Deserving of an epitaph, significant but sad,
Just the greatest England manager that England never had.

FANZINE SCENE

The very first fanzines (a word coined by combining 'fan' and 'magazine') were printed in 1949 by science-fiction enthusiasts. Pop music followed suit in the 60s and 70s, and by the 80s the 'voice of the people' phenomenon had been firmly taken up by football fans. Although Derby supporters were a little tardy in responding to the call, here are some titles either produced by Rams fans or which carry a Derby County link.

> **Up The Vine**
> **The Sheep**
> **Interesting, Very Interesting**
> **C-Stander**
> **We'll be back in '81**
> **Hey Big Spender**
> **Ivor Ram**
> **The Mutton Mutineer**
> **Ramlines** (Loughborough Branch Supporters' Club)
> **Good Bye Marco**
> **Bloomer Shoots, Shilton Saves**
> **Nor Ram** (Norwegian Branch Supporters' Club)
> **Capital Ram** (London Branch Supporters' Club)
> **West Country Ram** (West Country Branch Supporters' Club)
> **The Baseball Bat** (Internet fanzine)

A number of other club fanzines pay indirect homage to personalities at one time connected to the Rams – former assistant manager Dario Gradi is honoured by Crewe Alexandra's *Super Dario Land,* ex-Rams boss Jim Smith is immortalised at Newcastle United through *Jim's Bald Heed* and former Derby midfielder Gordon 'Sid' Cowans is fondly remembered by Aston Villa in *Missing Sid.*

OFF COLOUR

For many years the *Football Special* produced by the *Derby Evening Telegraph* on Saturday evenings has been something of an institution. Affectionately known as the '*Green 'un*' because it is printed on green paper, it suffered a sudden identity crisis in the early 1990s when, because of rising paper costs, its owners decided to print it on white paper. Only after readers expressed their horror at the shock colour change did it revert to its traditional hue, one correspondent even being moved to pen the following verse entitled *Paper Pigmentation Blues.*

> They mustn't let it die without a fight,
> Letters poured in – it just wasn't right,
> 'Financial considerations' the editor's comment said,
> That's why this faithful friend would very soon be dead.
> Paler it grew week by week,
> But what a shock when it finally came,
> At 6.15 one Saturday night,
> The colour drained from Derby's game,
> The day the 'Green 'un' changed to white!

A CAST OF SEVERAL

In recent years the sculptural arts and football have increasingly crossed paths as many football clubs have commissioned statues or memorials of their best-loved personalities. Derby County FC have been slow to follow the trend, so the limited cast of former Rams men appears largely courtesy of other clubs or individuals – this was the state of play in June 2006.

✪ On Monday 28 October 1996 a marble plinth depicting a relief portrait of the Rams all-time leading scorer **Steve Bloomer** was unveiled in Derby City centre. Club representatives attended the ceremony but funds for the tribute were raised by Bloomer's grandson Steve Richards, who sold some of the players' international caps to facilitate the project.

✪ In 1999 Nottingham Forest stole a march on the Rams by unveiling a head and shoulders sculpture of 'their' greatest manager **Brian Clough**. Modelled by an artist who also numbers Her Majesty The Queen among his subjects, it greets all visitors to the City Ground foyer and depicts a sweat-shirted 'Old Big 'Ead' bellowing instructions from the dug-out.

✪ On 14 September 2000 a memorial plaque to **Steve Bloomer** was unveiled in Cradley, in the Black Country, on a heritage trail close to where the player was born in 1874.

✪ On 19 January 2001 the Portuguese football legend Eusebio arrived at Bramall Lane, Sheffield, to unveil a bronze statue of the late **Jimmy**

Hagan, his friend and former manager at Benfica, who died in 1998 aged 80. Hagan played for Derby County in the 1930s but was unwisely sold to Sheffield United, where he starred for almost 20 years before his unexpected move into management abroad. The England international inside-forward is regarded as the best player in the Blades long history and the handsome figure stands in the club's box office.

☻ In 2003 the fan-led Rams Trust launched 'The Steve Bloomer Project', aimed at erecting a bronze statue of Derby County's greatest scorer at the club's Pride Park Stadium. The group thought big, seeking to raise £100,000 for a double life-size figure, but many supporters of cash-strapped Derby County expressed doubts about the validity of the idea and three years later the fund amounted to only a few thousand pounds.

☻ In June 2005 Nottingham Forest fans launched the Brian Clough Statue Fund to raise the £60,000 required to erect a figure in Nottingham city centre. By the summer of 2006 £40,000 had already been raised and a cheeky appeal appeared in the *Derby Evening Telegraph* asking Rams fans to dip into their pockets so the Forest-led target could be reached by the end of the year.

☻ Early in 2006 Middlesbrough Football Club announced that their own 'Cloughie' Statue Fund had reached £20,000. Should sufficient money be raised, the figure would stand in Albert Park near where Boro's prolific scorer once lived. A 'Blue Plaque' already adorns the Valley Road house where Middlesbrough's favourite son was brought up.

THE MOMENT IT CLICKED

Watching your team concede a costly late goal via the digital medium of Ceefax (it literally stands for 'See Facts') can be an agonising experience, but the click of a button once brought the former Derby midfielder Bruce Rioch worse news still. On 10 November 1997 Rioch tapped in 302 for the teletext football news only to discover he had just been sacked as assistant manager at Queen's Park Rangers. Nor was that the only managerial indignity suffered by the Scottish international – at the start of the 1986–87 season, while in charge at debt-ridden Middlesbrough, Rioch arrived at their Ayresome Park ground to find himself locked out by bailiffs after the club had been put into receivership. Then a struggling Third Division side, Boro were forced to play their opening games at Hartlepool's ground and Rioch was said to have parked his car over a manhole cover to prevent the electricity board cutting off the Ayresome Park supply!

CHALK AND CHEESE

Although Brian Clough's own taste in music was definitely Frank Sinatra rather than the Sex Pistols or Beethoven, the former Derby manager was the subject of two diverse musical tributes which embraced both the punk and classical scenes. In September 1989 the British punk band The Toy Dolls released their album *Wakey Wakey*, which featured a song called *Cloughie is a Bootboy*. The irreverent title referred to an incident in which the then Nottingham Forest manager had a scuffle with pitch-invading fans, an action which led to police cautions for all the parties involved followed by a famous 'kiss and make up' for the cameras. In 2000 Clough was honoured at the opposite end of the music spectrum when the modern classical composer Robert Steadman wrote a song called *Brian Clough's CV,* which was premiered in the Millennium Dome as part of an ensemble titled *The Nottingham Songbook,* a tribute to the city and its achievements. As for the great man's opinion of the 'chalk and cheese' offerings, it went something like 'I'd rather do it my way.'

OFF KEY PERFORMANCE

When the Rams winger Ivan Sharpe got married in 1913 he found the Derby County board were in generous mood – they gave him a handsome present of a piano. But after news of the expensive gift was reported in the local paper it struck a wrong chord with at least one churlish fan. During Derby's 1–0 home defeat to Aston Villa on 12 March 1913, a game in which the newly-wed Sharpe was way off-key, a lone voice rang out from the Popular Side for all to hear, not least the distinctly flat Sharpe – 'Go home and play that ******* piano'.

PRIDE PARK ANTHEM

A number of 'theme tunes' have traditionally been linked with the Rams, but since 1997 the song *Steve Bloomer's Watching*, written by Derby fans Mark 'The Tank' Tewson and Martyn Miller, has gradually assumed an official status. Australian visitors to Pride Park might find the tune itself oddly familiar, for it is that of *Up There Cazaly,* a song originally recorded by Mike Brady, which in 1979 topped the Aussie singles charts. That honoured the Australian Rules football legend Roy Cazaly, a star with St Kilda in the 1920s and 30s, and has become the much-loved anthem of the Aussie game. In consequence, when the re-worked version of *Steve Bloomer's Watching* was recorded by the Broadway star, actor and Rams fan Robert Lindsay, a certain amount of legal flak was encountered concerning copyright. But now the song has been loyally adopted by the Derby County faithful there is no going back – here are its full words:

Verse One -

Our history's full of legends,
And football played on high,
The names Carter and Doherty,
Made all opponents cry.

Now we all just love football,
But will we lift the crown?
The noise goes up, the Rams come out,
Onto the hallowed ground

– Chorus (home version) -

Steve Bloomer's watching,
Helping them fight,
Guiding our heroes,
In the black and the white,
For all teams who come here,
There's nowhere to hide,
Everyone is frightened,
Of that Derby pride.

Verse Two -

The Rams just play football,
That makes our heart so proud,
McFarland and Hector,
Names to thrill the crowd,
And if you love or hate us,
Depending on the score,

When the boys come out at kick-off time,
How the mighty roar...(crowd noise)

Chorus (home) again -
Chorus (away version) -

The Rams are a coming,
We're out there to win,
Playing like heroes,
They won't let 'em in,
Home sides be wary,
Of our heart and soul,
We're searching for glory,
And victory is our goal.
– Home chorus to end –

GOING...GOING...GONE!

The internet might well have given football fans an entertaining outlet through which to sing the praises of their club, but new technology cuts both ways. And for Derby County's beleaguered board known as 'The Three Amigos' that meant one more medium through which they could be roundly abused and humiliated!

After the cash-strapped club was bought by the three-man consortium for the nominal sum of £3 in October 2003, supporter concern soon turned to anger and despair as the debts continued to mount without further investment. When 2005 drew to a close with no sign of change, one disgruntled fan decided he had had enough, and on 5 January 2006 he placed Derby County up for sale on the internet auction site eBay. Item number 8746862171 – 'Famous old club going for £3' – was offered to the global market without reserve and there were over 3,000 viewers in the first day as news spread of the bargain sale. Potential purchasers posed many questions, one of the most pertinent being 'Will the buyer need to live in Derby, understand football and be willing to invest?' The seller's reply was unequivocal – 'No on all counts.' Much fun was had by Rams fans at the board's expense and bidding reached the heady heights of over £100 before the party-poopers known as the 'eBay police' rumbled the spoof listing and hastily withdrew it from the auction.

BLAME ELTON

It's never a bad thing to have a truly original excuse for a bad string of results, and they don't come better than this – Derby's equal-worst run of League defeats would never have occurred but for the legendary singer Elton John.

The chain of events for Arthur Cox's goal-shy side began in November 1987 when striker Bobby Davison was sold to Leeds United for £350,000. The plan was for Derby's 'multi-millionaire' owner Robert Maxwell to fund the purchase of another forward, but it all went pear-shaped when the obsessively acquisitive Czech, already involved with Derby and Oxford United, approached Watford's pop-superstar chairman with a view to part-acquiring the club.

Had Elton John had sense he would have told Maxwell to take a running jump, but as it was he welcomed him with open arms. And the deal failed to impress the Football League. Concerned that Maxwell now had effective control of three League clubs, they imposed a transfer freeze that prevented Arthur Cox bringing in the much-needed striker. If only Elton had said no things might have been different – as it was Derby embarked on a difficult run of fixtures with Phil Gee and Andy Garner as their twin strike force. Needless to say the results were predictable – between 12 December 1987 and 10 February 1988 Derby scored no more than a single goal in any game and the fearsome pair mustered just one strike between them as the Rams lost eight games in a row. There was an added spookiness to the losing run for it began after a 1–1 draw at home to Elton's beloved Watford and only ended when the Rams drew 0–0 at Oxford...could Maxwell have 'arranged' that long-awaited point?

Whatever the case, the run equalled the eight in a row suffered by Derby in the very first League season of 1888–89 and again over a two-season span covering the end of 1964–65 and the beginning of 1965–66.

STAR QUALITY

A number of Rams players have found themselves receiving nicknames which show a nod to television, 'show business' or fiction. Here is a half-decent squad of star-quality players all blessed with that rare capacity to entertain.

Colin Boulton – 'Bernie' in punning reference to the catchphrase 'Bernie the bolt' from the cult ATV game show *The Golden Shot*, a Sunday tea-time institution, which aired between 1967 and 1975.

Peter Shilton – 'Tarzan' after the ape-man literary creation of Edgar Rice-Burroughs – more muscle than brains.

Gary Charles – 'Ray' after the black American musician Ray Charles.

Mel Sage – 'Parsley' in allusion to the friendly but droll lion who appeared on the children's TV show *The Herbs* with an owl named Sage.

Rob Hindmarch – 'Rocky' after the tough film character boxer who never knew when he was beaten.

Michael Forsyth – 'Bruce' after legendary entertainer Bruce Forsyth.

Seth Johnson – 'Seth Lad' in roundabout allusion to *Emmerdale Farm* soap character Seth Armstrong, known for his quaint language.

Sean Flynn – 'Errol' after cinema legend Errol Flynn, despite not being blessed with quite such dashing looks.

John McGovern – 'George Formby' after the bashful and clumsy film comedian with the toothy grin for whom everything, as for McGovern, generally 'turned out nice' in the end.

Gordon Hughes – 'Charlie Drake' because of a passing likeness to the TV comedian – since Hughes played in the same 60s side as Norman Wisdom lookalike Billy Hodgson, it suited the crowd to have a pair of ready-made fall-guys in the team.

Grzegorz Rasiak – 'Rodders' after the nickname of the lanky and gormless character Rodney Trotter played by Nicholas Lyndhurst in *Only Fools and Horses*.

Kevin Hector – 'Zak' after the character Zak Bishop, star player with Brentwich United in the BBC One TV serial *United*, which ran for 147 episodes from 1965–67.

Billy Hodgson – 'Norman Wisdom' because the 60s left-winger was a dead-ringer for the knockabout film comedian.

Gordon Hill – 'Norman Wisdom' again, because it was Hill's party piece to do a very passable impression of the star.

Alan Hinton – 'Noddy' on account of a distinctive head motion when running, but the winger's nature also conveniently suited the lovable character created by Enid Blyton.

A CONTROVERSIAL ISSUE

Since the first known Derby County home programme was produced for a fixture against Wolverhampton Wanderers on 5 September 1903, the club's official organ has informed, entertained and occasionally irritated in peddling its predominately 'party line' to the paying punter. But on one infamous occasion it overstepped the mark to such a shameful degree that the loyal readers hit back with a vengeance!

The genesis of the scandal was in 1971–72 when Derby County radically changed the traditional programme format by issuing *The Ram*, a newspaper-style publication with a much more informal content. In those less politically-correct times the club ran an annual Miss Derby County beauty contest (Sheila Ann Walsh, Tarina Prince, Tracey Jayne Jessop and Mary McNulty were all winners) and liberal use of these and other 'glamour models' was made in the pages of *The Ram* to promote the club's merchandise. Sales of the paper proved very healthy indeed.

The photographs, although progressively more candid, were by today's standards very tasteful – at least until the issue of 24 August 1977 when all pretence of decency was cast aside. That day's programme revealed a nipple – only one, and in soft focus at that, but the offending item was unmistakeable.

An unwritten taboo having been broken, letters flooded in to the editor – one said 'there is no place for that in a family newspaper, especially one widely read by young boys' – and *The Ram* printed a grovelling apology – 'We have been abused by many women readers for the picture of an undraped lady in our Ipswich Town issue, and we can promise that on no occasion will it ever happen again.' That day's game ended 0–0 and the action was so dull that most of the 'innocent' young boys in the crowd soon buried their noses in the controversial 'nipple issue' – only to check the team changes, of course.

POPTASTIC

Thousands of youngsters left the official opening of Pride Park Stadium on 18 July 1997 believing they had seen a live performance by pop sensations The Spice Girls. In fact they were convincing lookalikes called the Spice-ish Girls. The programme made the subterfuge quite clear and anxious parents around the ground soon spread the word – 'don't tell the children'. A genuine pop concert was held at the stadium on Sunday 26 June 2005 when 60-year-old veteran rocker Rod Stewart became the first major performer to appear there, and the trend continued when the Red Hot Chili Peppers performed to a rather younger Pride Park crowd on 5 July 2006. Apart from anything else, that served as a good PR exercise – with the cheapest tickets priced at £40 football looked good value for the first time in years.

ON THE BIG STAGE

☺ *UP THE RAMS* by Bill Grundy – Performed at Derby Playhouse for two weeks from 22 September 1970, this long-lost musical revue celebrated Derby County Football Club and the stirring deeds of their manager Brian Clough but also took a swipe at some of the ills within the game and, according to the publicity, 'the fatheads who run it'. The playwright was better known as a Granada TV presenter, later moving to Thames Television where in 1976 he conducted a notorious *Today* interview with the Sex Pistols in which he goaded one member of the punk band into using the 'F-word' for the first time on prime time British television.

☺ *BY THE BASEBALL GROUND* by Tim Elgood – Performed only briefly during 1997, this community play with a 150–strong cast bade affectionate farewell to Derby's 102-year-old home pending the club's move to Pride Park. Although the playwright was based in Derbyshire, he confessed to being a Crystal Palace fan, but at least one of the cast had credentials much closer to home – the part of a lady football club manager was played by Libby Clough, daughter of the Rams former manager Brian Clough.

☺ *OLD BIG 'EAD* in *THE SPIRIT OF THE MAN* by Stephen Lowe – This tragi-comic tribute to the life of Brian Clough premiered at Nottingham Playhouse on 3 June 2005 then went on a highly-acclaimed national tour. The part of the man himself, who returns to earth after his death to 'sort things out', was bravely taken on by life-long Forest fan Colin Tarrant, best known for his role in television's *The Bill*. Although Clough's relationship with Peter Taylor was briefly explored, the script relegated Derby County to a minor role alongside main stars Nottingham Forest, a reflection of a sobering fact often overlooked by Rams fans...Clough spent six years at Derby and 18 at Forest. According to those who knew 'Cloughie' well, the performance was spot-on – former Derby winger John Robertson labelled the characterisation 'absolutely brilliant' while centre-forward John O'Hare seemed spooked by the whole theatrical experience – 'totally weird...at times it might really have been him on stage...really strange.'

NINE – THAT WAS THE
GAME WHEN...

A stirring victory will often stick in the mind, but there are some games which become celebrated, even folkloric, for different reasons altogether – like incompetent refereeing, pitch invasions, a bizarre own-goal, petty dispute or all-in fight. Whatever the incident, the encounters in this selection all left Derby County fans saying exactly the same thing – 'That was the game when...'

THEY WOULDN'T LET IT LIE

SHEFFIELD, JANUARY 1893

The mother of all sagas began on 21 January 1893. Derby County faced Sheffield Wednesday in a first-round FA Cup tie at Olive Grove. The Rams led 2–0 with only seven minutes to go – then disaster struck. Totally against the balance of play, Wednesday scored twice. The sides agreed to play extra-time, and Derby lost 3–2 to a last-minute goal. The 5,000 travelling Rams fans were gutted.

There was only one way to react after such a cruel defeat: don't accept it. Derby protested that Wednesday's Bruce Chalmers had not been properly registered. It was a technicality, but astonishingly the FA not only upheld the flimsy appeal but also switched the 'replay' to the County Ground. Wednesday went ballistic.

This time the Rams won 1–0 after extra-time. Now Wednesday appealed. Despite having labelled Derby's protest 'entirely foreign to the best interests of the game', Wednesday accused Steve Bloomer of 'illegally playing in a 6-a-side contest the previous summer'. As a failsafe they also added that '5 Derby players were ineligible.' It was almost comical, but again the FA amazingly upheld the appeal.

Now lots were drawn for venue. Olive Grove emerged from the hat and Wednesday won this third game 4–2. But Derby promptly lodged a further appeal – the Sheffield goalkeeper Allan 'had played 6-a-side last summer' – doubtless against Bloomer! Although no less valid a protest than the previous ones, the FA had to end the saga somehow. Wednesday were allowed through to face Burnley.

Yet it all came to nought for the Sheffield side too. They beat Burnley but lost 3–0 at Everton in the third round, even then only after Burnley had protested! And Wednesday also had one last try. They appealed against the Everton result because 'the Burnley hearing severely disrupted our preparations'. That was dismissed even without a hearing – no one in Derby shed too many tears.

There has been no more rancorous dispute in Derby's history. The 'single' Cup tie against Wednesday had lasted five and a half hours – and the fall-out even longer. Even over a century later, Derby County and Sheffield Wednesday could hardly be described as the best of friends.

TRY AND TRY AGAIN

SUNDERLAND, SEPTEMBER 1894

Having finished third in Division One the previous season, Derby County hoped to start their 1894–95 campaign brightly at Sunderland. As it was, Saturday 1 September 1894 turned out to be one of the darkest days in the Rams history.

The debacle began when the match referee Mr Kirkham failed to arrive on time. So the game kicked-off with John Conqueror (Southwick) taking control as his deputy. By the time Mr Kirkham showed up, the teams had already played 45 minutes, and Derby trailed 3–0. Common sense ought to have prevailed. But Kirkham was a stickler for correctness – he declared the first period null and void and astonishingly offered the Rams the chance to begin again. It took their captain John Goodall all of one second to accept. But as the Premiership goalkeeper Shaka Hislop once famously said – 'it was a case of déjà vu all over again'. Derby conceded another three in the 'second first half' and let in a further five in the 'first second half' – which of course was really the 'third third'.

Befuddled? Derby certainly were. They had conceded 11 goals in a single day without reply. The action lasted 135 minutes and was the longest single match in the club's history. The sole comfort for the punch-drunk Derby side was that the Football League correctly recorded the official score as 8–0.

After such a ludicrous start to the season, matters were only made worse by the ridiculous excuse made by Derby's England international goalkeeper Jack Robinson. He explained the debacle by his failure to consume rice pudding before the game – the only time he ever missed with his bizarre superstition.

The folkloric match soon became known as 'the game of three halves', itself a curious misnomer. As for the strange excuse, that cut no ice with Derby County fans – as fast as they could say 'Jack Robinson' all agreed there had been 11 puddings on the field at Sunderland that day. One for each goal conceded.

A DIM VIEW

COVENTRY, NOVEMBER 1921

Thick fog already enveloped Highfield Road when Derby County arrived there on 12 November 1921 for their Second Division game against Coventry City. All sane, rational and balanced human beings knew instinctively that the match should be called off without further ado. Then the referee arrived. Players and supporters were amazed that the dotty official considered beginning the game at all, and when he sanctioned the go-ahead not even the most optimistic of souls expected it to run its full course. Few were more sceptical than the reluctant reporter covering the fixture for the *Derbyshire Football Express*. His pen-name was 'County Onlooker' – but it might just as well have been 'Mere Onlooker' for all he managed to impart. The journalist told his readers:

'The fog was so thick prior to kick-off that it was impossible to discern the band which was discoursing music in the centre of the field. Indeed it was impossible to see more than a yard or two beyond the touch line. How many people were present it was impossible to say. It was also impossible to say who won the toss, for it was impossible to see the referee when he sounded the whistle.'

Only one thing wasn't impossible – for readers to guess that the disgruntled reporter would rather have been enjoying a quiet pint in a nice warm pub. Nor did his mood improve as his usual far-sighted analysis had to be abandoned – just like the game, which faltered to a conclusion as gloomy as it was inevitable:

'Muffled cheers were heard from a quarter of the ground which suggested that play was being concentrated in the vicinity of the Derby goal. At one point the sun tried to clear the air, but it hadn't the power. All I had to content myself with was an occasional glimpse of a couple of wingers running up and down the touchline. At the half hour the players left the field and on enquiry I ascertained that the game had been abandoned, and that there was no score. It has to be said that the proceedings were merely farcical.'

Five days later the Rams returned to Highfield Road for the rearranged game and won 2–1 under clear skies. But it was the eerie 30-minute affair that stuck in supporters' minds. The dullest match in Derby County's history became known as 'the game that shouldn't have started'. 'County Onlooker' had never seen one like it. In fact he never saw it at all.

A FRACTION OFF THE PACE

DERBY, MAY 1937

Football fans have forever urged players to 'slow it down' when the action gets too frenzied, but that was one cry definitely not heard at the Baseball Ground on a fine afternoon in May 1937 when a bizarre but much-loved annual tradition was enacted before 1,500 curious onlookers who had all the time in the world to peruse the studied play.

The occasion was the sixth annual 'Grand Walking Match' between the Derby and Crewe Railway Veterans Associations, the only hard and fast rule (or slow actually) being 'no running' on any account. Not that any of the participants were capable of much more than a trot, for all the players were older than 65 and the senior member of the Derby side, a man named Young, was 73.

A pacy affair it wasn't, even though an observer for the *Derby Evening Telegraph* suggested that during its most frenetic phase he had clocked the action at six miles per hour. There was more than a suspicion that he might have been hamming it up, for the reporter also informed his readers that 'the Derby winger, a 67-year-old youngster, put in some excellent walks down the left flank' and that the Crewe trainer had told one of his men to 'walk it off' after sustaining a knock.

But that was a rare clash, since most of the players couldn't get near each other – close marking was replaced by long-distance surveillance and surging runs gave way to the odd rolling amble or sneaky stroll on the blind side, a reminder too that many of the players wore glasses. The Derby referee Arthur Kingscott – a man who had officiated at two FA Cup Finals no less – certainly had no problems keeping up with play...and he was a pensioner too.

The most bizarre game ever played at the Baseball Ground ended in a 0–0 draw and the Cup was shared. As it was filled to the brim and passed between the sides, the gasping players had already begun to debate how next year's return game at Crewe might go. The Derby 'lads' certainly fancied their chances for they knew they had the younger side (average age only 68), but the Crewe 'boys' felt experience would count, for their average age was 69. Only one thing was certain as the gallant 22 shuffled off to the dressing room to wind down (and in several cases retrieve their teeth) – both sides would be a year 'older' next time round, provided none of them had been called up to a 'higher level'...and it came to them all eventually.

EGG ON HIS FACE

DERBY, MARCH 1970

The Easter Monday game against Leeds United at the Baseball Ground on 30 March 1970 was one Rams supporters had really been looking forward to – more than just a battle between two top First Division sides, it was a confrontation between two managers who came to detest each other. Brian Clough and Don Revie, although both born in Middlesbrough, were the chalk and cheese of football...and each loved nothing more than to see the other crumble under pressure.

The gates were closed half an hour before kick-off as 41,011 Bank Holiday revellers eagerly awaited the arrival of the teams. The Leeds side listed in the programme was known almost by heart to Derby fans, such was its pedigree – Gary Sprake, Paul Reaney, Terry Cooper, Billy Bremner, Jack Charlton, Norman Hunter, Peter Lorimer, Allan Clarke, Mick Jones, Johnny Giles, Paul Madeley and sub Eddie Gray...every single one an international, but many of them were not too popular with Derby fans. Few victories would be more satisfying if only the Rams could pull it off.

And pull it off they did, cruising effortlessly to a 4–1 win with goals from Frank Wignall, John O'Hare, Roy McFarland and Willie Carlin. But what the statistics fail to impart is that Derby fans booed and jeered throughout the game and trudged home bitterly disappointed with the day's sorry outcome. Nor did Brian Clough take an ounce of satisfaction from the win. True to type, the ever-deceitful Revie had pulled his most infamous fast one, for when the Leeds team changes were announced his revised side read like this – Harvey, Davey, Peterson, Lumsden, Kennedy, Yorath, Galvin, Bates, Belfitt, Hibbitt, Johanneson and sub O'Neill – a total clean sweep...the Rams had beaten nothing more than Leeds United reserves. No wonder their paying fans felt done.

Revie's reasoning for the unsubtle artifice was entirely in keeping with his character – selfish and calculated. Ahead of the Derby game his side lay second to Everton but trailed the Merseysiders by five points, a margin Revie considered too much to make up with only a handful of games left. So knowing that his side faced a massive European Cup semi-final against Celtic just two days after the Baseball Ground encounter, Revie effectively conceded the League title in favour of European glory. He also had his eye on an 11 April FA Cup Final date against Chelsea – so what did 40,000 or so Derby fans matter?

On April Fool's Day Revie's fully-rested team of internationals were beaten 1–0 by Celtic at Elland Road, and a fortnight later they lost the second-leg 2–1 at Hampden Park. Two weeks after that European Cup demise their dreams of Cup Final glory also crashed when Chelsea won a famous second replay 2–1 at Old Trafford, their winner headed by David Webb, who later played for Derby.

Having been in the running for three major trophies and not won a single one, Revie adopted his trademark set-jawed expression of a man who felt utterly dejected and cheated – 40,000 Derby County fans who knew exactly how he felt loved every single minute of it…and even better revenge was yet to come.

SECONDS OUT

DERBY, NOVEMBER 1975

The odd bout of fisticuffs is an occupational hazard for footballers. Most such encounters are 'handbags' affairs and few players ever get hurt. But 'Hunter v Lee' was the real thing, such a flurry of furious fists that the *Match of the Day* televised bout has become a vintage classic many times repeated. It took place on 1 November 1975…All Saints' Day! – League Champions Derby faced old adversaries Leeds United at the Baseball Ground, and even though the volatile Brian Clough and peevish Don Revie had departed the managerial hot seats in favour of the much calmer Dave Mackay and Jimmy Armfield, there was no love lost between the sides. This is the blow-by-blow account.

Trevor Cherry gave Leeds an early lead. Archie Gemmill equalised. Roger Davies came on for the injured Bruce Rioch. Then came the first flashpoint. Three minutes before half-time Francis Lee wriggled into the box and was challenged by Norman Hunter. Lee took a spectacular trademark dive and referee Derek Nippard of Bournemouth – described by the *Derby Telegraph* as 'steaming in from the middle distance' – pointed dramatically to the spot. Charlie George gratefully converted the penalty. Derby led 2–1. Hunter seethed as only Hunter could.

Seven minutes into the second half, after Lee had put in a shot at the Normanton End, Hunter clattered into him with a late challenge. Lee stood up to the bigger man and retaliated, although quite meekly. Hunter took his chance, landing a firm blow to Lee's lip which caused a deep cut requiring four stitches.

Nippard sent both men off, but as they trudged to the dressing room the real fighting began. Until that moment Lee hadn't realised the extent of his wound, later explaining that 'when I was able to push my tongue right through the hole I suddenly saw red.' Lee went for Hunter with fists flailing. Hunter fought back. Only when Leeds' Paul Reaney alerted the referee in the 'Look sir' manner of a schoolboy snitcher were the two combatants parted...but even then only after an unsavoury melée in which United's Billy Bremner took centre stage.

After 73 minutes Duncan McKenzie equalised for Leeds, but minutes from time supersub Roger Davies dipped inside from the right and belted an unstoppable left-foot winner past goalkeeper Harvey for a dramatic 3–2 Derby win. The Rams faithful felt justice was done, but there was fall-out yet to come. Lee was immediately suspended for Derby's next game, a second-leg European Cup tie at Real Madrid just four days later. Despite carrying a 4–1 lead into the tie, a weakened Derby lost 5–1 and crashed out. Then came insult to injury. Lee was punished with a hefty fine by the Football League. Hunter got off scot-free.

In 2003 the *Observer* placed the incident Number One in their Top 10 'Most Spectacular Dismissals' chart. Few would argue with the choice...although Norman 'Bites yer Legs' Hunter probably did.

A SPOT OF BOTHER
DERBY, APRIL 1977

When referee John Yates of Redditch was allocated Derby v Manchester City at the Baseball Ground as his last First Division game before retirement, he might well have imagined drifting gently into anonymity. But John Yates had forgotten the peculiar knack of Derby County for making headlines out of nothing. Almost 30 years later the hapless official is still appearing on video compilations of football's daftest moments – for he famously presided over the legendary interlude dubbed 'the saga of the missing penalty spot'.

Even without that episode the afternoon of 30 April 1977 was an eventful one. Although City lay second in the First Division and had every chance of beating Liverpool to the League title, they were taken apart by Colin Murphy's ailing Derby side and lost the game 4–0. They also lost their composure – on his 'quiet' afternoon Yates booked six City players and sent off Brian Kidd – and lost the title to Liverpool by a single point. Then there was that other spot of bother.

Derby already led 3–0 with only a couple of minutes remaining when Gemmill was adjudged by Yates to have been brought down (actually a blatant dive) in the Normanton End box. Mr Yates immediately pointed to the spot...or at least where the spot should have been, for the mud-baked Baseball Ground surface had rendered it entirely invisible.

Gerry Daly placed the ball at what he believed was 12 yards out. The City goalkeeper Joe Corrigan disagreed and paced out the distance – Daly looked to have pinched a couple of yards. But Yates booked Corrigan for his insolence and insisted Daly was right. Then on came the afternoon's unscheduled arbiter – the Derby County groundsman Bob Smith complete with bucket, paint brush and tape measure.

After a measuring ceremony which moved BBC *Match of the Day* commentator John Motson to new heights of incredulity Corrigan was proved absolutely right. On his swansong appearance Yates looked unutterably foolish and was only fortunate that the mildly comedic groundsman deflected some of the attention away from him – his huge flares, kipper tie and loud check jacket earned Bob Smith permanent celebrity status in the 70s TV archives.

Gerry Daly converted the penalty and that ought to be the end of the story...but remember this is Derby County. Losing the Normanton End penalty spot merely completed the set, for during the summer of 1975 when the Baseball Ground pitch was due to be replaced, an over-enthusiastic souvenir hunter equipped with a spade had broken into the ground at dead of night and stolen the spot from the Osmaston End.

If referee Yates had only done his homework he might have known that anything can happen in the strange-but-true world of the Rams – Derby County are thought to be the only football club in the world to have had both their penalty spots go missing.

SHORT TIME

DERBY, MAY 1983

Everybody knows that a football match must last a minimum of 90 minutes for its result to be valid – that's unless one side commits such a gross misdemeanour that the game is curtailed early and awarded to their opponents. But on 14 May 1983 against Fulham, the last game of the season, Derby County turned the whole thing on its head – they were the culprits who caused an early finish, yet the Rams still emerged victorious. But did the missing minute or so really matter? Fulham certainly thought so.

Derby had made a terrible start to 1982–83 under John Newman (sacked in November), and although his successor Peter Taylor staged a mini-revival the Rams still needed to beat Fulham at the Baseball Ground to be certain of avoiding relegation. Malcolm Macdonald's young Cottagers side also needed a win, one which would have earned promotion to Division One at Leicester City's expense. With so much at stake, the stage was set for a dramatic afternoon.

It was a tense affair, but after 75 minutes Bobby Davison swivelled to volley the only goal of the game. A small pitch invasion by celebrating Derby fans was quickly cleared, but the excitable supporters failed to get back over the barriers, indeed, the stewards had opened the gates of the perimeter fencing to prepare for the usual last-match pitch invasion. Fans were now gathering along the touchline several deep in front of the Pop Side. Suddenly a tight pitch looked even tighter – soon one touchline wasn't even visible, and on a foray down the left wing Fulham's midfield player Robert Wilson was 'fouled' by a spectator's outstretched leg.

The referee Ray Chadwick (Darwen) did his best to keep things going, but then did his absolute worst to bring things to a grinding halt – he issued a piercing whistle for offside. Thinking the game was over, the Derby fans swarmed onto the field to celebrate a 1–0 victory and survival for another season. Although referee Chadwick's watch still showed 78 seconds to play – time enough for Fulham to score twice, even though unlikely – the official panicked and took the teams off, a second Fulham player, Jeff Hopkins, being assaulted by a Derby fan in the process. Then a more stunning decision still – Chadwick elected not to bring the players back on.

What Derby's punishment would have been judged by today's standards can only be guessed at with trepidation – but back then they were allowed to keep the points and the only tangible outcome was that they had to erect better perimeter fencing. Soon after the game the furious Fulham manager Malcolm Macdonald demanded a replay, but his appeals to both the Football League and Football Association fell on deaf ears – Leicester City were promoted and Derby survived. As it was, other results dictated that the 'great escape' of Peter Taylor's side would have been pulled off even had Derby lost, but that was scant comfort to Fulham who finished a single point behind Leicester – a disillusioned Macdonald quit a season later and became a licensee in Worthing.

The game subsequently labelled 'The missing 78 seconds' is unique in modern British football – it has often been said that the Baseball Ground crowd was Derby's 12th man...on 14 May 1983 it proved absolutely true.

THE PERFECT STRIKE

DERBY, MARCH 1987

Only the most astute statistician would recall the score of Derby's home game with Blackburn Rovers on 18 March 1987. If you've just said 3–2 to the Rams then you are that anorak. But countless spectators departed the game with a memory that would never leave them – that of the own-goal scored by the Blackburn centre-back Glenn Keeley.

Most such self-inflicted wounds are inept affairs, but this one had brilliance written all over it. The reporter Gerald Mortimer described the strike as 'one of the most comprehensive own-goals of this or any other season' – and he's seen a few. No video compilation of 'bloopers' is complete without it.

Derby already led 1–0 when the head-clutching moment occurred. John Gregory hoisted a hopeful ball into space behind the Rovers' defence. Keeley was always going to be first to the ball, but the defender seemed unduly worried by the rapidly closing presence of Bobby Davison – not to mention the lurking menace of Phil Gee. The Blackburn man panicked – from well outside the penalty area he decided to attempt a toe-poked lob back to his 'keeper Vince O'Keefe, who was by no means badly positioned.

A player blessed with the combined talents of George Best, Matthew Le Tissier, Wayne Rooney and Thierry Henry could scarcely have judged it better. As the 'keeper frantically back-tracked, his arms flailing wildly, the ball described a perfect arc over his head and nestled in the Normanton End net. It was one of the most accomplished goals ever scored at the Baseball Ground.

By the end of the game it was only Keeley's lob that separated the sides, and the 3–2 victory took Derby to the top of Division Two that very day. Ten games later the Rams were promoted back to the big time as champions. The perfect strike had turned a great season into a truly memorable one – Glenn Keeley we salute you.

CODDINGTON'S MATCH
DERBY, APRIL 1992

There is nothing like a resounding victory to send the fans home happy. On 20 April 1992 Arthur Cox's high-flying Derby County beat Kevin Keegan's struggling Newcastle United by four goals to one. Yet even the Rams staunchest supporters left the Baseball Ground bitterly dissatisfied with the result. Two fearsome words explain the conundrum – Brian Coddington.

The Sheffield referee didn't begin well. After only three minutes he controversially adjudged Newcastle's Kevin Brock to have handled a goal-bound header. Brock was dismissed and Paul Williams put Derby 1–0 ahead from the resulting penalty. Derby fans were happy; Newcastle fans were not.

Coddington needed to restore calm. After 16 minutes he spotted Terry McDermott berating a linesman. Keegan's assistant was immediately banished to the stand. Seven minutes later Paul Kitson put Derby 2–0 ahead. Derby fans were still happy. Newcastle fans were still upset, but now even more so.

The game needed stabilising. After 26 minutes Marco Gabbiadini was brought down by United's Kevin Scott, who had already been booked for felling Ted McMinn. Coddington knew how to handle it. He reduced Newcastle to nine men by sending off Scott. Now even Derby supporters were becoming upset. They wanted to see a contest. Newcastle supporters were now apoplectic.

Amazingly the Magpies rallied after the break. Four minutes into the second half they mustered a goal through Gavin Peacock. At only 2–1 down and playing well, their fans sensed an amazing comeback. Even when Craig Ramage increased Derby's lead to 3–1 on 70 minutes the visitors looked in with a chance.

Codddington was having none of it – after 72 minutes Newcastle's Liam O'Brien fouled Tommy Johnson. It was little more than a clumsy hack, but the official dismissed O'Brien from the field. Not surprisingly the eight men were unable to prevent a second Ramage goal shortly before time.

Coddington had achieved the ultimate in refereeing incompetence. He had upset both teams, both managers and both sets of fans. Newcastle supporters threw seats as the game drew to a close, and the Derby faithful felt they had been cheated of their admission money – they knew the 4–1 victory was a hollow one.

Having etched his name in the memories of everyone present, the terrified-looking referee positioned himself close to the tunnel before bringing the game to a close. He retired to the refuge of his dressing room and remained there for some time. All those who witnessed the frightening ineptitude on display in 'Coddington's Match' rather wished the infamous official had retired altogether.

BLOW-OUT

DERBY, AUGUST 1997

Not even the most superstitious or pessimistic soul in the Derby County ranks had the least qualm about the first ever League match at Pride Park being scheduled for the 13th of the month. For once the 'unlucky' club had covered every option ahead of the Wednesday evening blockbuster opener against Wimbledon on 13 August 1997 and only nine days earlier a full floodlit rehearsal against the Italian club Sampdoria had been heralded a brilliant success.

The lights had been especially remarked upon, and the signing of a £10 million share deal with an investment company named Electra seemed clever work indeed as the stage was set to perfection. Nothing could go wrong on what would be a truly memorable night in the Rams great history, one when the grand old club would once again be in the national spotlight...and for all the right reasons.

But their finest hour proved neither fine nor even an hour, for the showpiece game was abandoned after 56 minutes. But how brightly it had started – Ashley Ward put the Rams ahead with what he fondly imagined would be recorded as the first ever League goal at Pride Park, and though Wimbledon equalised Derby moved 2–1 in front through Stefano Eranio and seemed well in control.

Then it happened...just short of the hour mark the gleaming new Pride Park stadium was plunged into darkness as the floodlights failed. Uriah Rennie, refereeing his first Premiership game, took the players off and gave Derby's mystified and panic-stricken electricians 10 minutes to resolve the problem...then another 10 minutes...and then a final deadline of 9.30.

Wimbledon started to get changed. They knew the score...2–1. Rams manager Jim Smith bawled 'buy me some time'. Director Peter Gadsby raced around the stadium like a man possessed. Chief executive Keith Loring bore the expression of a man about to be repossessed. A wag in the crowd yelled 'put another 50 pence in the meter'. But the deadline passed and the game, like Ward's 'historic' opening goal, was declared null and void.

At 9.33 the lights came back on again. Three minutes too late...but at 9.35 they flickered off again for good. Just as well they hadn't restarted. All sorts of theories were put forward, including one that a far-eastern gambling syndicate had nobbled the lights to land an audacious bet, but the club electrician made everything clear – 'a variable setting fuse with a tolerance of between 160 and 420 amps had been left set at its minimum level and a new external light we'd installed after Sampdoria purely to light up the Ram logo took it just beyond the threshold.' Loose translation...it blew it, and so did we.

The farce was completed when the club were unable to apologise to spectators because the PA system had been commandeered by police 'for safety reasons'. On the way in supporters had remarked that the stadium rose from the ground like some giant glowing spaceship...and now a disembodied voice sounding for all the world like E.T. in a grumpy mood brought the disastrous evening to a close – 'Go home. Go home please. Go home.' – and that was that.

Next day Derby County got the spotlight treatment they had craved – all the national newspapers covered the antics and one ran the headline which the club has never lived down – 'PRIDE DARK'.

A COMPASSIONATE AFFAIR

GRIMSBY, AUGUST 2002

Derby County folklore has it that Grimsby Town are one of the nicest clubs to visit. The players of old particularly enjoyed their annual jaunt to Blundell Park. So much so that when Derby won there on 21 February 1948 the Rams team were visibly crestfallen – they realised they had just condemned the Mariners to relegation.

Maybe this was explained to Fabrizio Ravanelli – for when Derby County played at Grimsby on 17 August 2002 the emotional Italian displayed such compassion to the Mariners' cause that he pleaded for the game to be abandoned.

In the ninth minute there was a sickening clash of heads between Rams defender Danny Higginbotham and Grimsby striker Steve Livingstone. The forward stayed down, patently unconscious. Medical staff, officials and players gathered around the stricken player – blood trickled from his ear and he struggled to breathe. Ten minutes later he had barely moved.

Ravanelli could stand no more. In a scene that might have been from an Italian opera, he moved his hands together as if in prayer. Then his features contorted, and like some mediaeval serf begging for mercy he implored the referee Tony Leake to end the game there and then. Rarely had football seen such histrionics – at least in favour of the opposition.

Supporters too feared for Livingstone's life, but referee Leake remained steadfast and continued the game after the Grimsby man was carried off on a stretcher and taken to hospital for a brain scan.

Ravanelli seemed badly affected. On several occasions afterwards he spurned easy chances. A total of 14 minutes was added to the first half, which lasted a minute short of an hour – the longest in Derby's history.

The drama eventually concluded with the Rams emerging 2–1 victors thanks to a double strike from Adam Bolder. Steve Livingstone made a full recovery. So did Derby's most emotional player of all time.

NAKED AMBITION

COVENTRY, DECEMBER 2002

It's not every day that Lady Godiva gets a mention in a Derby County match report. That explains why the Rams away game against Coventry City on 21 December 2002 has remained in the memory of those who were there.

Normally it would have been instantly forgotten as another sorry away defeat. John Gregory's desperate Division One strugglers were humbled 3–0 by a Coventry side allowed to play with total freedom. So perhaps it was appropriate that one liberated spectator celebrated as she did.

When Gary McAllister scored the first with a screaming volley past Lee Grant, an 18-year-old barmaid named Amy Freeman showed her appreciation in a novel way. Clad only in a red and white Santa skirt, the topless blonde broke from the crowd amid huge festive cheers and gave a seasonal hug and kiss to Coventry's Mo Konjic. Most newspapers featured the photographs, and Amy was in great demand for post-match interviews – 'I did it for charity', she said, 'but it was very cold out there'. Having enjoyed an outstanding close-quarters view, a beaming Konjic was well able to corroborate the fact.

Three years later Rams fans with good memories (very good for those that had used binoculars) recalled the streak when Derby again travelled to Highfield Road and were hammered 6–2 in what was the last League game ever staged there. Much of the blame was heaped on that man Mo Konjic, who was by then a Derby County player. Supporters joked that the memories of Amy Freeman might have disturbed his concentration, for the big Bosnian floundered his way through a performance which many travelling fans considered to be the most inept ever given by a Rams defender.

Amy was one of a rare breed in Derby County history, but she was by no means the club's first such exhibitionist. Pride Park had one of its own on Sunday 3 March 2002, and on that occasion the game itself was memorable too. Derby drew 2–2 with Manchester United and were denied a dramatic win only because Malcolm Christie's last-gasp 'hat-trick goal' was disallowed by referee Steve Dunn.

The raider that day was a naked male who swung on the crossbar before planting a kiss on the billiard ball head of the United goalkeeper Fabien Barthez. Despite the obvious gender difference, there was one similarity to the Coventry streak: a mocking chant echoed around the stadium as police led away the intruder while covering his embarrassment – 'What the ******* hell is that?' Once again it was a very cold day.

THE CUP THAT CHEERED

DERBY, MARCH 2004

Most League clubs have at least one Cup in their trophy cabinet, but Derby County are the only one to have a coffee cup, and a pretty naff plastic one at that. Yet it is signed by the Rams striker Paul Peschisolido and is looked upon by supporters privileged to visit Pride Park's inner sanctum with a reverence approaching awe. For this was the celebrated receptacle – salvaged by a quick-thinking steward with a sense of both occasion and humour – that helped the Rams to a famously thumping victory over their arch-rivals Nottingham Forest.

The game that made the cup's name – later christened 'Cuppie' and emblazoned on mugs and replica shirts – took place at Pride Park Stadium on 20 March 2004. Derby desperately needed a win – not least to climb away from the Division One relegation scramble but also to enable their fans to claim the all-important bragging rights from their Forest counterparts.

It couldn't have gone better. On a fiercely blustery day on a pitch littered with rubbish Derby stormed into a 3–0 lead after 37 minutes, and it was the bizarre second goal that really set them on their way. An innocuous back pass by Wes Morgan bobbled up off the Kenco coffee cup, causing the embarrassed Forest goalkeeper Barry Roche to miscue the ball off his shin straight into the path of an amazed Peschisolido, who stroked the ball coolly into an empty net.

Although Forest pulled back to 3–2 in the second half, the famous 'Cuppie' goal always separated the sides, and Marcus Tudgay wrapped up a 4–2 win eight minutes from time. The newspapers had a field day – the *Daily Mirror* ran with 'THE COFFEE HORROR SHOW' while another suggested Derby had found the right blend at last…most had 'stirring encounter' and 'sweet' finish somewhere in their reports…and a 'bitter aftertaste' for Forest naturally.

Derby ended the 2003–04 season only one point ahead of the relegation places – no wonder their surprise 12th man entered the club's folklore.

END TO END STUFF

Derby County have been on the end of some strange refereeing decisions in their time, but few have been more bizarre than the one that occurred at the Britannia Stadium on 30 August 2004. Stoke City were the fortunate beneficiaries. The Rams were the outraged victims.

The score stood at 0–0 after 65 minutes when Stoke won a corner. The ball was swung across and somehow scrambled into the net by the Potters striker Ade Akinbiyi. The Stoke players peeled away to celebrate the goal and conducted an elaborate pre-rehearsed routine on the pitch perimeter close to the corner flag.

It looked to have cost them dearly. Having become so engrossed in the weird gyrations they completely failed to notice that the referee Neale Barry had disallowed the strike. The eagle-eyed official had spotted an earlier push on the Derby goalkeeper Lee Camp.

As more than half of the Stoke side continued their cavorting, Derby reacted as any professional side should. They played to the whistle. They took the free-kick quickly and swept downfield past the three or four Stoke players still offering resistance. The swift move finished with Adam Bolder planting the ball in the net. Derby's army of travelling fans rose to acclaim the goal.

But Barry sensed trouble from the Stoke crowd – what should he do? The answer came quickly – the official bottled it. He disallowed the Derby goal and ordered the Rams to re-take the free-kick back in their own box! Two goals had been disallowed within a matter of seconds, almost certainly a record.

Once he'd had time to think of an excuse, Barry explained it was because the initial free-kick had 'not travelled out of the penalty area' – strictly correct if it was true, but Derby's furious players and fans remained unconvinced.

Even so, the Rams continued to dominate the game as they pushed forward looking for the decisive goal. In any case, a 0–0 draw was still a good result. But Barry had one last ace up his sleeve. He added on three minutes to compensate for Stoke's celebratory delay. And how it counted – Marcus Hall scored Stoke's winner in the final second of the 93rd minute. Neale Barry was not the toast of Derby that night – or any other night for that matter.

TEN – CURIOUS CONNECTIONS...

Derby County have an uncanny knack of making 'unscheduled appearances' in sensational or unusual stories, often those linked to rival clubs or to particular personalities and organisations. There appears to be no limit to where the club's name might surface – the United States, Bury, Germany, Wolverhampton, Spain, Newcastle, Italy and the island of St Vincent are all featured here. So too are the diverse worlds of deep-sea fishing, Nazism, railways, terrorism, stamp collecting and the brick industry! Here is a random selection of links from the alternative world of the Rams.

BADLY SHAKEN

Bury hold a remarkable record which is unlikely to be beaten. But the Shakers owe it entirely to Derby County. The occasion was the FA Cup Final played at the Crystal Palace on 18 April 1903, a game which has entered the history books as 'the worst Cup Final of all time'.

Derby went into the game without the injured Steve Bloomer, but goalkeeper Jack Fryer opted to play despite a severe groin strain. It proved a catastrophic decision. Fryer was 'on' then 'off' then 'on' again – the 'keeper conceded three soft goals before limping away for good after 68 minutes.

Left-back Charlie Morris then took over in goal. His tally for the afternoon was also three. Then right-back Jimmy Methven became the third Derby 'keeper when he relieved the disconsolate Morris for the final 10 minutes. Methven kept a clean sheet but the damage had already been done. The Rams had been an absolute shambles and the final score read Bury 6 Derby County 0.

It remains the record margin of victory in an FA Cup Final. The *Daily Chronicle* described the match as 'a fiasco' and the *Sheffield Independent* labelled it 'the tamest and dullest Final ever played.' Neither newspaper was exaggerating.

Derby's lame showing was inexcusable. But even then some superstitious fans looked to blame their shirts. Due to a clash both sides changed from their usual black and white. Bury played in blue and Derby County donned the red of their arch-rivals Nottingham Forest. Was that why they were so off-colour that day?

As for Jack Fryer, his feeble performance proved his last ever for Derby County – he was transferred to Fulham without further ado. Meanwhile Bury milked the victory for all they were worth. Celebratory postcards poking fun at the Rams were produced within hours, a mocking testimony to the sorry day when Derby County were the shame of the football world.

SUCK IT AND SEE

The illustrious Everton Football club glories in two recognised nicknames. Officially the team are the Toffees, but they are often referred to as the School of Science. That unusual moniker was coined in the late 1920s to reflect the club's intelligent style of play and meticulous preparation.

They owe the classy label to the Rams legend Steve Bloomer. In 1928 he wrote in the *Derbyshire Football Express*: 'Everton worship at the shrine of craft and science. They always manage to serve up football of the highest scientific order.' Journalists respected Bloomer's opinions. They picked up the phrase and pared it down. The new name stuck. What chance of back-dated royalties for the Rams?

GENEROUS ACT

When Nottingham Forest met Derby County in the FA Cup Final on 16 April 1898 both sides attended the official photo-call prior to kick-off. It was a very overcast day and the designated snapper was concerned that Forest's deep-red shirts would contrast badly against the dark background. So he made a suggestion – they should borrow their opponents' tops.

Thus it was that Nottingham Forest appeared in their official 1898 Cup Final photograph resplendent in the white shirts of Derby County. To add insult to injury, the Reds (or should it be whites?) then donned their own attire and beat the highly-fancied Rams by three goals to one. That's gratitude for you.

TOP OF THE BILL

Stockport County suffered a gross indignity on 7 May 1921 in which Derby County proved willing accessories. The official crowd for the Hatters home game against Leicester City that day was the lowest ever recorded at an English League game – only 13 lonely souls!

But all was not as it seemed. Stockport's own ground had been closed by the Football League following crowd trouble, so the Leicester fixture was held at Manchester United's Old Trafford as part of an unusual 'double-header'.

First up was the Division One game between Manchester United and Derby County, which United won 3–0. Then on came Stockport and Leicester for an encore. Close to 10,000 were there for the first game, including canny Stockport fans keen to make the most of their money. Several thousand stayed on for the second match but only 13 'new arrivals' actually paid admission for that game alone.

The Football League stubbornly insisted that 13 must be entered as the official crowd. Evidently Leicester City weren't a great attraction that day. Having played second fiddle to City far too often, this was one occasion when the Rams were undeniably top of the bill.

A SAINTLY INFLUENCE

The Spanish giants Real Madrid have an illustrious history but there are several embarrassing blots in their record books which can never be erased. Their first major stumble occurred on Sunday 4 May 1924 when they were beaten 1–0 in the Final of the prestigious King's Cup by the small-town amateur side Real Irun. What made it worse was that the minnows came from the Basque region of Northern Spain whose tough folk loved nothing more than to steal a march on the softies from the Spanish capital.

But the big boys soon manufactured an opportunity for revenge. Irun were invited to Madrid to play two friendlies over Christmas 1924, but it was obvious that presents weren't on the agenda. Everybody in Madrid and the rest of Spain expected a sack full of goals, and they certainly got them. The games finished 3–0 and 7–0…to Real Irun!

Genuine shockwaves were felt throughout Spanish football. The press described the results as '*una sensacion*' and dubbed Irun's wonder manager 'a saint'. This would have nothing to do with Derby County but for the fact that the manager in question was Steve Bloomer. The Derby marksman is suitably honoured in the Basque club's official history – *Historia del Real Union Club de Irun*. Those famous Rams get everywhere.

MOST VALUABLE EXPORTS

A large number of Derby County players have exported their skills to the United States, but two made a bigger mark than any. The first to make a genuine impact was the former Rams striker Bill Paterson, who in 1928 signed for Providence. The move not only changed the New England side's luck, but his too.

While with Derby, between 1921 and 1924, the Scot had scored a creditable 24 goals in 68 appearances, but at Providence he attained the Holy Grail of more than one a match as he netted 78 times in 75 games. His overall record in the American Soccer League was an impressive 151 goals in 212 appearances.

Many years later the legendary Rams winger Alan Hinton also crossed the Atlantic to great effect. In 1978, playing for Vancouver Whitecaps in the NASL, he smashed the assists in a season record by laying on 30 goals in just 29 games. The previous record was a paltry 18 held jointly by two former internationals who were unable to match Hinton's unerring delivery – their names were George Best and Pelé.

HEIL KIRBY

Adolf Hitler has an indelible link with Derby County, but he was never a secret Rams fan. The Nazi leader is said to have attended only one football match in his life – Germany 0 Norway 2 in the 1936 Berlin Olympic Games – and he walked out 10 minutes from time. But his indifference to the sport didn't stop him demanding that overseas football teams should publicly recognise the Nazi regime, and Derby County were put to the test early.

In May 1934 they played four exhibition games in Germany, and the Rams players were instructed to give the Nazi salute before each one. Despite the Derby men's great unease, the British Foreign Office ordered them to follow Hitler's dictate for fear that a refusal would create an 'international incident.'

All except one player complied. Overseal-born goalkeeper Jack Kirby steadfastly kept his hand down when the time came and even turned away in a public show of marked disinterest. Others had to grin and bear it – photographs of the tour capture Rams' directors posing with German officials who are proudly displaying the swastika emblem.

The goalkeeper's defiance didn't extend to keeping clean sheets. Derby failed to win a single game against their German hosts and twice conceded five. Even so, Kirby's stubborn stand in the face of a threatening regime was brought fully into perspective five years later. Once war was declared in September 1939 Rams fans were proud to give a salute of their own – to Jack Kirby.

INSPIRATIONAL STRIKER

Not content with leaving his mark on Spanish football, Steve Bloomer also gets an honourable mention in the history of the Italian game. The story concerns Vittorio Pozzo, a revered figure known as 'The Father of Italian Football'. It was Pozzo who laid the foundations of the modern game in Italy, while serving as national manager during the 1930s. Under his guidance Italy won both the 1934 and 1938 World Cups and an Olympic title. Rock-solid defending allied to attacking flair was his side's watchword.

Pozzo once revealed where much of his early inspiration came from: 'When I was a young man, just prior to the First World War, I went to England to work as a language teacher. I lived for a time in a town called Derby and sought out the great international Steve Bloomer. I enjoyed several long discourses with him about how the game should be played and the words of helpful advice he gave were invaluable in showing me the way to go.'

Italian football seemed reluctant to return the favour. In 1973 Derby County's European Cup dreams were shattered by Juventus. Twenty years later the Rams were beaten by Cremonese in the Anglo-Italian Cup Final. Finally they got some sort of payback – in 1997 the stylish duo of Stefano Eranio and Francesco Baiano arrived at Pride Park. But the favours were merely temporary – in August 2001 the nation to whom Derby County had shown the way sent them Fabrizio Ravanelli.

THE WRONG TRACK

Sunderland have become unwittingly associated with one of those conundrums that do the rounds of Derby's hostelries from time to time. On how many occasions have Derby County been to Wembley? Fans who know their stuff will generally plump for four.

✪ 27 April 1946 – Derby County 4 Charlton Athletic 1 – FA Cup Final.
✪ 9 August 1975 – Derby County 2 West Ham United 0 – FA Charity Shield.
✪ 27 March 1993 – Derby County 1 Cremonese 3 – Anglo-Italian Cup Final.
✪ 30 May 1994 – Derby County 1 Leicester City 2 – Division One Play-off Final.

But the devious questioner has one more date up his sleeve – the day Sunderland beat Preston North End 3–1 in the FA Cup Final – 1 May 1937. The answer lies in trains. In March 1936 a Gresley B17 'Sandringham' class steam locomotive was built for the London and North Eastern Railway. The fiery beast was named *Derby County* and sported two huge nameplates to prove it – but the train was 'borrowed' to carry fans from Sunderland to Wembley in 1937. So Derby County has been to Wembley five times!

But it doesn't do to get too deeply involved in this type of thing for there's always someone who will seek to count Derby's regular appearances during the 1970s at the *Daily Express* five-a-side tournament held at the indoor Wembley Arena – the Rams won the contest in 1973.

So let the official answer rest at FOUR – it has been so for over a decade and may yet remain that way for many years to come.

GOING DOWN

There were many unlikely links established between football clubs during World War Two, but one not featured in the official record books concerns the time York City joined forces with Derby County to take on the Germans. This unusual alliance occurred on Friday 15 December 1939, but the encounter didn't take place on a football field. Both *Derby County* and *York City* were former fishing trawlers pressed into war service as Anti-Submarine vessels. The two craft detected the presence of a German U-boat in the English Channel and launched a joint attack with depth charges. The German opposition retreated before the twin-strikers registered a hit.

Derby County had been launched on Saturday 26 August 1933 as the third boat in a 39-strong 'football fishing fleet' conceived by Consolidated Fisheries Ltd of Grimsby. The company hit on the novel idea to engender a spirit of friendly competition between the vessels' captains. Catches were recorded by weight and a League table kept. In the inaugural season *Derby*

County suffered suction-pump trouble and finished mid-table. Later they netted more regularly and did quite well.

Derby County returned to fishing duties as soon as the war was over, but the proud vessel was eventually scrapped in Belgium in 1964. It was a dignified end compared to the fate suffered by some of its rivals – *Notts County*, *Aston Villa* and *Lincoln City* all went down in the face of German attacks.

However, the stormiest passage of all was suffered by a trawler launched in 1960. First the club's chairman complained that the ship had been 'incorrectly named'. Then its crew staged a mutiny. Next the skipper provoked a strike by fishing illegally in Icelandic waters. Finally a deck-hand drowned at sea in 'suspicious circumstances'.

In between times the unlucky vessel spent many months languishing in dry dock after suffering regular storm damage. Strangely it appeared that the world of fishing was mirroring that of football to perfection – the curse of the fleet was the ill-named *Notts Forest*.

FALL GUYS

Derby feature in a truly sensational entry in the Wolverhampton Wanderers record books, but unfortunately not in the way they would have liked. The Rams were the visitors for a Football League North game on 21 November 1942. The Wolves centre-forward that day was Jack Rowley, a guest player then resident in Ireland but registered with Manchester United.

Rowley was on two weeks' leave when he casually agreed to 'have a run out' at Molineux. And the Rams obligingly made sure he enjoyed the break – Rowley 'bagged a quadruple brace' in Wolves crushing 8–1 win. In plain English the man on his holidays scored all eight goals! Bill Townsend was the shell-shocked Derby 'keeper.

Although Jack Rowley remains Derby's greatest nemesis in a single game, another high-scoring feat which present-day Rams fans might actually recall occurred in a Division Two clash at Ewood Park on 10 September 1983.

On that occasion Blackburn Rovers hammered Peter Taylor's Derby County by five goals to one, and the *Derby Telegraph* reporter Gerald Mortimer was moved to describe the Rams' entire performance as 'quite disgraceful'. Few who witnessed the debacle will wish to recall the name of the man who scored all five Rovers' goals. For the record it was Simon Garner.

GLAZED OVER

Crystal Palace would never have made it into the *Guinness Book of Records* but for a terribly dozy start by the Rams. One of the three fastest ever authenticated League goals was scored by Keith Smith in a Division Two game against Derby County on 12 December 1964.

Many of the 11,828 Baseball Ground crowd were caught napping, as was the Derby centre-half Ray Young. Straight from the kick-off he let the ball slip under his foot, and Smith put the Glaziers ahead in six seconds dead. After such a terrible start it was to the Rams' credit that they recovered from a 3–1 deficit to draw 3–3. Eddie Thomas scored the first two before Ray Young atoned for his early Christmas gift by snatching the equaliser 12 minutes from time.

OLD BIG 'EAD

Tussaud's waxworks in Blackpool had every reason to be grateful to Derby County during 1973. Their takings took a healthy leap. In January of that year the company announced that the football genius and world-famous superstar George Best was being thrown out and melted down in favour of a figure described in a press release as 'someone even better known'.

The papers were full of it, since the new figure was the Derby County manager Brian Clough – 'He is certainly no dummy', said a Tussaud's spokesman. 'No one else in sport has quite the same aura of attraction. Everybody knows Mr Clough – he is a wizard of the football world'.

The model cost £300 and included real human hair. When it was finished thousands of visitors paid 20 pence to look 'Cloughie' straight in the eye. And for once he remained silent. The ultimate fate of the celebrated figure is unknown – rumours that the head was melted down to make models of Henry VIII and his six wives remain unconfirmed.

FAMOUS FIRST

Juventus were custodians of a proud Italian record when they entertained Derby County on 11 April 1973 for the first leg of the European Cup semi-final. Since the competition began in 1955, no English club had scored a European Cup goal on Italian soil.

But what countless stars had failed to achieve in 18 years, Kevin Hector managed in just 30 minutes. When Altafini put the Zebras ahead on 28 minutes, the record looked set to continue. But two minutes later Hector struck for the Rams and left legendary 'keeper Dino Zoff flat on his backside for good measure.

The 72,000 in the Stadio Comunale were stunned. No matter that the Rams lost the game 3–1, or that they went out of the competition two weeks later after a goalless second leg. A seemingly impregnable record had been expunged from Italian history with one sweet strike from the boot of 'The King'. No one in Turin that spring afternoon had seen anything like it before – and for once that's no exaggeration.

NO GOING BACK

Newcastle United have had many newsworthy encounters with Derby County, but none with such a strange aftermath as the Division One game played at the Baseball Ground on 27 August 1975.

Gordon Lee was Newcastle's manager and in his team that day was midfielder Terry Hibbitt, who Lee regarded as a troublemaker. Unknown to the player, Lee had already arranged for Hibbitt to be sold to Birmingham City. Now all the manager had to do was make it known – which he did in no uncertain terms.

There are various versions of the story, but the consensus is that Hibbitt's boots were secreted in a paper bag and shoved into the dressing room waste bin. By the time he'd found them, the team bus was already pulling away from the Baseball Ground with Hibbitt trailing in its wake waving his arms for it to stop. Gordon Lee sealed the transfer by yelling 'drive on'. The dejected player was left behind.

Poor Terry Hibbitt moved to Birmingham City the very next day. No opposition player can have had such a sad memory of the Baseball Ground. To add insult to injury the Rams ran out 3–2 winners.

BLACK HUMOUR

Portuguese champions Benfica fell easy prey to punning journalists when on 8 November 1972 the legendary Eagles were sent plummeting out of the European Cup by Derby County. A 0–0 draw in Lisbon was all it took since the Rams had already won the home leg of the second-round tie 3–0 – McFarland, Hector and McGovern scored the goals on a memorable night in Baseball Ground history.

Benfica's shock exit in front of 75,000 fans in Lisbon wasn't the reason for the pun-fest – that was down to a 17th-minute floodlight failure, which occurred just as Eusebio was bearing down on the Derby goal. The 'Black Panther' blindly stabbed the ball past Rams 'keeper Colin Boulton only to see it had rolled wide when the lights came back on five seconds later.

Of course, the punsters knew full well that Benfica's imposing bowl of an arena was the Estadio da Luz... 'The Stadium of Light'.

DEFENSIVE WALL

When Derby's fierce rivals Leeds United ran out at the Baseball Ground on 12 February 1977 they got rather a shock. Jimmy Armfield's boys did a worried double take when they saw that the Osmaston End goal was completely bricked up. Derby's allies in the subterfuge were the match sponsors Butterley Bricks, who had created the impenetrable barrier using 1,320 of their most durable product.

At least it appeared so from a distance, but the wall was mere painted plywood. It was carted off just before kick-off. Leeds overcame the psychological barrier to breach the Rams real defensive wall on one crucial occasion. Joe Jordan headed the only goal of the game after 83 minutes.

It was a typical Leeds display. Derby duo Steve Powell and Jeff King both looked like they'd been 'bricked' that day – each suffered a broken nose in the face of stubborn Yorkshire resistance. Derby have often cried out for a truly solid defence – unfortunately the experimental Butterley system remains illegal.

FIRST OR SECOND CLASS?

The Rams were big news in St Vincent in December 1987 when the tiny Caribbean island issued a postage stamp featuring that season's official team photograph of Derby County. Arthur Cox's newly-promoted side were valued at $2. That just about reflected their worth on the field that season – able to stamp little authority on opponents, the Rams finished 15th in Division One and posted only 10 wins. They were even licked home and away by Nottingham Forest.

It isn't the club's only philatelic link – a number of first day covers celebrate key games in Derby's history, but catalogue records suggest that only one Rams player has featured on a postage stamp in his own right – Raich Carter, a member of Derby's 1946 FA Cup-winning side. For reasons which remain obscure, the England international was selected by the Republic of Equatorial Guinea to appear on a 35 peseta World Cup issue in 1974.

The two-goal hero of that 1946 Cup win must also get a mention – centre-forward Jackie Stamps was so determined to make a play of his distinctive surname that in retirement, more out of desperation than inspiration, he erected a sign naming his Burton-upon-Trent bungalow 'Stamps Album'.

Finally on this postal tour, one man able to give chapter and verse on the subject is international stamp expert Ian Kellock, whose knowledge of philately is only matched by his unerring support of the Rams. When the club faced a winding-up order in the High Court in 1984 Kellock was in the public gallery to follow every twist and turn of the nail-biting hearings, an act of dedication that won him the Supporter of the Year award. He attended every session before Mr Justice Mervyn Davies blessedly lifted the petition at the eleventh hour – Kellock later said all the sessions were tense but the most enjoyable was the marathon one in Ye Olde Cheshire Cheese in Fleet Street celebrating the Rams survival.

CAREER CHANGE

The *Match of the Day* pundit Mark Lawrenson isn't everybody's cup of tea. Many viewers find his forthright brand of analysis hard to bear. Derby County must shoulder a large part of the blame, for 'Lorro' might never have turned to punditry but for a draconian act by Rams chairman Robert Maxwell in October 1988.

Lawrenson was in his first managerial post at Oxford United when Maxwell senior agreed with his son Kevin, the United chairman, that Welsh international striker Dean Saunders would move to Derby for £1 million. The deal was done entirely without Lawrenson's knowledge.

He immediately threatened to quit, but Maxwell wouldn't hear of it. He told Lawrenson 'No one resigns on the Maxwells', and the next day he was sacked. Although the chastened manager dabbled briefly with a number of other clubs, he was so disillusioned that he decided a media career was much safer. So next time the controversial pundit says something unutterably outrageous we know exactly who to blame: that man Robert Maxwell.

FANTASY FOOTBALL

On 17 April 1997 Arsenal endured a total nightmare when they lost 8–0 to Derby County. Reports of the game made it clear that the Rams triumph had been no fluke: 'Derby were simply unstoppable, and the ball never entered the Arsenal half once in the first period of play.' What made the result even more amazing was that all eight goals came in just 40 minutes.

There is no mention of this epic victory in official Derby County statistics. Unfortunately the teams in question were playing 20 minutes each way in the under-10 section of the Ansonia Soccer League in Connecticut, US.

The side is one of a number worldwide to have assumed the name of Derby County – in the youngsters' case they lived near Derby in Connecticut, and the club's founder was a Rams exile. There was no contest in choosing a name.

The Arsenal result was one of a number of eye-catchers that season – only a week before thrashing the Gunners, the all-conquering Derby County had beaten the mighty Juventus 2–1. It mattered not that the Ansonia League lacked a team named Nottingham Forest – the genuine Derby County can take care of that lot for real.

RETURN TO SENDER

Derby County fan Andrew Cooper made global headlines during the 2002 World Cup. The patriotic Rams supporter planned to watch England in a warm-up game in South Korea before moving on to the group matches in Japan. In every media report of his eventful journey, Derby County received an honourable mention. Or dishonourable to be fair, for Cooper never saw a single ball kicked.

Instead he endured the shame of becoming the first supporter denied entry into a host nation. On arrival at Incheon airport from Frankfurt, he was deported by South Korean officials and sent back to Germany on the same plane.

The 37-year-old Derby County fan had been placed on a World Cup blacklist after serving a four-month prison term in 1999 for unlawful possession of tear gas. One day the club might make headlines of the right sort – 'RAMS STRIKER WINS WORLD CUP FOR ENGLAND' – it could be a long wait.

CONTROVERSIAL BOOKING

This was one story Derby County wanted no part of. Omar Bakri was the sort of man no family club would wish to be associated with, for the radical Muslim leader of the militant al Muhajiroun group held some very extreme views indeed.

As self-appointed British spokesman for Osama Bin Laden, the controversial Bakri was known to actively encourage suicide bombers and had publicly praised terrorists for 'justified attacks' in New York and Madrid, which killed thousands of innocent people.

On Sunday 21 March 2004 he peddled just such messages to a meeting of 800 Muslims, at which videos were shown of terrorist attacks on American buildings.

'Suicide bombers will be guaranteed a place in paradise,' he promised. The gathering made national headlines – all of which was very embarrassing for Derby County since the meeting was held in a suite at their Pride Park Stadium.

A spokesman for the club was left to issue a fudged statement as protests poured in: 'Derby County Football Club respects freedom of speech, but we are keen to ensure our name is not used to endorse any political or religious views.' There have been many controversial bookings at Pride Park – this one must rank as the worst of all.

ELEVEN – TRIUMPH AND TRAGEDY...

Triumphant hat-tricks were once commonplace at Derby County, but as season 2005–06 ended it had been fully 10 years since any Rams player had performed the feat. Here are some to fall back on until the next time.

- No player scored more hat-tricks for Derby County than **Steve Bloomer**. In two spells between 1892 and 1914 he performed the feat 18 times and is the only Rams player to net a double hat-trick – his 'six in a game' came on 21 January 1899 in a 9–0 First Division win at home to Sheffield Wednesday.

- The only Rams player to score a hat-trick on his Derby County debut is **Ted Garry**. The ultimate in dream starts came on 2 September 1907 when Derby beat Lincoln City 4–0 at home in the opening game of the season.

- **Jack Bowers** lies second to **Steve Bloomer** in the Rams hat-trick stakes but holds the record for the most triples in a single season. In 1930–31 he scored three goals or more on a remarkable five occasions, all in League games.

- After **Keith Havenhand** scored a hat-trick against Bristol Rovers in a 4–1 away win in November 1961, his teammates joked that they expected a repeat performance at the Baseball Ground in the return fixture. Amazingly, although never a prolific scorer, the inside-forward obliged to the letter – in March 1962 Rovers were again beaten 4–1 and Havenhand grabbed himself another hat-trick.

- The rare feat of three separate hat-tricks in a game has been achieved only once by Derby County, in a first-leg UEFA Cup tie at the Baseball Ground on 15 September 1977. The Irish club Finn Harps were humbled 12–0 as **Charlie George** and **Leighton James** helped themselves to conventional hat-tricks while **Kevin Hector** made up the triple-triple with a personal haul of five. For once the absentees were the losers – only 13,353 witnessed the amazing game.

✪ The youngest player to score a Derby County hat-trick is **Andy Garner**. He was 18 years 30 days when he netted all the goals in the 3–0 home win against Crystal Palace on 7 April 1984. In contrast, the oldest to perform the feat was aged 38 years 261 days – **Steve Bloomer** on 9 November 1912 in a 5–1 home win against Sheffield United.

✪ It was a case of 'once you get one you'll get more' for the Rams striker **Kevin Wilson**. On 29 August 1984 he scored four in Derby's 5–1 League Cup win at home to Hartlepool and again nabbed a hat-trick four days later in a 3–2 home win against Bolton.

✪ Of the last six Rams hat-tricks up to the end of 2005–06, four were by men named Paul, three by one player, two against the same team and one in a defeat in which another Paul (Williams) went in goal as an outfield stand-in.

Paul Simpson on 8 April 1996 in a 6–2 home win v Tranmere Rovers
Paul Simpson on 22 January 1995 in a 3–0 home win v Portsmouth
Paul Kitson on 6 September 1994 in a 6–1 home win v Cesena
Marco Gabbiadini on 3 January 1994 in a 4–0 home win v Tranmere Rovers
Mark Pembridge on 23 January 1993 in a 5–1 away win at Luton Town
Paul Simpson on 6 September 1992 in a 3–4 home loss to Bristol City

THEY DIED TOO SOON

✪ The only Derby County player to die as a result of an incident on the pitch is **William Cropper**. Having left the Rams, the 26-year-old was playing for Staveley against Grimsby Town in January 1889 when he was accidentally caught in the stomach by the Grimsby defender Dan Doyle. He died the following day of a ruptured bowel.

✪ The career record of left-back **Phillip Bloomer** stands in stark contrast to that of his older brother Steve. He played once for the Rams in September 1895 but died aged 21 the following summer, a victim of peritonitis.

✪ England right-back **Tommy Cooper** played 266 games for the Rams from 1925–34 before meeting a tragic end. In June 1940, while serving as a sergeant in the Military Police, he was killed aged 36 when his motorcycle collided with a double-decker bus in Aldeburgh, Suffolk.

✪ Two members of Derby's 1946 Cup-winning side died within six months of each other in 1955, while still playing. **Chick Musson** and **Leon Leuty** both fell victim to leukaemia aged 34 and 35. Some superstitious fans said the infamous gypsy curse had struck after all.

✪ The Scottish international centre-forward **Hughie Gallacher** led a turbulent life off the field. In June 1957, while facing a charge of cruelty to his son, the 54-year-old former Derby star threw himself in front of the Edinburgh–York express train at a spot known as Dead Man's Crossing in Gateshead. He is the only Rams player known to have committed suicide.

✪ Few Derby defenders have been as inspirational as centre-half **Rob Hindmarch**, a giant in the Arthur Cox sides of the 1980s. He had been running soccer schools in the United States when he died from motor neurone disease in November 2002 at the age of 41.

✪ When Derby became League Champions in 1971–72, their classy left-back **John Robson** missed only one game. Barely six years later his career was ended by multiple sclerosis, and in May 2004 he became the first member of that legendary side to pass away, aged just 53.

✪ Two Derby County left-wingers had their careers tragically affected by early deaths of the cruellest kind. **Frank Middleton** had moved to Leicester Fosse when he dropped out of the team in 1907–08 following the loss of one of his children. Seven decades later the Rams favourite **Alan Hinton** mustered only five substitute appearances in 1975–76 after the tragic death of his young son Matthew.

INSULT TO INJURY

Accidents and injuries are an occupational hazard in football, but a number of Rams players have suffered more unconventionally than most.

✪ In an 1890s exhibition game the Rams' **John Goodall** had two teeth knocked out by the giant fist of the famous Sheffield United goalkeeper William 'Fatty' Foulke. In a subsequent match at Aston Villa, Goodall's dentures popped out and the game was held up while the players grovelled in the cloying mud to retrieve the missing choppers.

✪ When left-back **George Birdsall** joined the Rams in 1921, it was nine months before he made his debut after falling prey to a debilitating bout of 'ptomaine poisoning'. He remains the only Rams player credited with that sinister-sounding complaint...the old-fashioned term for food poisoning. A more quaint condition once kept **John Goodall** out of the side in the 1890s – he was reported to be 'suffering from a severe quinsy', in fact nothing more than a throat infection.

✪ In 1918 winger **Alf Quantrill**, one of two Rams players born in India (the other was midfielder **Don Masson**), suffered recurrent bouts of malaria while serving in Salonika with the Derbyshire Yeomanry, but he made a remarkable recovery to resume his Rams career a year later. He later played for England, and in 1921 he married the eldest daughter of his Rams coach Steve Bloomer.

✪ Many players take a jaundiced view of the game once they retire, but in **Mike Smith**'s case it was more than a figure of speech. The Rams centre-half was forced to retire in 1961 following a genuine attack of jaundice.

✪ A game against Scotland on 18 May 1974 proved to be the last of only five England appearances for the Rams classy left-back **David Nish**. He missed a tour to Eastern Europe after suffering a perforated ulcer which required immediate surgery and was never selected again.

✪ On 20 November 1976, following Derby's 2–0 defeat by Everton at Goodison Park, the Rams midfielder **Bruce Rioch** turned to shake hands with an opponent, accidentally trod on his foot and turned his ankle. Fans were mystified as Rioch, who had been running strongly at the final whistle, was helped off the pitch by two Derby players – much to his embarrassment the handshake ankle sprain kept the Rams hard-man out of the next game.

✪ England striker **Trevor Whymark** arrived at Derby County on loan in December 1979 but was withdrawn on Boxing Day after an hour of his second game. Glandular fever was diagnosed, and he never played again for the Rams.

✪ On his Rams debut in October 1980 **Frank Sheridan** scored twice from midfield in a 3–3 home draw with Queen's Park Rangers before ending up on the treatment table suffering from 'post-match emotional exhaustion'. Nor was that his only unusual complaint – having moved to Torquay

United in 1982 the unfortunate player suffered a ruptured spleen, which ended his League career.

⊕ When **Charlie George** signed for Derby County for a second time in March 1982 there was definitely something missing. Many trivia lists say he lost a toe while cutting his lawn but in fact the severed digit was the first finger of his right hand. The bizarre accident happened on 14 April 1980 when he was a player at Southampton.

⊕ In January 1997 rock-solid Danish defender **Jacob Laursen** was carried off injured during the pre-match warm-up of a home FA Cup game against Aston Villa. Both **Wayne Sutton** and **Marino Rahmberg** were summoned over the Pride Park PA system, but Rahmberg claimed the unexpected place on the bench as Derby reshuffled and won the game 3–1. The Rams goalkeeper that day was **Russell Hoult**, known as 'Hot Dog' because he once received a similar late call-up for Leicester City while munching a Frankfurter in the stands.

⊕ When Derby beat Crystal Palace 2–1 at Pride Park in March 2006 a classy strike by **Inigo Idiakez** led to an unusual injury. As the Spanish midfielder curled in the Derby equaliser, the Rams caretaker manager Terry Westley celebrated with such abandon that he pulled a calf muscle.

⊕ The most poignant 'injury' to befall a Rams player was that suffered by former winger **Ted McMinn** after his playing career had ended – in 2005 a mystery infection led to the 42-year-old favourite having his trusty right leg removed below the knee. McMinn faced the ordeal with the rare courage and good humour for which he was known as a player, but he wasn't the first Rams player thus tested – in 1952 the club's first ever signing **Haydn Morley** was forced to give up working as a solicitor after his leg was amputated when a scratch became infected. There was only one small difference – Morley, who died the following year, was a sprightly 91 at the time.

WORLD WAR ONE DISPATCHES

Football initially adopted a 'business as usual' approach when World War One broke out in August 1914, but by the time the four-year conflict ended there had been some unfortunate consequences for the Rams.

✪ **Jimmy Methven**'s stylish Derby side were crowned Second Division champions in the first wartime season of 1914–15, but League football was then abandoned for the duration. It changed the club's history – by the time the Rams played their next League game on 30 August 1919 many of their past and present personnel had suffered cruel fates on foreign fields unrelated to football.

✪ In July 1914 **Steve Bloomer** took up a coaching appointment in Berlin. On 6 November Derby's record scorer was arrested and held captive in a civilian prison camp at Ruhleben until 22 March 1918. After a further enforced stay in Holland, he arrived back in Derby on 22 November 1918 having not seen his wife and family for almost four and a half years.

✪ Two members of the Rams 1914–15 Second Division Championship side survived the war to the eleventh hour before meeting remarkably unfortunate ends. Fifteen-goal forward **Tommy Benfield** was killed in France by a sniper's bullet on the eve of Armistice Day, but his teammate Lance Corporal **George Brooks** suffered a crueller fate still. The Derby wing-half escaped death until the very last day of fighting but was killed in France on the morning of 11 November 1918 only minutes before the armistice took effect. He was the only professional footballer killed on that day and is believed to be the last British casualty of the entire conflict.

✪ **Bernard Vann** led Derby's attack three times in 1906–07. The graduate of Jesus College Cambridge was an ordained minister, but his high connections were unable to save him from being killed in action in October 1918. Vann had already received the Military Cross and the French *Croix de Guerre* and was posthumously awarded the Victoria Cross for his last brave acts at Ramicourt. Only one professional footballer is recorded as having received the VC – Donald Bell of Bradford Park Avenue – since Derby County's own war hero is classed as an amateur, having never played for money. Bernard Vann remains the most decorated player in Rams history.

✪ Tough centre-half **Frank Buckley** had a fine Rams career before joining the 17th Middlesex Regiment – known as the footballers' battalion. he was promoted to major and proudly used the rank for the rest of his life, becoming best-known as the innovatory manager of Wolves in the 20s and 30s.

✪ A Derby County player born in June 1916 suffered a lifetime of war. **Verdun Jones** was named after the World War One battle and later had his career badly interrupted by World War Two. He played twice for the Rams in 1937–38 but was then 'rested' and next resurfaced 10 years later in May 1948 on the books of Southend United. By then he was a little short of match practice, and his two Derby County games proved the only League outings of a sad career which was both long and short at the same time.

WORLD WAR TWO NEWS

✪ When war was declared in September 1939 the League was abandoned after three games of the 1939–40 season. The expunged results were a 3–0 defeat at Sunderland and home wins against Portsmouth (2–0) and Aston Villa (1–0). When the League resumed in 1946–47, exactly the same fixture list was used and history repeated itself as Derby lost at Sunderland and again beat Portsmouth 2–0. But spoilsports Aston Villa were no fans of symmetry – seven years after their original defeat they returned to the Baseball Ground and won 2–1.

✪ In the absence of organised football, the Baseball Ground was put to good use. When it was taken over by the military, the pitch was used to train volunteers for the Home Guard, and at one point sheep grazed on the turf once reserved exclusively for Rams.

✪ In January 1941 the Osmaston Stand at the Baseball Ground took a direct hit during Derby's heaviest air raid of the war. Perhaps it was no surprise, for the German Luftwaffe had used an aerial photograph of the ground and its surrounds to identify nearby industrial targets. Not that Rams fans were daunted by the strike – a crowd of 31,795 attended the Cup tie against West Bromwich Albion on 26 January 1946, and many put themselves at grave risk by crowding into the still-ramshackle structure to witness a vital 1–0 win.

✪ Derby County's **Jack Stamps** had a harrowing war. He had enlisted in the Royal Artillery and was sent to France. When the British Expeditionary Forces evacuated from the Dunkirk beaches in 1940, Stamps found himself near the end of the queue for a ride back to England. As he attempted to board an overcrowded boat after hours in the water, Stamps was threatened by a British officer – 'stand down or I'll shoot you' – but the burly centre-forward risked it and hauled himself on board. Six years later he scored two goals in Derby's 1946 Cup Final win.

⚽ Many Derby County players joined the forces during the war but only one who had appeared in the first team was killed. **Arthur 'Rasher' Bacon** was serving as a special policeman in Derby when he lost his life on 27 July 1942. Bacon's unlucky end came when a lone Dornier flew over the town and bombed the Rolls-Royce factory close to the Baseball Ground, where the striker had been a player in the 1920s.

⚽ Derby County maintained an enduring link with the war by adopting the rousing *Dambusters' March* as their matchday signature tune. The bouncing bombs used in the legendary raids on German dams in May 1943 were the invention of Ripley-born Barnes Wallis, and the daring mission had been perfected in dummy runs at Derbyshire reservoirs. To complete the hat-trick tribute, the engines of the 617 Squadron aircraft which pulled off the raid were the celebrated Merlins by Derby-based Rolls-Royce. Some patriotic Rams fans still call for the *Dambusters' March* to be reinstated, and it is sometimes played on special occasions.

ODD ENDS

⚽ Only one Derby County player is known to have died during a match. Hard as nails half-back **Ernest Hickinbottom** survived countless bruising games from 1888–93 but was less resilient to the rigours of spectatorship. He passed away at the Baseball Ground aged 74 on 2 September 1939 while watching the Rams beat Aston Villa 1–0 in the final League game before World War Two.

⚽ The wife of the former Rams player and manager **Jimmy Methven** found the excitement of the 1946 Cup Final all too much. While listening to the radio commentary of Derby's 4–1 victory over Charlton Athletic, 77-year-old Agnes Methven suffered a heart attack and died two days later.

⚽ **Raich Carter** played in Derby's 1946 Cup Final victory unaware that his father-in-law Edgar Marsh had died shortly before kick-off. In telephoning Wembley to inform Derby officials, Mrs Marsh insisted that her daughter and son-in-law should not be given the sad news until after the final whistle.

DERBY COUNTY MAD

It's been said in jest that only the mad would throw in their lot with the Rams, but for Derby's England international wing-half Ben Warren it was no joke. The Newhall-born man died aged 38 on 15 January 1917 after spending time in an institution for the certified insane. His lowest point was reached when he was found wandering along a Derby street naked except for a collar and tie. Nothing in the Rams constitution covered that sad eventuality, but the club did make provision for directors of the same breed. Derby's official Articles of Association drawn up in 1896 state that 'a director may be disqualified if found to be a lunatic or of unsound mind'. Strangely the clause has yet to be invoked. Meanwhile the official title of the establishment in which Ben Warren was incarcerated had no connection with the club, although some would say it was well-named – it was The Derby County Lunatic Asylum.

FINAL WHISTLE

A bitterly-disputed goal in Derby's home third-round FA Cup tie against Plymouth Argyle on 20 February 1909 had far more tragic consequences than anybody could have realised. The score stood at 0–0 in the final seconds when the Rams were awarded a free-kick, and the ball was flighted into the box for Alf Bentley to head a dramatic winner. But just as it entered the net the referee chose to blow for full-time, and the Plymouth players believed the goal would be disallowed. When it became clear that the goal stood, the Argyle team surrounded the official and he had to have a police escort from the pitch.

That might have been the end of the affair, but the mood in the Argyle camp remained unsettled. While most of the Plymouth party travelled straight home after the game, a breakaway group were given permission to stay in Derby for some 'refreshment', and on their 11.30 train journey back to Devon an argument broke out over a game of cards in which the Argyle trainer Nick Wallis was struck a violent blow by one of the players, Edward McIntyre. Wallis's jaw was broken in two places, and he died a few weeks later after complications had set in. McIntyre was duly charged with manslaughter. The referee's disputed blow had led to a second fatal one, and if only the official had whistled at a more sensible time the tragic consequences of that late Derby winner might well have been avoided.

THE BRAINS TRUST

It has become something of a tired cliché to suggest that footballers are deficient in grey matter, but there are always exceptions to the rule. Here are some Derby County players who defeated the stereotype by demonstrating they had brains in their head as well as their feet.

Percy Exham (1884)
The Cork-born left-half, who also played cricket for Derbyshire and Ireland, was a Cambridge graduate and a master at Repton public school for 36 years.

Aubrey Howard Fabian (1931–32)
The Cambridge graduate and public schoolmaster at Highgate, London, was also a leading journalist and the author of *Constructive Football* (1950), for many years a standard coaching work. Football was not his only sport – he was a fine cricketer and thrice winner of a national 'fives' championship.

Ray Wilkins (1949–53)
When the ex-Rams centre-forward returned to Derby with Boston United for an FA Cup tie in 1955, he scored two in the Pilgrims' amazing 6–1 win. The feat met with ambivalence from certain junior members of the crowd – some cheered the opposition man 'as a friend', but others weren't so sure, for the hero who hit the back of the net on Saturday might easily have been the villain hitting their backsides on Monday – Wilkins had trained as a PE teacher and become the headmaster of a Derby school.

Glenn Skivington (1980–82)
After 43 games with Derby, the midfielder's talent for multi-tasking was put to good use in the lower Leagues. In 1989–90 he became an England non-League international and helped Barrow to win the FA Trophy...all while studying for a law degree.

Andy Hill (1981–83)
The scorer of a famous goal that clinched victory over Forest in the 1983 FA Cup later swapped crunching tackles for crunching numbers – he was an accountant by profession and became audit manager for a borough council.

Steve Biggins (1984–85)
Even with the best will in the world, it would be impossible to say the striker was a qualified success at Derby, although he was elsewhere – Biggins was a late-entrant into League football after first qualifying as a teacher.

Andy Comyn (1991–92)
The thinking man's central-defender understood the bounce of the ball better than most – before signing for the Rams, Comyn had taken the unusual step of leaving Manchester United to pursue a physics degree at Birmingham University.

HIGH OFFICE

A number of Rams men have been appointed to administrative positions of authority within the game – here are some who 'went upstairs' to good effect.

☻ When Derby County appointed their first official manager in 1900, their secretary, **Harry Newbould**, a qualified accountant, was an obvious choice. The highly capable administrator went on to became the long-term secretary of the Players' Union, the forerunner of today's PFA, and his bullish approach did much to improve the lot of early footballers before his untimely death in 1929.

☻ Although the Rams winger **Sammy Crooks** was known as everybody's friend, the former miner from a huge family of 17 certainly knew his rights – ideal qualifications for becoming chairman of the Professional Footballers' Association, a position he filled to lasting good effect from 1937–46. A *Pathé News* interview with Crooks in that capacity, which can be viewed on the internet, is thought to be the earliest surviving sound footage of a Rams player.

☻ Had **Jim Smith** been more of a 'suit', he would never have become manager of Derby County. In March 1995, having been sacked by Portsmouth, Smith 'retired' from team management and became chief executive of the League Managers' Association, a job ironically offered to him outside the Baseball Ground following a reserves game. A few months later he was back there as Derby County's new manager, having realised a 'shirt and tie' job just wasn't him. Smith once again donned shorts and sweatshirt to take the Rams into the Premiership in his first season.

❂ A curious hat-trick was effected by PFA executives when they appointed three chairmen in a row who have Derby County credentials. Former Rams defender **Warren Barton** became PFA chairman in 2003 but announced his retirement a year later and handed over the reins to **Dean Holdsworth**. But when Holdsworth became Derby's assistant manager in August 2005 he too resigned from office, and his replacement as PFA chairman was the former Rams full-back Chris Powell. All future applicants desirous of landing the role are advised to include Derby County somewhere in their CV.

CUP FINAL QUIRKS

❂ Saturday 27 April 1946 was a memorable day in Derby County history – when the Rams beat Charlton Athletic 4–1 in the FA Cup Final – but the match might have been sensationally called off. A few days before the Final the Derby players threatened to boycott the game when their wives and girlfriends were allocated uncovered seats instead of the more expensive covered ones given to the directors' wives. When the furious players told the board 'No new tickets, no Final' the better tickets magically arrived in a flash.

❂ Derby were allocated 12,000 tickets, but 250,000 letters were sent to club secretary **Jack Caterall** requesting one million tickets in all. Stamp machines in Derby ran dry, and the players were drafted in to help sort the applications.

❂ A fabled Romany curse was said to have been placed on the Rams in 1895 when the club turned a band of gypsies off the Baseball Ground. It was thought Derby would never win the Cup until the curse was lifted, so a few days before the game the Rams captain **Jack Nicholas** visited a gypsy camp to have his palm crossed with silver – the result speaks for itself.

✪ The team's secret hideaway was the Glen Eagle Hotel at Harpenden, which still stands. The village was festooned with Rams colours, which explains why a number of older Harpenden residents support the club to this day.

✪ Luckiest fans at the game were airmen Lesley Ball (25) and John Purcell (22) who were arrested in Derby on Friday night for being drunk and disorderly. Only when they showed their match tickets were the fortunate pair granted bail to travel to London.

✪ Unluckiest supporter was Littleover confectioner Ernest Powell. On his way to Wembley the motorcycle he was riding pillion on crashed near Kettering. He died aged only 36 from his head injuries, leaving his heartbroken widow grieving his loss while the rest of Derby celebrated the club's triumph.

✪ The 1946 FA Cup was unique for being played on a two-leg basis up to the quarter-final. To win the trophy Derby played a record 11 matches unbeaten and scored 37 goals to only eight conceded. Their triumph seemed only right, for Charlton had actually lost 2–1 to Fulham in the second leg of the third round.

✪ The supporter with both the sorest feet and most feeble brain was 43-year-old Thomas Perrins, who walked all the way to Wembley from his home in Bilston near Wolverhampton despite having no ticket.

✪ Match referee Mr E.D. Smith of Whitehaven was a former footballer, rugby player and star athlete but was still heavily criticised by the Rams no-nonsense inside-forward Raich Carter for not keeping up with play.

✪ When the famous ball-bursting incident occurred with the score at 1–1, Princess Elizabeth was most amused. Perhaps getting confused with cricket, she turned to the Mayor of Derby and asked him 'Do you think the new ball will make a difference?' The future Queen Elizabeth II proved an astute pundit – with the replacement the Rams scored three extra-time goals.

✪ The Wembley triumph should have been recorded on canvas for posterity. Derby-born artist Frank Beresford RA intended to depict the scene in a large oil painting but the picture was never done – he became so engrossed in the action that he neglected to do even a single sketch.

TWELVE – RANDOM RAMBLINGS...

———————— TRAVELLERS' TALES ————————

✷ During a tour of Scotland in the 1890s Derby County became the first (and probably only) football team to walk across the newly-opened Forth Rail Bridge. Full-back **Jimmy Methven**, who arranged the rare privilege via a friend working on the railways, recalled 'Whenever a train rushed by we clung to the sides for dear life. Some of the boys put pennies on the track for the fun of seeing them flattened, but the Scots among us were accused of using halfpennies to make them into pennies.'

✷ After 27 May 1936 **Steve Bloomer** found himself all at sea. But this is no slur on the great man's ability to cope with advancing years, for when the *Queen Mary* made its maiden voyage on that date the former Rams striker's image adorned a mural of sporting celebrities in one of the luxury liner's elegant public rooms. But in 1938 Bloomer found himself at sea for real when, because of failing health, a subscription fund was launched to send him on a four-month recuperative cruise to Australia and New Zealand. Although he enjoyed the once-in-a-lifetime trip immensely and was fêted at every port of call, he had a relapse the day after his return and died three weeks later, aged 64.

✷ When **Alf Quantrill** received an emergency summons to play for England against Wales in March 1921, his mercy dash to Cardiff was fraught with delay. Having raced the final few miles from the railway station by taxi, he arrived at the ground only minutes before kick-off, but the Rams winger's patriotism was thrown back in his face when the FA refused to reimburse his taxi fare...the grand sum of 3s 6d (17.5 pence).

✷ Petrol rationing both during and after the war made travel to games a real problem. In May 1945 magistrates fined a Horsley Woodhouse coal merchant £1 10s (£1.50) for 'wasting petrol' after he had driven to watch Derby play at home, strangely enough a complaint not uncommon among Rams fans even today. A rather cannier tradesman earlier employed an ingenious ruse – throughout the war, each time Derby played at the Baseball Ground, he travelled from Belper and back carrying a piano in his van. Had the police stopped him, he had a ready excuse – black and white scarf or not, he was simply delivering a piano.

☺ Although winger **Sammy Crooks** missed the 1946 Cup Final because of injury, he was a driving force in the build-up to the Rams victory. A few days before the game, Crooks calmly took the wheel of the team's Trent bus to take the players from their Harpenden HQ for a relaxing round of golf after the regular driver had been given permission to go sightseeing in London.

☺ When Derby crashed out of the UEFA Cup to the little-known Yugoslav side Velež Mostar in December 1975, the Rams striker **Francis Lee** joked on the return flight from Dubrovnik that only a plane crash could further darken the sombre mood. At which point the aircraft hit a massive air pocket and plunged 600 feet without warning. The entire squad was left unnerved by the incident, but it was said that the whitest face of all belonged to the joker himself.

☺ When Derby County struck a sponsorship deal with Saab in 1977 each of the Rams squad was given one of the aptly-named (baas backwards!) cars. The cream-coloured SDT-registration fleet soon became a familiar sight around town, but although player-spotting had never been easier one man never seen behind the wheel was young full-back **David Langan** – the crestfallen Irishman wasn't offered one of the shiny new vehicles because he couldn't drive.

☺ An unusual 'death' occurred on Wednesday 23 March 1977. As the *Ramaway* train carrying Derby fans to a key relegation battle at Tottenham came to a halt in St Pancras Station, the Derby faithful disembarked to find a macabre token of welcome had mysteriously attached itself to the engine's front – a large wreath carrying the message 'RIP Derby County.' Whichever Spurs fan did the deed wasn't laughing later – the very much alive Rams cruised to a 0–0 draw and embarked on a good run to finish in 13th place in the First Division…four points ahead of Spurs who were dead, buried and relegated.

☺ **Charlie George** and **Igor Stimac** both suffered car crashes on signing for the Rams. After falling asleep at the wheel of a borrowed Jaguar XJ6 on his way up to Derby, George was very fortunate to survive unscathed after a high-speed smash on the M1 in which he ploughed through road works and on to the hard shoulder. Meanwhile, on only his second day in England, the super-cool Croatian defender Stimac drove on the wrong side of the road, with inevitable consequences, while trying to negotiate a Derby retail park. Both recovered fully but the Rams 1970s goalkeeper **Graham Moseley** had a much worse experience behind the wheel – while playing for Cardiff City in 1986 he was injured in a car accident and forced to retire for good.

☙ On 26 September 1987 spectators at Derby's home match with Oxford United witnessed a surreal sight as new Rams chairman **Robert Maxwell** arrived at the Baseball Ground by helicopter to watch his first ever game there. But by the end of a dire 1–0 defeat the only 'Blades' in sight was the Rams defender Paul – true to form, 'Mad Max' had sneaked out before the final whistle.

☙ The second leg of Derby's 1993–94 play-off semi-final victory at Millwall made national headlines after Rams players were attacked during two violent pitch invasions, which caused a 32-minute delay. Nothing was sacred at The Den that shameful night – after the game a quaking commentary trio found their BBC Radio Derby car had been trashed and turned onto its roof!

☙ Derby County are the only football club to have 'lost' a Spitfire, a Hurricane and a Lancaster bomber. The three World War Two aircraft were scheduled to make a dramatic flypast over Pride Park on the day of its opening in July 1997. When a designated 'spotter' gave the signal that they were on their way, the *Dambusters' March* was played and the announcer bade the capacity crowd to 'look skywards for a big surprise'. The surprise was that nothing happened, since the spotter had panicked and been mistaken – in truth the aircraft were grounded in Lincolnshire by fog and a fax cancelling the appearance had failed to reach officials at 'high-tech' Pride Park because the machine had been left behind at the Baseball Ground. It could only happen at Derby County.

☙ When the former Rams winger **Ted McMinn** had his right leg amputated below the knee in October 2005, he might well have sat back and felt sorry for himself. But that wasn't the 'Tin Man's' style – instead he got on his bike for charity and cycled all the way from Glasgow to Derby, more than 300 miles. Along with a posse of outriders, including former Rams striker **Bobby Davison**, he began the epic journey at Rangers' Ibrox Stadium on 8 April 2006 and breezed into Pride Park six days later having raised more than £15,000.

☸ On 2 June 2006 Derby County scored a theatrical first when their new manager **Billy Davies** dramatically arrived at the club for his introductory press conference by helicopter. But surely it had been done before? Not quite like this though, for the female pilot of the craft was the Rams own commercial director Jill Marples. True to Derby's usual form, the ambitious stunt went mildly awry when the conference's scheduled 11am start was delayed 15 minutes due to the chopper's late arrival. As Radio Derby stood by to cover the event a desperate presenter filled in with an ungallant suggestion – 'I reckon she's got lost and can't find a parking space.'

CUP CAPERS

☸ No wonder supporters believed the tale of the Gypsy Curse, thought to have been put on the Rams in 1895. It was said that Derby would never win the FA Cup as long as they tried – and so it began to appear. Starting in 1896 they reached four semi-finals in a row, reaching the Final twice but losing on both occasions. Nor did a new century banish the curse – from 1902 the Rams reached another three semi-finals in a row, but after only one more outing in the Final – a record 6–0 defeat by Bury – the trophy dubbed the 'Little Tin Idol' still eluded them. They also fell in the semis in 1909, 1923 and 1932 and by then, including replays, had taken part in 13 semi-final ties. Only when that unlucky figure was surpassed in 1946 did they finally lift the FA Cup.

☸ Derby's FA Cup semi-final replay against Birmingham City on the afternoon of Wednesday 27 April 1946 helped sound the death knell for midweek afternoon games as the government feared chronic absenteeism was affecting industrial output. An astonishing 80,407 were at Manchester City's Maine Road to see the Rams win 4–0 after extra-time, and so many men asked for time off to attend 'funerals' that the day was dubbed 'Grandmothers' Wednesday'.

☸ But for Adolf Hitler Derby might never have won the FA Cup. Former Sunderland player Raich Carter, one of the Rams' star players in the 1946 Final, signed for Derby only because he took refuge there at his in-laws' home in Chaddesden after his house in Sunderland had been flattened during a German air raid in 1943.

✪ When Derby played Manchester United at Hillsborough in the semi-final of the 1948 FA Cup, thousands of fans were left disappointed as they were unable to obtain a precious ticket. But one applicant whose polite written request to Derby proved unsuccessful had far more reason than most to be disgruntled – he was 88-year-old **Haydn Morley**, the Rams first ever signing, whose brother and father **William Morley** and **William Morley senior** had been co-founders of the club.

✪ Derby's 4–1 home victory over Manchester United on 8 August 1970 made them winners of the first sponsored Football League competition, the Watney Cup. Twenty years later the Rams 'regained' the handsome trophy in unusual circumstances – they 'borrowed' it from Whitbread Brewery to display at an exhibition and have quietly hung on to it ever since!

✪ When Derby beat Burnley 2–0 in an FA Cup replay on 25 January 1992, the celebrations from supporters were the most extraordinary ever seen at the Baseball Ground – because it was the Burnley fans who were cheering! After the final whistle the Clarets army stoically refused to budge from the Osmaston End and began a round of relentless ritualistic chanting that continued for almost 20 minutes. Only when the Burnley players and their manager Jimmy Mullen came out to plead with them and say thank you did the 'best losers ever' head back north to their beds.

✪ Derby lost three FA Cup Finals in the first 20 years of their existence – 1898 to Nottingham Forest, 1899 to Sheffield United and 1903 to Bury – but there was a healthy consolation for the descendants of at least one supporter who went to the games and resisted the temptation to tear-up his programmes in a fit of rage. In 2003 the three original programmes were sold at a Sotheby's auction for a combined figure of £21,120 despite being in poor or incomplete condition – time to search that attic!

✪ Good deeds sometimes backfire. When Colchester United faced a third-round FA Cup tie at Sheffield United in January 2006, the Derby manager **Phil Brown** allowed the Essex side to use the Rams Moor Farm training facilities to prepare for the big clash because he counted their manager Phil Parkinson as a good friend. United beat the Blades 2–1 and by coincidence next landed a plum tie at home to Derby. The reward for Phil Brown's generosity was that his side were dumped out 3–1 by his chum's ruthless outfit, and after the game the beleaguered Rams boss was roundly abused by an irate fan while conducting a live interview on Radio Derby. The most helpful manager in the game was sacked two days later after just seven months in the Derby hot seat.

ALL A MATTER OF TIME

☺ Derby County once clinched a Championship title with a very late victory. After they drew 1–1 with West Bromwich Albion on 30 April 1894 a replay was required to see who would emerge 1893–94 United Counties League champions. Due to fixture congestion the game was put off until 1 October 1894 the next season, all of five months later. The Rams triumphed 2–1 to lift the 1893–94 title...the only side ever to win a Championship in the wrong season.

☺ Derby supporters enjoyed a huge surprise on Christmas Day 1920 – **George Thornewell** and **Noah Burton** scored in a 2–2 draw at Bradford City. What made it so unexpected was that it had been eight whole games since Derby had scored a single goal, the last strike also belonging to Thornewell in the home game against Arsenal on 23 October – the two months and two days goal drought which lasted for 720 minutes of playing time was the longest in the Rams' history and not surprisingly the 1920–21 season ended in a sorry relegation to Division Two.

☺ The second round of the FA Cup in 1923–24 saw Derby County and Newcastle United become engaged in a marathon. The fun began with a 2–2 draw at Derby on 2 February 1924 followed on the sixth by another 2–2 draw at Newcastle after 30 minutes' extra-time. Five days later the teams tried again at Burnden Park, Bolton, but once more the game ended 2–2 after extra-time. As the FA despaired of ever finishing the tie, lots were then drawn for the venue and Newcastle got lucky. On 13 February at St James' Park the Second Division Rams finally succumbed 5–3 to their top-flight opponents after seven hours play and 20 goals over 11 days.

☺ Delaying a kick-off due to crowd congestion is one thing. Bringing it forward for the same reason is quite another. But that's exactly what happened when a record 75,118 packed into Roker Park on 8 March 1933 to see Sunderland and Derby contest an FA Cup sixth-round replay. The gates were locked well before kick-off and when the game started early four trainloads of Derby supporters were already heading home having been turned back just outside Sunderland. Two men tragically died in the crush as the Rams won 1–0 through a Peter Ramage goal.

⊙ Senior supporters are inclined to moan that today's close season is far too short, but their memories of the good old days seem to fail them. In fact the shortest close season in Football League history was just after the war. Because of prolonged bad weather, Derby played their last game of 1946–47 on 31 May, but the League season didn't officially end until 14 June. When the Rams began their 1947–48 campaign on 23 August the summer break had lasted only 70 days.

⊙ After Derby drew 0–0 at Airdrie on 26 January 1972 in the first leg of the Texaco Cup Final, their fans were kept on tenterhooks for fully three months as the second leg was played at the Baseball Ground on 26 April – thankfully the long wait proved thoroughly worthwhile as goals from **Alan Hinton** and **Roger Davies** saw a well-oiled Rams side cruise to a 2–1 aggregate victory.

⊙ When **Brian Clough** replaced his great rival Don Revie as manager of Leeds United in 1974, he quickly set about upsetting people. After telling the players to 'throw your medals in the bin because you didn't win them fairly' he was famously given the sack after only 44 days in charge. But that was a lifetime compared to another Rams manager's brief reign at Exeter City – when **Tim Ward** joined them in March 1953 he stayed just eight days.

⊙ Up until the dying moments of their game at Middlesbrough on 15 January 1977, Derby County had gone an impressive 449 minutes without an opposition player scoring against them. The near five-game shutout – four League games and one FA Cup – began against Arsenal on 15 December 1976. It almost ended sooner in the Middlesbrough game but the first of their two goals was credited as a **Charlie George** own-goal – only when Boro scored the clincher in the last minute was the stubborn Derby defence breached by an opponent.

⊙ In May 1991 a Derby County time capsule laden with memorabilia was ceremoniously buried at the Osmaston End of the Baseball Ground with the declared hope that 'future generations may one day learn something of the club's magnificent heritage.' But after Derby moved to Pride Park and the Baseball Ground was set for demolition, the capsule was wearily dug up in 2003 by some of the very same people who had gravely buried it only 12 years earlier.

COLOURFUL HISTORY

While Derby County's traditional colours are black shorts and white shirts, they have played in many alternatives, of which here is just a sample.

☻ In 1884 the newly-founded side adopted colours based on those of Derbyshire County Cricket Club – white shorts with chocolate and blue halved shirts and amber sleeves. Although they soon ditched the scheme in favour of white shirts and black shorts, the original colours made a nostalgic comeback a hundred years later as a 'flash' on the club's 1984 centenary shirt.

☻ In 1890–91 Derby adopted cardinal (bright red) shirts and black shorts, the archaic name deriving from the colour of the vestments associated with the Catholic church. In their first outing in the new garb Derby conceded five goals at home to Blackburn Rovers, but there was a suggestion of divine intervention as they won the amazing contest by putting eight past the dazzled visitors' defence, the first five coming in the opening 10 minutes.

☻ In 1893–94 Derby's ongoing predilection for the unspeakable hue of Forest saw them play in red and white halves, a scheme verified only recently when an original shirt worn by captain **John Goodall** was unveiled by a descendant.

☻ The club's dogged insistence on wearing red was finally halted after a colour clash led the team to again don shirts of that colour in the 1903 FA Cup Final against Bury – after a shameful 6–0 defeat the faces of the Derby men were barely distinguishable from their shirts.

☻ Derby's most frequent second strip from the 1890s to 1920s was black and white stripes, firstly as a home change but then as an away one when in 1924 the Football Association introduced a new regulation stating that the visiting side must change in the event of a clash.

☻ In the early 1960s Don Revie famously changed Leeds United's yellow and blue 'peacock' colours to all white in a bid to emulate Real Madrid. Less well known is that Derby also dallied with the same 'Lillywhite' scheme in 1965–66 – alas the Spanish touch eluded them as 'Real Rams' put in some very 'unreal' performances and finished eighth in Division Two.

🟣 On 12 April 1969 Derby arrived at Millwall with white shirts not realising they would face a colour clash. They borrowed their opponents' red away shirts resplendent with a Millwall badge, and a **Willie Carlin** goal gave an unfamiliar-looking Rams a 1–0 victory.

🟣 Derby broke with tradition in 1971–72 by adopting navy blue shorts instead of black when manager **Brian Clough** said 'I fancy the sight of England running out every week.' The new colour stuck and only after the Annual General Meeting of November 1988 was a resolution passed to revert to the fans' favoured black.

🟣 A strange one-season rule gave an odd look to the Derby v Leeds sixth-round Cup tie played at the Baseball Ground on 17 March 1973. The FA required both sides to wear away kits in the event of a colour clash so Derby donned all blue and Leeds all red – a Peter Lorimer goal sealed a 1–0 win for United.

🟣 Although black and white has remained Derby's first-choice strip for many seasons, a vast range of different coloured away shirts have been sampled. They include yellow, lemon, gold, black, orange, black and blue stripes, blue and white 'Argentina' stripes, blue checkerboard, baseball-style pinstripe and the infamous broad and narrow black and white stripes from 1989–90, which the Rams long-suffering shirt enthusiasts dubbed the 'barcode kit'.

🟣 At the start of the 1971–72 season the Manchester United winger Willie Morgan said that if Derby finished above United in the First Division he would wash the Rams kit. When the Rams failed to beat United in two early games Morgan looked safe, but the Manchester club finished a mediocre eighth and Derby County won the League Championship. Rams fans called for the pledge to be honoured, but club officials were more generous – although Morgan's agent contacted the Rams, the relieved player was allowed to keep his dignity…what was left of it.

✪ In 1977 the vehicle manufacturer Saab became the first company to emblazon its name on a Derby County shirt, but the move badly backfired when the Football League refused the team permission to wear them. One of the reasons stated was that they wished to preserve the 'sanctity' of the game, so instead the new kit's exposure was restricted to a string of glamour models draped over car bonnets on the erstwhile hallowed Baseball Ground. By the time the Rams were permitted to play in sponsored shirts in 1980–81, their travelling aspirations had gone sky high – the message they carried read 'Fly British Midland'.

BADGE OF HONOUR

✪ Derby first sported a standard badge on their shirt in 1924–25, and then only for two seasons. The design was based on an idea produced by the supporters' club – a three section shield depicting a ram's head, the rose and crown emblem of Derbyshire and the Derby Borough arms of a buck in the park. From 1926–27 the players' shirts remained unadorned until after the Cup Final of 1946 when a surge of pride led to a new design being unveiled and worn on the shirts for the first time in the cup-winners' official team photograph.

✪ Although it seems to have been around forever, Derby's distinctively-styled snorting ram logo was conceived only in 1971–72. It was created by the Derby company Product Support (Graphics) Ltd. and took 240 hours of work and 40 variations before the final image was decided upon. The brief was to create something which typified the attacking progressive spirit of Derby County, and to that end the angular beast first faced forwards with eyes right. However it soon did an about turn before again adopting a more positive direction in the 1980s, but in 2006 it was once again facing left, heading in the wrong direction. The perversity of the creature is arguably no surprise, since its main creator was a Leeds United fan.

✪ Quick-thinking photographers got the shot of the century on 1 May 2006 when Derby Legends drew 3–3 with Rangers Legends at Pride Park in a benefit game for both clubs' former player **Ted McMinn**. That the ex-Forest star Nigel Clough should open the scoring in a Derby shirt was surreal enough, but the truly iconic moment came when 39-year-old Forest legend Stuart Pearce slotted home the second – after giving his trademark 'clenched fist and snarl' salute, Pearce grabbed his shirt and kissed the Rams badge like he truly meant it. The jaw-dropping moment left the Derby faithful not knowing whether to cheer or jeer.

FAMOUS FIRSTS AND LASTING LASTS

✪ In their historic first ever fixture on 13 September 1884 Derby were beaten 6–0 at the Bolton club Great Lever. The Rams made an even more inauspicious start to their FA Cup quest – in their very first tie on 1 November 1884 they lost 7–0 at home to Walsall Town. Thirteen goals without reply in those two symbolic games might have seen some clubs fold at the very outset – but the redoubtable Rams were made of sterner stuff.

✪ The first FA Cup Final held outside London was hosted by Derby County. The game took place at the County Ground on 10 April 1886, a replay between Blackburn Rovers and West Bromwich Albion after the first game at the Kennington Oval had ended 0–0. A crowd of 15,000 saw Rovers triumph 2–0 after an unseasonal snowfall had put the game in jeopardy and almost landed the hosts with an unwanted place in the record books. As it was, the sun came out and all went perfectly, the *Sports and Pastimes* newspaper reporting that 'the sight of the Derby County Ground was a most imposing one all round.'

✪ Although Derby were victorious in their first ever Football League game – a 6–3 away win at Bolton Wanderers on 8 September 1888 – their supporters had to wait almost four months to see the first League win at home. It finally came on 22 December 1888 when Notts County were beaten 3–2 in the 12th game of the season.

✪ The honour of scoring Derby County's first ever League goal – in the opening game against Bolton – fell to their second ever signing **George Bakewell**. He first took up the game seriously as a pupil at Derby School, one of the key pioneering establishments in Derbyshire football at a time when many other top schools insisted on pursuing rugby.

✪ On 3 October 1908, four games into Tottenham Hotspur's first season in the Football League, Derby County entered the Spurs record books by becoming the first ever team to take a point in a Football League match held at White Hart Lane. The meeting, which ended 0–0, was also the first between the two clubs and the point pilfered by the Rams was the first ever dropped by Spurs.

☺ At Highbury on 26 September 1936 the celebrated England cricketer and Arsenal footballer Denis Charles Scott Compton made his Football League debut in a game against Derby County. The man known as the original 'Brylcreem Boy' proved a slick opponent – playing on the left wing, he scored the opener in a 2–2 draw.

☺ According to the book *Relics of the Rams,* Derby's first official home friendly match against English opposition did not take place until 11 August 1965. The programme dubbed it a public practice match and the visitors were Sheffield United.

☺ A surprising number of games finished 10 against 11 prior to substitutes being permitted in Football League matches in 1965–66. Derby's first substitution came after only 15 minutes of the opening game against Southampton on 21 August 1965 when injured full-back Geoff Barrowcliffe was replaced by Bobby Saxton – the Rams lost 3–0. Scottish football was a year behind, the first sub appearing on 13 August 1966 when St Mirren brought on the future Rams player Archie Gemmill in a League Cup game against Clyde. It was even longer before Derby fielded a genuine 'supersub' since their first to actually score was **Richie Barker** – away to Plymouth Argyle on 20 January 1968, Derby had trailed 3–1 before late entry Barker netted two minutes from time to pinch a dramatic 4–3 win.

☺ The Spurs and England legend Jimmy Greaves scored a record 266 goals in 379 matches for Tottenham, the very last of which, a rare header, was glanced past the Derby 'keeper **Les Green** at White Hart Lane on 10 January 1970 – the Rams obligingly gilded the historic moment by losing 2–1.

☺ In 1971 Derby County became the first club to involve themselves in a major sponsorship project when the Texaco Oil Company bought their ground rights over a two-year period, transforming the Baseball Ground overnight as it became emblazoned with Texaco hoardings. A year later Derby were the first club to sell a game to an individual sponsor – the Derbyshire company Cox Moore of Long Eaton – who were 'pleased to bring the Rams and their supporters all that is best in men's knitwear from the region's top brand leader'. A pioneering hat-trick was completed in

April 1977 through a deal with Saab when Derby became the first Football League club to be fully sponsored.

✪ There was a satisfying sense of order and finality about Derby's home game with West Brom on 1 May 1971. It was the last game of the season, the last time **Dave Mackay** played for the Rams, and the only time in his long career that the 'Iron Man' had been ever-present for a season. After Derby had won the game 2–0 Mackay left the Baseball Ground for the final time as a Rams player with that definite 'job done' feeling.

✪ The Rams striker **Francis Lee** knew how to do things in style. When Derby played at Ipswich on 24 April 1976 – his 500th and last game in League football – Lee had only two minutes of his career remaining when he signed off with two late goals to seal a memorable career and a thumping 6–2 win.

✪ On 24 September 1977 Liverpool played a young debutant defender against Derby at Anfield. The Reds won 1–0 and the super-cool Scotsman, who went on to play 434 games for the club, cites that first appearance as the most memorable moment of his career – his name…Alan Hansen.

✪ Although the Rams were beaten 1–0 at Liverpool on 1 May 1990, they enjoyed the privilege of sharing in an iconic moment. After 72 minutes the 39-year-old Liverpool manager Kenny Dalglish brought himself on as a substitute to thunderous applause – the surprise appearance, the last of his career, was his first for 19 months after the Anfield legend had long since announced his retirement as a player.

✪ The last ever first-class game at the Baseball Ground was a Premier League match against Arsenal on Sunday 11 May 1997. Although Ashley Ward netted the opener to become Derby's last ever scorer at the famous old stadium, 10-man Arsenal (Tony Adams had been sent off after 11 minutes) calmly pooped the party as two goals from Ian Wright either side of a clever strike by Dennis Bergkamp earned the Gunners a 3–1 win. Derby County legends from far and wide had come to say farewell to the 102-year-old celebrity, and supporters travelled from Europe, America and even Australia especially for the occasion, but one man sent his apologies – **Brian Clough** was 'suffering from flu'.

✪ The first ever game at Pride Park Stadium was a friendly against the Italian club Sampdoria on 4 August 1997. A capacity crowd saw the visitors, including German superstar Jürgen Klinsmann, win 1–0, but the result was incidental on an occasion when around 50 ex-Rams stars took to the pitch in an emotion-packed curtain-raiser to the main event.

☻ When **Branko Strupar** scored for Derby 108 seconds into the home game against Watford on 3 January 2000, he nabbed a widely-reported place in the record books – the scorer of the first Premiership goal of the new millennium.

☻ On Sunday 15 October 2000, bottom-of-the-Premiership Derby County entertained Liverpool at Pride Park. When England striker Michael Owen left the field with a head injury after only 22 minutes, the Rams defence heaved a huge sigh of relief and relaxed a little – just enough to concede four goals without reply and to allow Emile Heskey to score his first ever hat-trick.

SCORING FOR FUN

☻ Derby set to work quickly in establishing the club's scoring records. On 6 September 1890, the opening game of only their third Football League season, they beat Blackburn Rovers 8–5 at the County Ground. It remains the highest aggregate score in a Derby County Football League match, one ahead of their 9–3 hammering of West Bromwich Albion at the Baseball Ground on 8 December 1935.

☻ After Derby lost 8–0 at Blackburn Rovers on 3 January 1891 the Rams captain **John Goodall** called for 'a response' in their next game at home to Wolves just a week later. He got it – in an amazing turnaround in form Derby landed their record League victory in a 9–0 triumph. They again won 9–0 at home on 21 January 1899, when Sheffield Wednesday were the victims and **Steve Bloomer** nabbed a club record six, but the magic double figures in a League game have continued to elude them in over a century of trying.

☻ Derby fans who witnessed the 3–2 defeat at Aston Villa on 3 February 1900 returned home chuntering like never before or since. Robbed just wasn't the word – they ought to have seen a high-scoring away win, but with the Villa crowd baying for every decision the 'homer' officials duly obliged by disallowing five Derby 'goals'.

❧ When a German international side first visited England they received a hot welcome from the Rams striker **Steve Bloomer**, who captained the Professionals of England in an unofficial international held at Manchester City's Hyde Road ground on 25 September 1901 – after scoring a brace Bloomer expressed himself pleased with the result...England 10 Germany 0.

❧ When **Jimmy Bauchop** scored against Gainsborough Trinity on his Derby debut on 1 September 1909 he was only doing what came naturally. The prolific inside-forward clocked up a magnificent seven by also netting in his debut games for Celtic, Norwich, Crystal Palace, Spurs, Bradford and Lincoln City. For the Rams he was that rare commodity 'a one-in-two man', hitting 72 goals in 135 games.

❧ In 1891–92 the Rams forward **John Goodall** scored in every one of the first six League games of the season. The dream start record was not matched until **Horace Barnes** repeated it in the first six matches of 1913–14. **Eddie Thomas** did something similar by netting in his first six appearances of 1964–65 after missing the opening two fixtures of the season. But the rarity of any six-in-a row feat was brought home when it took another 33 years before it happened again – this time the Italian **Francesco Baiano** equalled the club record when he netted in six League games running in September and October 1997.

❧ In 1920–21 **Jack Atkin** did what no other Rams full-back has ever managed – he scored four goals in successive matches. But 40-yard screamers they weren't – two were penalties and the other two were own-goals scored for the opposition!

❧ Only six players have achieved the rare feat of scoring five or more goals for the Rams in a single League match. **Sandy Higgins, Johnny McMillan, Jimmy Moore, Hughie Gallacher** and **Roger Davies** all settled for 'going nap' (the old slang for scoring five), but **Steve Bloomer** kept going and netted six. Even so his feat didn't match Jimmy Moore's for timing – in 1922 'Gentleman Jim' scored the first five in a 6–0 home win over Crystal Palace...on Christmas Day.

❧ From 1921–25 Derby-born **Frank Keetley** scored only eight goals for the Rams in 82 appearances, so the club let him go. Only then did the forward find his touch, and in January 1932 he scored six goals in 21 minutes for Lincoln City against Halifax Town. Keetley was one of an astonishing family of nine brothers living in Derby who were all signed by professional clubs at some stage, and in February 1929 Tom Keetley also scored six in a single game for Doncaster. But all the brothers except Frank were allowed to leave their home town right under the noses of the Derby scouts.

⊛ Bristol City were anything but ship-shape when Derby visited them for a Division Two game on 29 September 1923. **Harry Storer** scored four as the Rams sailed to their record away win by a thumping 8–0 margin.

⊛ The saying 'it's goals that count' has never been more appropriate for Derby than in 1923–24. Needing to win the final game against Leicester City by at least 5–0 to gain promotion to the First Division, the Rams stormed into a sensational 4–0 lead after 65 minutes and missed out to Bury on promotion by 0.015 of a goal.

⊛ It is every manager's dream to have a 30-goal-a-season striker in his side, but Derby County have landed only five of that rare breed in their entire history, and not one in the last 50 years. **Steve Bloomer** set the ball rolling with 31 goals in all matches in 1896–97, followed by **Alf Bentley** with 32 in 1908–09. Bentley again hit 30 a season later and **Harry Bedford** matched him in 1929–30 before **Jack Bowers** netted 39 in the following campaign as a prelude to bagging a club record 43 in 1932–33. The last man to achieve the prolific feat was **Ray Straw** in 1956–57 – his 37 goals were all in the League, equalling the club League record first set by Bowers in 1930–31. The chances of the magic mark ever being achieved again seem somewhat remote.

⊛ The best consecutive scoring streak for an individual Derby player in all competitions belongs to **Jack Bowers**. From 3 January to 14 February 1931 he netted in seven games in a row, six League and one Cup. His tally during his 'magnificent seven' run amounted to an astonishing 17 goals including four braces, two hat-tricks and one instance of four – the double brace return against Portsmouth might easily have been five, but Bowers was denied the rare chance to go nap when the Rams were awarded a penalty and **Sammy Crooks** grabbed the ball instead.

⊛ Some might say he was a mercenary, but certainly the least discriminate scorer in Derby County history was **Peter Doherty**. The Irish international was much in demand as a wartime guest player and rarely declined an invitation to turn out for whoever wanted him – so much so that from 1939–45 he scored for 10 different clubs and wrote in his autobiography that he 'once played for six different League teams in little over a week.'

☮ Derby players familiar with cricket slang might well have shouted 'Nelson' at the end of the 1956–57 season when the Rams tally of League goals in their 46 matches reached the magic combination of uni-digits, which is 111. It remains Derby's highest League tally for a season but their overall best return came in the previous campaign when, aided by two own-goals, the ram-raiders hit the back of the net a remarkable 118 times in 49 League and Cup games.

☮ Derby's leading scorer in 1956–57 was former Ilkeston miner **Ray Straw**, but some credit must go to his brother for providing an unusual incentive. He had offered Straw half-a-crown a goal and 10 shillings for every hat-trick – and boy did he pay for it. Straw bagged three triples and equalled the club record of 37 League goals for a season before calmly trousering his spoils – six pounds two shillings and sixpence.

☮ The former Derby Boys star **Peter Newbery** was given only five games for the Rams but the young centre-forward still found himself making unexpected headlines for unwittingly reaching a club landmark. Statisticians were beside themselves when at Leyton Orient on 10 September 1960 Newbery's first ever goal for the Rams proved to be the 4,000th League goal in their history. The youngster enjoyed the attention so much he scored again in the very next outing – they were the only two goals he ever scored in League football. A rather more prolific scorer netted Derby's 5,000th League goal – it came from **Kevin Hector** in a 1–0 win over Arsenal at Highbury on 8 November 1975 – and **Paul Kitson** hit the 6,000 landmark in April 1994 against Leicester City.

☮ When **Brian Clough** became manager of Derby County he had earned the right to tell forwards where to stick the ball…and that wasn't always in the net. In 274 games for Middlesbrough and Sunderland between 1955 and 1964 he scored a remarkable 251 goals and reached both the 200 and 250 mark in the fastest time in Football League history. Only a bad cruciate ligament injury sustained when he was 27 prevented the goal-machine from adding many more, and he was forced to finish playing after his comeback lasted only three games.

☮ For part of two consecutive seasons Derby literally couldn't stop scoring. In 1960–61 they netted in every League and Cup game from 3 December

1960 until the season end in April. The following campaign they picked up where they had left off, scoring in each of the first six games before finally drawing a blank at Leyton Orient on 9 September 1961. Although the thrilling 33-game run is the best consecutive scoring sequence in the club's history, it masks a sobering truth. Only 13 of the games were won, since the cavalier approach resulted in the Rams defence leaking 71 goals during the same period, an average of more than two a game.

☺ Brighton & Hove Albion leaked goals at an alarming rate in 1973–74. Shortly after the arrival of a prestigious new management team, the struggling Third Division club were beaten 4–0 at home in the FA Cup by non-League Walton & Hersham. That was followed by a shameful 8–2 home defeat by Bristol Rovers, and the Seagulls finished the season in a sorry 19th place. Who were the incompetent managers? None other than the brilliant **Brian Clough** and **Peter Taylor**, who had arrived at the lowly club after leaving the First Division Rams. As the saying goes…that's football Brian.

☺ In December 1990 the Sheffield Wednesday full-back John Harkes scored a 40-yard Goal of the Season at the Baseball Ground past the Rams legendary goalkeeper **Peter Shilton**. The wonder strike helped dump Derby out of the League Cup 2–1, and Harkes gained a winners' medal at Wembley as Wednesday went on to lift the trophy. Yet after the American star later joined Derby and converted to midfield, he was unable to score from only a couple of yards out when Derby visited Wembley to face Leicester City in the 1994 First Division Play-off Final. As a consequence, Derby also lost that one by two goals to one – they may say 'it's a funny old game', but whoever wrote the Harkes script had a pretty warped sense of humour.

☺ Supporters have always called for players to shoot more, but the recent advent of detailed statistics has lent more weight to their case. In 1998–99 Derby's tally of 156 on-target shots for the season was the lowest in the entire Premiership. But the critics were soon confounded – despite their shot-shy approach, the Rams finished eighth, their best Premiership showing to date.

☺ In March 2003 *Match of the Day's* football sage Albert Sewell came up with this little gem for his 'Ask Albert' slot – only five players had scored in the Premiership for five different teams. Two were Stan Collymore and Mark Hughes, but remarkably the other three all counted Derby as one of their clubs – **Dean Saunders**, **Ashley Ward** and **Benito Carbone**.

BY ROYAL APPOINTMENT

☻ Derby County's longest mid-season League break attributable to factors other than weather was 28 days. On 19 January 1901 they drew 0–0 at Wolves and their next League game was a 1–1 draw at home to Newcastle on 16 February. The unscheduled interval occurred following the death of Queen Victoria on Tuesday 22 January when, as a mark of respect, all FA Cup games scheduled for the following Saturday, the day of the funeral, were postponed until 9 February. The first Edwardian Derby County side lost their tie 1–0 at Bolton before resuming their interrupted League programme a week later.

☻ One of the scarcest items of memorabilia owned by Derby County is a two-handled Spode-Copeland porcelain 'Loving Cup' presented to them to commemorate the Coronation of King George VI and Queen Elizabeth in May 1937. Only First Division clubs and FA dignitaries received the gift, and the example held at Pride Park is numbered 16 out of a Limited Edition of only 30. Tradition has it that club directors should toast the reigning monarch by drinking from the cup, and evidence suggests that other clubs may have pursued the practice rather too vigorously – of the 30 original examples, all but four are believed to have been broken!

☻ In the summer of 1954 the former Rams winger **George Davis**, who in 1912 had emigrated to Canada and made his fortune in the hotel business, caused quite a stir when he came back to Derby for a visit. At great expense he had shipped over his magnificent limousine, a 20-foot long Lincoln coupé which had been used by Princess Elizabeth during her tour of Canada with the Duke of Edinburgh before she became Queen. Rams players have driven some snazzy cars in their time, but no set of wheels turned more heads than the one driven by self-made millionaire George Davis.

☻ Although Her Majesty Queen Elizabeth II has never gone public on her football allegiance (all celebrities have to have one these days) it has been conjectured that she would either support Reading (the Royals) or her local non-League club Windsor and Eton (the Royalists), whose staunch patron is her husband, the Duke of Edinburgh. But a perusal of the archives suggests there may be a split in the royal household. The first professional football match ever attended by Her Majesty (then 20-year-old Princess Elizabeth) was Derby's 1946 Cup Final victory over Charlton Athletic. The boys in black and white must have impressed her, for in 1984 she remembered to send the club a congratulatory telegram on their 100th birthday. Then in 1997, surprising even her own aides, the busy monarch cheerfully agreed to open Pride Park Stadium, the first such ceremony the Queen had ever carried out at a football ground. And finally she returned to Derby County's home in 2002 for a grand celebration of her Golden Jubilee. Let there be no more doubt about it...Her Majesty Queen Elizabeth II is a Rams fan through and through.

☸ With the above in mind, an intriguing *Guardian* newspaper headline in 1970 suggested a spat over split loyalties – 'QUEEN IN BRAWL AT PALACE' is a classic of its genre, but in fact referred to the sending off of the Crystal Palace striker Gerry Queen. The robust centre-forward played against Derby later that season and there was more fun to come – other headlines to boost paper sales were 'QUEEN IS KING' and 'PALACE SELL QUEEN FOR £70,000.'

☸ Although not quite royalty, the official patronage of Derby County by the Duke of Devonshire once lent a distinct touch of class to the Rams list of 'officers'. And when Derby won promotion in May 1987 it seemed he had laid on a rare treat. A roadside sign in Belper read – 'Duke of Devonshire's Topless Barmaids Congratulate The Rams' – but in truth his grace's personal serving wenches remained safe at Chatsworth House, while the novel pint-pullers at the Duke of Devonshire pub actually came from Ripley.

☸ Derby County's first win at Pride Park was the 1–0 Premiership victory over Barnsley on Saturday 30 August 1997, but the celebratory mood was quickly dampened when news broke early the next morning that Diana Princess of Wales had died in a car crash. By chance, no Premiership fixtures had been scheduled for the day of the funeral, Saturday 6 September, but after all other British games were cancelled as a mark of respect Derby picked up the threads a week later with a 3–1 home win over Everton. The mass postponements provided a sharp contrast to Saturday 30 January 1965 – on that historic date a full fixture list went ahead and 14,765 saw Derby beat Manchester City 2–0 at the Baseball Ground only hours after the day's main event...the State Funeral of Britain's greatest wartime leader Sir Winston Churchill.

☻ Fresh from polishing off their Christmas Day lunches in 1997, countless Derby County supporters could scarcely believe their eyes as the Rams manager **Jim Smith** scored a football first by making a surprise TV appearance during the Queen's Christmas Message. Her Majesty had agreed for the 'highlights' of a tragic royal year to be uplifted by a brief clip of the day she officially opened Pride Park Stadium – so having already been treated to a fat, plucked turkey, her millions of loyal subjects around the world enjoyed the unexpected bonus of a plump Bald Eagle.

THE DREADED DROP

Whether it's called relegation, dropping down a League or demotion, there are few worse fates for a football club than tumbling through a gaping trapdoor into a lower Division. While tradition has it that Derby County fans are more long-suffering than most, the records confirm that the Rams have endured the torture of the dreaded drop only nine times in the 119 years since the Football League began. Here is the evidence to be grateful for.

Season	Division	Manager in charge
1906–07	First to Second	Jimmy Methven
1913–14	First to Second	Jimmy Methven
1920–21	First to Second	Jimmy Methven
1952–53	First to Second	Stuart McMillan
1954–55	Second to Third North	Jack Barker
1979–80	First to Second	Colin Addison
1983–84	Second to Third	Peter Taylor then Roy McFarland
1990–91	First to Second	Arthur Cox
2001–02	Premiership to Division One	Jim Smith then Colin Todd then John Gregory

Former player Jimmy Methven is the undisputed 'king of the drop', but it is testimony to both his great popularity as a loyal club servant and his yo-yo ability to bounce back through promotions that he was allowed to continue so long in the manager's role. The figures suggest that turning to such former players or old favourites may be counter-productive – six of the 10 managers complicit in relegation seasons had at one time played for the Rams, while Peter Taylor had previously served as assistant to Brian Clough. Only Colin Addison, Arthur Cox and Jim Smith came with no Rams baggage at all. One other lesson can be learnt from the list – it doesn't pay to have two managers in one season, while three is a recipe for certain disaster!

GOING UP

Although the saying 'what goes up must come down' usually proves true in football over a long period, an adage that holds better is 'what goes down must come up'. While certain big clubs have held on to their top-flight status for many years without ever knowing the heartbreak of relegation, most clubs who do suffer that fate show a remarkable tendency to regain their status via promotion. Here is a rundown of the seasons when Derby County proved their bounce-back-ability.

Season	Division	Manager in charge
1911–12	Second to First	Jimmy Methven
1914–15	Second to First	Jimmy Methven
1925–26	Second to First	George Jobey
1956–57	Third North to Second	Harry Storer
1968–69	Second to First	Brian Clough
1985–86	Third to Second	Arthur Cox
1986–87	Second to First	Arthur Cox
1995–96	Division One to Premier	Jim Smith

The eight promotions against nine relegations ensured that Derby began 2006–07 one level below where they started in 1888, when they were one of just 12 founder members of the single Division Football League. An 'equaliser' is long overdue.

FABLED FIXTURES

☉ Beginning in 1919–20 and lasting until 1923–24, the Football League fixtures took on a monotonous feel as teams played each other home and away either in successive games or at fortnightly intervals. The odd system (which afforded the opportunity for immediate retribution between feuding players) was most noticeable in 1923–24 when Derby played no fewer than 18 of their 21 League opponents in successive games only seven days or less apart.

☉ Rams fans wanting to travel to Derby's away clash with West Ham on 24

May 1925 were advised to set off in particularly good time, but even the most intrepid supporters considered the long journey to be scarcely worthwhile. But wasn't London only 128 miles from Derby? It was, but the unusual away game was an exhibition friendly played at the Ajax stadium in Amsterdam!

☺ The name of Derby's opponents for a friendly game held at the Baseball Ground on 14 February 1955 seemed to suggest they might be a team of mixed character. And that's exactly how it proved – early in the second half, when the game seemed on the point of boiling over, the over-robust Austrian visitors suddenly put the lid on their aggression to sportingly take the heat out of the contest. As the team from Vienna left the field, the Rams players raised a tribute in the time-honoured fashion – 'Three cheers for Sporting Simmering'.

☺ Derby County's battling spirit has sometimes been called into question, and a series of friendly games held at the Baseball Ground in 1941–42 in aid of the War Fund seemed to suggest that the Rams weren't always up for it against well-drilled opposition. On Christmas Day 1941 they found their opponents far too good in the air and were soundly beaten 3–1 by an RAF XI. Shortly afterwards they were outgunned 4–1 by Anti-Aircraft Command before salvaging a modicum of pride in a 3–3 draw against the Belgian Army...or 11 of them at least. But there was one victory...and what a win it proved. On 10 January 1942 the Rams routed the Czechoslovakian Armed Forces by 11 goals to four.

☺ There is seldom any place for shared honours in Derby County v Nottingham Forest encounters, but on one occasion a 2–2 draw saw both teams and both sets of supporters trip off home with joy in their hearts. The friendly took place at the Baseball Ground on 9 May 1945 – the day after VE Day – to celebrate the official end of six long years of war in Europe.

☺ Schools and factories in the Derby area noted unusual levels of absenteeism on 29 February 1972 when Derby's fifth-round FA Cup replay at Arsenal was played in the afternoon due to floodlight restrictions necessitated by a miners' strike. The faithful Rams supporters who had taken advantage of the 'free' day afforded by a Leap Year were rewarded with a fighting 0–0 draw – but a cruel 1–0 defeat in the second replay at Leicester City's Filbert Street ended the Cup dream for yet another year.

⚽ Friendly games and European competitions have given Derby the opportunity to play against some top-quality non-English sides in their time, including seven who won the European Cup – here is the pick of the bunch. Real Madrid, Benfica, Barcelona, Juventus, Celtic, Atletico Madrid, Ajax Amsterdam, Athletic Bilbao, AEK Athens, Real Mallorca, Spartak Moscow, Feyenoord, Hibernian, FC Bruges, Panathinaikos, Rapid Vienna, Dukla Prague, Moscow Dynamo, Sampdoria and Lazio. The debate over who is the best side Derby ever played might rage forever, but one big gun they never played was Santos – Derby were set to face the Brazilian giants on 20 August 1990, and a programme was printed, but the prestigious friendly was cancelled at the eleventh hour.

⚽ Derby County were in such demand to play pre-season friendly games that on 3 August 2000 they fulfilled two fixtures in one day. One team took on KSTVV in Belgium while the other Derby County played Hayes in Middlesex. Although the extent of the club's squad made the double bill perfectly possible, the programmes for the games suggest the Rams were a little stretched – Richard Jackson, Paul Boertien and Adam Murray were listed as substitutes for the game in Belgium but were named in the starting line up against Hayes.

⚽ On 17 July 2004 Derby notched up 'a cricket score' against Team Halden on the last game of a pre-season tour of Norway. Halden, a representative side from three lower Division teams, battled gamely but were 5–0 down at half-time. Then the Rams manager George Burley made changes, and Brazilian substitute Junior seemed to have a point to prove – he hit six second-half goals as Derby cruised to a 15–0 win and hit the woodwork five more times. It had been a total mismatch, but none of the 300 spectators would ever forget it. Even the *Derby Evening Telegraph* entered the fun spirit, using a neat retro headline gleaned from a vintage TV programme – 'Junior Showtime'.

RECORD BREAKERS

It would be unthinkable for it to happen now, but there were once occasions when Derby County actually broke the British transfer record when purchasing and selling players. Here is a list of those rare deals which made the Rams the talk of the football world.

Fee	Player	From –To	Year
£2,500	Horace Barnes	Derby–Manchester City	1914
£15,500	Billy Steel	Greenock Morton–Derby	1947
£24,500	Johnny Morris	Manchester United–Derby	1949
£225,000	David Nish	Leicester City–Derby	1972
£2,900,000	Dean Saunders	Derby–Liverpool	1991

The likelihood of such a thing ever happening again, either on an incoming or outgoing basis, seems remote indeed, and few transfer deals at any clubs will create the stir caused by Derby's sale of Horace Barnes on the eve of World War One. The fee of £2,500 was then considered outrageous and sparked a moral debate about the value of a single human being when lives were being lost to war so cheaply. The Arsenal manager Leslie Knighton captured the nation's mood in his book *Behind the Scenes in Big Football,* the quote bringing home that while attitudes may not have changed, the magnitude of the figures certainly has:

'Men argued with each other in pubs up and down England, not about the menace of the Kaiser's steel-helmeted hordes but about the price paid to Derby County for Horace Barnes.'

THIRTEEN – ALL
CREATURES GREAT AND
SMALL...

Although the Derby County mascot Rammie reigns supreme, a whole menagerie of creatures has strayed into Derby County territory over the years. Here are some stories of the 'strange but true' variety that made the news.

RAMMIE

Derby County's official mascot Rammie first appeared to his adoring public at the Baseball Ground in 1991. Six years later the club became the first to make the mascot job full-time when they appointed Burton-based fan Dean Mottram in the role. In his time the local icon has won the Mascot Grand National, been voted Best Mascot in the Premiership, released his own DVD and supported a wide variety of community initiatives and charities. Unlike most of his breed, he sports 'proper boots' and has the sweetest left foot in the mascot kingdom.

An experimental mating programme with a female partner Lambie was short-lived – the pair failed to bond and the planned progeny (Prammie) never materialised. There were hopes of a fresh liaison when Derby found themselves in the 2005–06 FA Cup draw with non-League Tamworth, but the dream tie of the Rams v the Lambs never came off. Instead of a first date with Tammy the lamb, Rammie was landed with old adversary Bertie Bee from Burnley.

The most famous ram in Derbyshire looks set to be king of the beasts for many seasons to come. During staff cutbacks in 2005 a club spokesman confirmed that the role was safe: 'Rammie does a tremendous all-round job both on and off the field. The fans can be assured there are no plans to put him out to grass.'

DERBY DOG

According to the *Oxford English Dictionary,* a 'Derby dog' is an age-old racing phenomenon – they define it as 'the proverbial stray which invades the course just as "The Derby" is about to begin'. But the breed also inhabits football, and what more appropriate place for a run-out than Derby's own Baseball Ground.

On 19 April 1969 Derby County played Bristol City in the final Division Two game of the season. The Rams were briefly assisted by a speedy mongrel (black and white naturally), which broke from the vicinity of the boys' pen. After a good midfield run and a series of nifty feints, the plucky pooch was nabbed by a quick-handed policeman and carried from the field to hearty cheers from the crowd.

Although its name went unrecorded, it might well have been Lucky. Derby's performance that day was described as 'one of the most complete in the club's history.' A hat-trick from Alan Durban plus a goal each from Kevin Hector and Alan Hinton gave Brian Clough's side a resounding 5–0 win. The Rams were promoted by a mile and three seasons later became League Champions for the first time in the club's history. Although long since departed to the great kennel in the sky, the most authentic Derby dog of all was photographed for posterity.

NICE SWAN CYRIL

In January 1999 Derby County travelled to Third Division Swansea City for a fourth-round FA Cup tie. There is little to say about the match itself. Derby substitute Kevin Harper nodded the Rams ahead after 82 minutes. The Swans responded by bringing on the aptly-named A. Bird. But flying headers there were none. Derby won a dour contest 1–0 and the team were hissed from the pitch by a Vetch Field crowd utterly unimpressed by their Premiership visitors.

The press agreed with the locals – which is why Derby County suffered the gross indignity of being denied the headlines in favour of a mascot. So entertaining were the touchline antics of Swansea's manic Cyril the Swan that the *Sun* awarded the 9ft tall, beady-eyed bird the Man of the Match accolade.

Few locals were surprised, for Cyril had shown FA Cup form previously. Only a month earlier, in the first round of that season's competition, referee Steve Dunn reported Cyril for an on-pitch fly-past in celebration of a goal against Millwall – having stuck his neck out once too often the swan was charged by the FA for bringing the game into disrepute. Swansea were fined £1,000, while Cyril's bad-bird image secured him his first CD release – *Nice Swan Cyril* sold 2,000 copies.

Derby's 1998–99 FA Cup dream ended in the quarter finals at Highbury when a disputed last-minute strike by Kanu gave Arsenal a controversial 1–0 victory. The referee was that man Steve Dunn. Derby's furious fans could again have done with Cyril to mark the official's card – preferably from a great height.

A DAY AT THE RACES

Footballers have been likened to racehorses. Both breeds need careful handling. Each needs to be fed right, trained hard and rubbed down afterwards. Some become finely-tuned specimens that turn into winners. Others lose form and fall at the first hurdle. All are put out to grass eventually. But one management team took the comparison far too literally. In July 1970 Brian Clough and Peter Taylor took their entire squad to Nottingham's Colwick Park Racecourse – not to watch the races, but to run around the course itself!

A photograph of the most unusual pre-season training session in Derby's history shows a bunched field of 36 led by trainer Gordon Guthrie. Most of the players seem to be finding the going heavy. Alan Hinton, handicapped by extra weight, brings up the backmarkers. Needless to say, there were only two declared non-runners at that day's meeting – Brian Clough and Peter Taylor watched from the rails.

THE WHINNYING GOAL

Derby County players have never been big on distinctive goal celebrations. The 'shirt over the head' routine patented by Ravanelli was a rarity – not least because he only got a chance to do it 16 times. In stark contrast, the ever-modest Kevin Hector scored a net-busting 201 goals, but a minimalist arm-raise generally did the job for 'The King'.

Steve Bloomer occasionally got carried away, once using his momentum to complete a spectacular cartwheel even before the ball had trickled over the line. 'It wasn't arrogance,' said Bloomer – 'I just knew it was in.' Steve could be forgiven for showing off – his 332 goals for the Rams remains the club record.

But none of these three takes the honour for the best goal celebration of all time, for that accolade falls to an unlikely spectator. On 30 January 1893 a County Ground crowd of 15,000 saw Derby County beat Sheffield Wednesday 1–0 after extra-time in an FA Cup tie, a result later expunged following a Wednesday protest. The *Derby Express* reported on the extraordinary scenes 'Several times the encroaching crowd had to be controlled by mounted police. In fact the horses enjoyed the excitement as much as anybody. When John Goodall scored the County goal one of the fiery steeds did a caper on its hind legs in the centre of the field.'

The creature evidently knew that its celebratory invasion of the hallowed turf was fully justified, for the County Ground also served as Derby Racecourse. It seems unlikely that such horseplay will ever be bettered.

NATURE'S GENTLEMAN

England international forward John Goodall was labelled 'nature's gentleman' by his Rams colleague Steve Bloomer. He was also dubbed 'Johnny Allgood' – his honest personality enhanced the reputation of the professional game at a time in the 1890s when playing for money was still considered by critics to be vulgar.

Goodall was a keen amateur naturalist who loved wildlife and the countryside. In retirement in Hertfordshire he bred canaries, kept a pet fox and ran a bird shop. Displaying unusual eloquence and sensitivity for a footballer, he once said:

'Fishing and nature, especially birds, I have loved, although the one passion of my life has been football – the most exhilarating game I know, and the strongest protest against selfishness, without sermonizing, that was ever put before a thoughtful people.'

It must be the most erudite quote ever to issue from a Derby County player, and one unlikely to be matched by the modern breed who might well expect a 'naturalist' to go without clothes.

ABSOLUTE MAYHEM

The most surreal game ever associated with Derby County took place at Pride Park Stadium on 1 August 2002. For a start it was a friendly played on Thursday lunchtime – yet 27,000 fans crammed into the ground in pouring rain to watch it.

Neither team showed any regard for the rules. Each fielded 30 players at a time and played across the pitch rather than up and down. The odd player moved with a swagger, but none could be accused of being too big for their boots – in fact their boots were too big for them. Catching the eye were an owl, a robin, a fox, several lions, two cats, a super-cool hippo and a rather ponderous moose.

Yet strangely the crowd watched this unique mascots' exhibition game as intently as any Derby County encounter, even berating the referee when a surprisingly nimble pig was scythed down by a lumbering bulldog – surely proof positive of the old saying that Derby is a real football town.

Perhaps they had also come to see what followed. At 2.45pm Her Majesty Queen Elizabeth II arrived at the stadium. Although sporting neither huge feet nor a foam rubber head, she received loyal applause from the crowd. The visit was part of Her Majesty's Golden Jubilee celebrations and 18,400 gold balloons were released to mark the occasion, one for each day of the 50-year reign.

Although the mascots mustered not a decent goal between them, the crowd went home safe in the knowledge that they had seen a right royal game to remember.

JACK THE LAD

No Derby player has pursued 'the art of procreation' with more obvious enthusiasm than Jack 'Pimmy' Davis (1904–09). His never-ending supply of willing females made him the constant butt of dressing-room banter. Once when two of his 'ladies' were about to give birth, his teammates arranged for a telegram to be delivered to the Baseball Ground – 'RETURN CODNOR SOONEST – FANNY & ETHEL SERIOUSLY ILL'.

Cox rushed home only to find it was a practical joke – though not quite in the bad-taste that it seemed. Fanny and Ethel were sows, for Jack Davis was one of Derbyshire's leading pig breeders and an ardent member of the Jacksdale Pigkeeping Club for nearly 50 years.

A century later another Rams player revealed a similar passion in a candid interview: 'Ever since my childhood in Lambeth, I've never been able to resist the birds,' said Darryl Powell. And to prove it he obligingly caressed his current favourite for the camera. The Rams captain was an incurable pigeon fancier.

PESKY FOXES

It was the Foxes who inflicted what many fans consider the most disappointing defeat in Derby County history. The Division One Play-off loss against Leicester City at Wembley on 30 May 1994 – Foxes 2 Rams 1. The cruel late winner was too much to bear – Tommy Johnson cried buckets and most of Derby with him.

Two years later real-life foxes caused more trouble. In autumn 1996 a whole pack of the creatures began digging holes in the pitch. As a deterrent, the club sprayed perimeter fencing with an odious chemical, but made the mistake of doing it on a windy day. The chemical drifted and 10 female workers from a nearby underwear factory were hospitalised. One tabloid newspaper ran the best headline on the story – 'A PANTS DAY FOR THE RAMS'.

THE PERFECT STOPPER

Harry Storer (1955–1962) was one of Derby County's most feared managers. By all accounts, he had no need of a ferocious sidekick – but he had one all the same. His constant working partner was Bill, who stalked the Baseball Ground corridors keeping a lookout for troublesome players. Bill was always seen in the same thick coat and never spoke a word. He also had terribly bad breath, four legs and a tail.

The hound's favourite repose was at the bottom of the steps leading into Storer's office. It proved a good positional strategy for only the bravest players dare ask for a wage rise – stepping over Bill was a highly dangerous manoeuvre in shorts. No wonder the club's overdraft was halved during Storer's tenure.

Some said Harry's bark was worse than his bite. With Bill it was the other way round. But the partnership worked – when Storer took over Derby languished in the Third Division North bereft of spirit, yet they won promotion in his second season. Perhaps there is a lesson in this shaggy dog story. Any Rams manager might do well to take a lead from Harry Storer – one with a fearsome defender attached to it.

WORDS OF WISDOM

Found scrawled on a toilet wall at Pride Park – an anonymous but almost erudite proverb from which long-suffering Derby County fans might take comfort:

'IT IS BETTER TO LIVE ONE DAY AS A RAM THAN 100 AS A SHEEP'.

THE INSIDE TRACK

On Monday 7 November 2005 Derby County took on Leicester City. The very same evening Derby also faced Notts County, Mansfield Town and Burton Albion. The conundrum isn't so mysterious for all the 'teams' were dogs racing each other in the inaugural event of the Greyhound Football League in Nottingham.

Supporter reaction to the sleek-looking speed merchant was entirely predictable. When the dog made a celebrity appearance at Derby's home game against Ipswich Town five days earlier, many suggested the muscular specimen should play up front. But the lugubrious West Stand really summed up the mood. After seeing Ipswich snatch a late equaliser in an alarmingly open 3–3 draw, many headed for the exits muttering that Derby County had gone to the dogs long ago.

FOLLOW THAT CAMEL

The overseas players dubbed the Rams Foreign Legion are no longer a novelty, but when the first of the bunch arrived from Sporting Club Cairo in 1920 he caused quite a stir. Presenting himself at the Baseball Ground entirely unbidden, the Egyptian Tewfik Abdallah uttered only three words – 'Foot the ball'. The Rams manager Jimmy Methven spent some time trying to sell the exotic visitor a season ticket before realising he wanted a trial.

Once Abdallah became accustomed to playing in boots (barefoot had been his practice) he made it into the first team and quickly became a crowd favourite blessed with the nickname 'Toothpick'. Nifty control and a nice turn of speed earned the likeable forward 15 appearances with one goal.

Footballers being what they always have been, the Egyptian soon got on the end of dressing-room banter – witness this tale related by author Andrew Ward (son of Rams manager Tim Ward) in *The Manchester City Story*:

> 'Abdallah made his Derby debut on 9 October 1920 at home to City. He was told to mark the famous Irish international Mickey Hamill, a man he had never met. It's said that Abdallah wandered around the Baseball Ground pitch for the first few minutes apparently shouting "where's mi camel?...where's mi camel?" – in fact, since numbered shirts had yet to be introduced, he was merely enquiring "Where's Mick Hamill?"'

Apocryphal possibly, but the Egyptian certainly had the last laugh – Hamill got the hump, while Abdallah scored his only goal for the Rams in a stirring 3–0 win.

SWINGING IDEA

Dynamic Derby County Secretary Stuart Webb was a real trailblazer in the 1970s. Many of his innovations were inspired by trips to America. In the *Ram* newspaper for 3 September 1977 Webb outlined his latest series of ideas for promoting the game. Blessedly, not all of them got the go-ahead.

'At Dallas Tornados their live chimpanzee mascot named Deena is fettered to the opposition goal and is released to do gymnastics on the woodwork whenever Dallas score. The Americans go wild for it'.

The Rams directors quickly scotched the idea, but even so the chimp still had Derby County to thank for much of its regular exercise. The man dubbed the 'King of Dallas' that season was the Rams export Alan Hinton, whose classy play and record-breaking assists regularly made monkeys of the opposition.

THE B-TEAM

Of 226 League and Cup goals scored by Derby from 1908–09 to 1910–11, an amazing 183 were netted by players whose surname began with 'B'.

The free-scoring Bentley, Bloomer, Barnes and Bauchop were quickly dubbed the 'Busy Bees' and the pun-loving *Derbyshire Football Express* soon had them 'buzzing around the opposition' and sending in 'stinging' shots from both wings.

Manager Jimmy Methven began the B-fest when he brought back old boy Bloomer from Boro – on his 'welcome home' against Lincoln City on 1 October 1910, Steve and Jimmy Bauchop bagged a brace each and Horace Barnes blasted in a beauty to complete a 5–0 win.

Methven decided to stick to the winning formula. By April 1912 his side to face Wolves at the Baseball Ground included Barbour, Buckley, Bagshaw, Bloomer, Bauchop, Barnes and Betts. Unfortunately Bentley had by then been sold... naturally to Bolton.

Methven's B-team secured promotion to the top flight in 1911–12, but in 1913–14, even with the addition of Bowler to the squad, the honeymoon was over – Derby finished bottom. Methven left quietly in 1922 having loyally served the club as player and manager for 31 years – despite his peculiar alphabetic fixation, there was nothing B-list about Jimmy Methven.

AND FINALLY

It's a sad fact that there is almost certainly not a single morsel of trivia in the strange world of the Rams that at least one fan wouldn't already know. But here's one that may have escaped the sane majority. Derby County are the only club to feature twice on television in the company of a ring-tailed lemur.

In the BBC One documentary *Back to the Wild* on 23 August 1998, presenter John Cleese watched a playful group in Madagascar and told viewers: 'What I like about lemurs is that they've got bags of attitude. They remind me of football fans on their way to a match all waving their scarves at one another.' Then he added as one sauntered into shot – 'there goes Derby County'.

Seven years later the Rams achieved their unique double. On 22 December 2005 ITV's *Central Soccer Night* ran its *Beat the Monkey* betting slot in which a ring-tailed lemur named Jim from Drayton Manor Zoo was invited to select one of three predictions for forthcoming games.

One of the options was Derby County to draw with Luton Town in the upcoming Boxing Day clash at Pride Park, but Jim looked it over and stubbornly refused to place the bet. It was a bad mistake, for four days later a trademark free-kick conversion by Inigo Idiakez earned Derby a 1–1 draw.

All of which proves that true Derby County fans, ring-tailed lemurs included, are not prepared to back their side for anything but a win.